Old Friends and New Music

OLD FRIENDS

and

NEW MUSIC

by

NICOLAS NABOKOV

An Atlantic Monthly Press Book

Little, Brown and Company · Boston

1 9 5 1

FIRST EDITION

Published January 1951

ATLANTIC–LITTLE, BROWN BOOKS
ARE PUBLISHED BY
LITTLE, BROWN AND COMPANY
IN ASSOCIATION WITH
THE ATLANTIC MONTHLY PRESS

*Published simultaneously
in Canada by McClelland and Stewart Limited*

PRINTED IN THE UNITED STATES OF AMERICA

Born into a wealthy Russian family in the early
years of this century, young Nabokov was particularly well-placed to indulge his love for music.
Affectionately he describes his first memorable
performance of Glinka's A Life for the Tzar at
the sumptuous Mariynski Theater and talks of
the music-making which went on in his family.

After the Revolution, the aspiring composer
found himself in Paris, then the cultural capital
of the Western World. It is at this point in his
autobiography that Mr. Nabokov cheerfully
yields the center of the stage to the magnificent

Nabokov, Nicolas. Old friends and new
music. 1951. 294p. Little, $3.50.
These personal reminiscences of boyhood in
pre-revolutionary Russia and of associations
in music and ballet circles of Europe and
America since the 1910's are seasoned with
trenchant comments on music in general.
Sketches of personalities as well as musical
comments are candid and the author's favorite subjects are his fellow Russians, notably
Diaghilev, Stravinsky, and Prokofiev.
B   Musicians—Correspondence, reminiscences, etc.
51-176

Nabokov's long friendship with Stravinsky has
provided new material for a stimulating study of
this great composer and his music, and the author's account of his recent visit with Igor Stravinsky in his California home is both delightful
and instructive.

Since the early '30's, Mr. Nabokov has been
writing and teaching in this country. New compositions of his have been commissioned by the
Koussevitzky Foundation and have been played
by the Boston Symphony, the Philharmonic in
New York and other leading American orchestras. He has become an American citizen and
during the war served as a "cultural" officer attached to the army. His particular concern was
the musical life of Berlin after the surrender and
his experiences there attempting to co-operate
with the Russians close this absorbing memoir.

Contents

Old Friends and New Music

I

The Picnic

WAIT a minute . . . don't be impatient," said my
mother as she sat down at the piano and started
sliding the rings off her fingers.

I, a plumpish boy of five in a French sailor suit, stood by
watching the rings drop into the cup formed by the palms
of my folded hands.

"What do you want me to play?" she asked, while I carried the rings to the music rack and deposited them carefully
in a glittering heap on the top shelf.

"Don't tell me it's Rachmaninov again," she said with a
teasing smile.

"Oh yes, please," I exclaimed, "please play *The Elegy*, or
perhaps that other thing . . . the one that is fast in the middle and noisy at the end . . . you know . . ."

"You mean *The Prelude*," said my mother, "*Noo Khorosho*.
Only sit quietly and don't fidget around."

She picked up the music from the top of the piano, opened
it and began rubbing her hands together as if she had just
returned from a brisk wintry walk. After a great deal of rub-

(3)

bing, adjustment of the piano stool and a few preliminary arpeggioed chords, in the now obsolete fashion of the nineteenth-century virtuosos, she finally started playing.

Curled up near the bass end of the keyboard on one of those double-decker contraptions called "poufs," which populated most of the drawing rooms of my childhood and consisted of two voluminous damask-covered and ornately betasseled cushions, I listened intently to the music which was coming out from under her fingers. Gradually a state of total rapture, a blend of amazement and delight, took hold of me, making ripples down my spine and stopping the air in my lungs. By the time she had turned the first page nothing seemed to exist in the world except those round hands ("My hands are like those of a fat bishop," she used to say) with their quick fingers moving up and down the keyboard like thousands of vanishing question marks.

How easily she could reach broad expanses of intervals and chords (involving those perilous black keys on which my own rubbery digits always stumbled) and how neatly she struck those juicy bass tones which resounded like deep mellow bells and supplied such a warm, such a solid foundation for the tender flow of the melody! And above all, how well she knew how to make the music sing, cry and laugh, grow bigger, fatter, richer, more intense and more voluptuous as the piece progressed towards its inevitable center climax.

Yes, indeed, her hands were a miracle of agility and adroitness, far more adroit, I thought, than the hands of the magician who came once to our villa in Dresden and pulled an egg out of my nose and two lovebirds out of my brother's ears.

But the greatest thrill always came over me at the same

(4)

moment, when her hands took a run across the full expanse of the keyboard, anticipating the climax. Then the left hand would have repeatedly to cross over the right and, at a constantly accelerating speed, reach for, or rather aim at, the highest note of the keyboard, which it would catch and slap down with its index finger as if it had killed a mosquito.

As always, I waited impatiently for the run, preparing myself to relish every bit of it. For that purpose I had crawled up on my knees, leaning with both hands and chin against the edge of the piano.

"Here, here it comes," I thought excitedly, remembering each turn of the music. . . . Already the left hand had struck the big black note right under my nose and paused a moment waiting to start its run upward. Its partner-competitor, the other hand, was high up in the air ready to dart at the keyboard and at the proper instant support its perilous musical race.

But suddenly, while my mother was waving her little finger on that black note in the futile attempt to extract from it a belated tremolo, something snapped and her hand jerked and fluttered like a wounded bird.

"*Aie*," she exclaimed and stopped playing. She pulled back her left hand and clutched at the aching finger.

"God, how it hurts," she whimpered. "I must have broken something." Tears came into her eyes as she swayed back and forth on the piano stool. "Go, quickly, dear," she said to me, "and fetch Fräulein Abzieher."

Instead, I emitted a howl and with tears streaming down the collar of my sailor suit rushed to my poor, dear tremolo victim and buried my face in her lap.

(5)

Thus in the summer of 1908 were formed and ended the first and fondest musical memories of my childhood. Never again was I to spend those enraptured hours on the pouf. My mother had injured her little finger badly enough to keep it in a cast (a tiny white casket, as I imagined it). She wore her arm in a sling for several months and when she finally resumed practicing the doctor would not let her play anything that involved technical exertions. Thereafter her injury became in my mind as permanent a feature of her personality as the large round birthmark on her right wrist and the tiny pleats which formed themselves near her eyes when she smiled.

I have always assumed, although no one has ever suggested it to me, that during those hypnotic sessions at her piano side my mother must have concluded that I was a born composer and hence should immediately begin to take piano lessons. Several weeks after her accident she persuaded our Austro-American governess, Fräulein Abzieher, to teach me, against the determined opposition of my stepfather and my matronly Aunt Carolina, a distant relative of ours who had lived with us since time immemorial and played the role of a "deputy matriarch" whenever my mother was absent.

I remember well those first tortured, exasperating sessions with Fräulein Abzieher at our funereal concert grand.

The good Fräulein would perch over me hopelessly trying to make my wrists remain at a level with my fingers.

Soon, I would burst into tears, while Fräulein Abzieher or Miss Slipcover (the English equivalent of her name, which we called her behind her back), an insistent being and a disciplinarian, would call me a *Kleiner Dummkopf* and threaten to deprive me of dessert if my hands did not behave before the end of the hour.

I would rush out of the room to the understanding expanse of Aunt Carolina, to weep out my misery and be consoled by several peppermint fondants of which she always had a profuse store. Aunt Carolina in turn would make protestations to my mother, urge her to stop "torturing the poor child with those silly lessons" and forbid Miss Slipcover, that "heartless beast of a governess," to bully the "little angel."

Yet, despite the discomfort and the suffering incident to my unhappy pianistic honeymoon with our old Bekker (which despite its Teutonic name was a product of a St. Petersburg piano manufacturing firm), I soon began to enjoy my lessons. My fingers began to lose their wobbliness, my wrists were gaining a sense of co-ordination with the movements of the fingers, and by the middle of September I was able to extract timid but fairly accurate sounds from the white teeth of the gleaming black monster.

I even started to practice the first number of Schumann's *Children's Album*, which, it was hoped both by Miss Slipcover and by me, I should be able to offer to my mother in lieu of a more tangible Christmas present.

Of the three autumn and winter seasons of my life that I spent in the Russian countryside this first remains clearest in my memory. I am perhaps not able to reconstruct an orderly succession of events from the dozen or so images neatly framed in my recollection, but the intense radiance, the depth and lucidity, of those few images are such that whenever they are evoked it seems as if that early part of my Russian childhood came back in all its sweetness, brilliant with a thousand mysteries and surprises.

Before that first winter in Russia, I had lived abroad with my family, brought up by a heterogeneous troupe of foreign nurses and governesses. When I returned to my native land in 1908, I barely spoke its language and as means of interfamilial communication employed an inadequate blend of pigeon German and English or, on more select occasions, very old-fashioned and hopelessly homespun French.

Our house in the northwest corner of Byelorussia — between Minsk and Pinsk — stood on a moated mound overlooking the sedate waters of the Niemen, which tortuously winds its way from the northern tip of the Pripet Marshes through the perennially antagonistic lands of Byelorussia, Lithuania, Poland and East Prussia until it reaches the Baltic Sea at the ancient city of Memel.

I remember my stepfather's remark, a few days before the First World War, as he looked from the terrace of our house at the lacy curlicues of the Niemen: "This river is a miracle of diplomacy. Look how unconcernedly it travels through so many countries without a passport!"

The Niemen emerged some two miles to the north of our house out of a dark rim of forest that stretched all the way from the eastern to the western horizon. The river flowed straight towards my mother's estate, but just before reaching it, as if making obeisance, it genuflected sharply westward at the point of the tiny harbor inhabited by a kindly old excursion steamer which my Aunt Carolina liked to refer to as "our yacht." From thence, the Niemen looped extravagantly through a marshy, bright green pastureland as if it were groping for the sun at the point of its setting.

Beyond the garden of our house stood the church, the police station, the post office and the various houses, shops and barns of the village Lubcza, which, following the river's course, stretched for more than a mile westward, past the precarious floating bridge which united the two banks of the river that always groaned and spluttered water under its heavy, variegated traffic.

Behind the village the marshy plain soon became a hilly countryside whose valleys contained the habitual North Russian log cabin villages, their drab poverty somewhat enlivened from a distance by the golden onions: the Greek Orthodox Church cupolas.

Our house, or the *Zamok* (castle) as it was called (it was built on the foundations of a medieval castle which burned down during the Napoleonic Wars), occupied the northern, river side of the quadrangular mound. It was a rambling two-story stone mansion with a high main house and two lower and narrower eastern and western wings. Like so many Russian country houses, it was covered with a creamy coat of yellow stucco and had eight Moorish towerlets rising from its roof, supported by thin minaretlike spires. Two of these towerlets were permanently occupied by nests of highly prolific stork families whose discourteous bathroom habits disfigured the stucco around their nests and whose noisy rattle during their mating and nesting seasons used to wake me up shortly after sunrise.

Aside from these two Victorian features — the Moorish minarets and the untidy storks — the house was utterly styleless. It was barely sixty years old, yet one of the two massive towers near the house dated back to the thirteenth century and thus was the oldest stone structure of the region, built by the first rulers of Lithuania, the Yagelons.

There, so the legend goes, high up in the ancient octagonal tower, in an enormous round room where eight Romanesque lookout windows peered through six-foot walls at the four corners of the horizon, I was born on the night of April 4, 1903 (according to the faulty calculations of the Julian calendar). A resounding welcome was provided by a brood of storks which had nested precariously around the lightning rod right in the center of the tower's roof.

The life of the children in this spacious country house of my mother's was like that of most children of well-to-do Russian families whose homes were filled with tutors, governesses and servants, whose stables were bristling with horses and carriages and whose estates were able to provide them with all kinds of pleasures and luxuries undreamt of by the majority of the Russian people.

Only later, after the outbreak of the First World War, did I begin to realize the singular injustice of our carefree life, with all of its ill-deserved privileges and unmerited, leisurely security.

At that time, however, in my early boyhood years, the outer world seemed as intangible as the mirages in the South Russian steppes which, in the scorching heat, bathe ephemeral villages in nonexistent lakes. There were many absorbing pleasures and occupations. In the summer we went on long walks in the forest, to pick berries or mushrooms, or to hunt for the moths and butterflies with which my brother and Tze-Tze had started a token collection. Piotr Sigismundovich Tzetzenyevsky (Tze-Tze, for short) was our new part-Polish, part-Russian tutor, to whom we had both taken a great liking. On celebrations, like my mother's or stepfather's birthday, an elaborate picnic was held, followed in the evening by an equally elaborate display of fireworks. From the terrace of our house we could see star-filled rockets burst over the Niemen with a hollow report and follow the blue Bengal lights as they floated downstream and died on the glossy surface of the river.

The picnics were carefully prepared and planned long in advance by a self-appointed conspiratorial committee consisting of Aunt Carolina, the hunchback housekeeper Maria Filipovna, the old cook Elizabeth and the haughty and imposing-looking head butler Nikifor, the "wolf" of our village girls, whose graying whiskers and double-barreled, strawberry-scented beard used to tickle my neck when he served at the table.

The committee meetings took place in the greatest secrecy in Aunt Carolina's private study. No one was allowed in. The picnics were supposed to be a total surprise to everyone in the family outside of the members of the committee. But fortunately our keyhole intelligence was always able to penetrate Aunt Carolina's security curtain and hence know exactly on what day, at what time and where the picnic would be held.

Early on the morning of the picnic I would slip out of my bed and tiptoe through a dark corridor up a narrow, winding staircase to the attic. From there, out of a bull's-eye window, I would watch the servants loading a large cart with chairs, tables and baskets filled with china and food, and large boxes holding various cooking utensils, and an enormous copper samovar. An hour later I could see the cart being drawn by a pair of horses across the roadless pastureland that separated our house from "the Oakwoods," that is, from that part of our forest under each of whose ancient oaks Napoleon was supposed to have slept during his Russian campaign.

The picnic party would not take off until noon because of the vast amount of ceremony which preceded our departure and which was endured by all concerned with resignation as if it were an immutable, sacred ritual. The ceremony began in my mother's boudoir with the birthday greetings and presentation of presents by the children. While we were paying our studied birthday compliments and handing over our gifts, Clara, my mother's chambermaid, dressed my mother's hair. Clara served as a kind of Greek chorus, commenting about the beauty, the usefulness and the quality of our handicraft gifts. "*Ach*, Madame," she would exclaim, looking at a carved picture frame displaying the color-pencil drawing of a red-headed toadstool. "Look! How finely carved are all these twists and turns in the wood and how lifelike this lovely mushroom!" Or with equal enthusiasm she would greet a paper weight inlaid with a swallow-tail butterfly, and weighted with lead. The lead plates for these paper weights were secured by Dr. Silberstein, our visiting dentist, who came to us once a year from Vilna and peddled for five days his awesome dental gear in my stepfather's study. After the children's birthday greetings were complete, and the hair had been dressed in a smooth coiffure garnished by several diamond-studded combs, my mother would descend past the elk and boar heads, the stuffed grouse and various other hunting trivia that decorated the wall of the stairway leading to the entrance hall of our house. There she would receive the birthday greetings of the priest, the police chief, the postmaster, the rotund village horse doctor, the emaciated rabbi, the permanently ill-shaven and ulcerous-looking superintendent and various other village notables, in addition to the many relatives and friends who were living or visiting at our home. After these birthday greeting ceremonies, which took some two hours, there followed the hour-long ordeal of the *Molyeben* (the Greek Orthodox equivalent of the *Te Deum*). This was usually celebrated in the main drawing room and required from those attending it an intemperate amount of kneeling, self-crossing and bowing. The *Molyeben* was sung, or rather bleated, in the goaty tenor of Father Basil, our cachectic village priest, in an incongruous antiphon with his enormous deacon, whose bottomless bass seemed to emerge from a fifty-ton barrel in a Munich *Brauhaus*. Towards the end, the *Molyeben* became a procession, carried through all the rooms of our house, with copious aspersion of the walls and the furniture with holy water. Upon the return of the procession to the drawing room, it came to a close with a general anointment of all foreheads with myrrh. This was accompanied by the distribution to each of a handful of *Prosphora* (sacrificial bread) cut up into neat, tiny cubes and the passing of the silver cup containing a dilution of sacrificial wine and warm water called *Tyeplota* (warmth), both of which, according to Greek Orthodox tradition, are symbols, or "friendly reminders," of the Eucharist and represent a survival in diminutive of the *agapae*, the "love feasts" of the early Christians.

By the time my moist palm received its share of *Prosphora* and my mouth was given a sip of the wine and water mixture, I was so hungry, so thirsty and so relieved that the *Molyeben* had come to an end that ever since the taste of unleavened bread and diluted wine has remained the most *final* and savory in the world.

The disposition of forces invading "the Oakwoods" was as follows:

FIRST CARRIAGE. A fancy victoria upholstered in dark red morocco containing Anton, the chief coachman, in the box, wearing top hat, blue livery, white kid gloves, holding the reins of a pair of overfed, roan Arab horses in black patent leather and silver harness.

The Passengers: My mother and stepfather facing the two boys, my brother and myself, and our nets, green metal insect boxes, baskets and other entomophilical equipment.

SECOND CARRIAGE. Equally a victoria, but less fancy.

Passengers: Aunt Carolina, squeezing Miss Slipcover into one quarter of the back seat. Opposite them, Mlle. Vérrière, the French governess and old family friend, and my older sister, Onia.

THIRD AND FOURTH CARRIAGES (a trim French cabriolet on high rubber wheels and an enormous, squeaky Russian gig) contained the rest of the permanent or temporary inhabitants of our house, such as the visiting guests and relatives, the housekeeper, Tze-Tze, and usually one or two village dignitaries including, of course, the priest and his gigantic collaborator, the deacon.

The four carriages started rolling away in quick and orderly succession. The horses' hoofs thundered across the bridge, arousing flocks of tar-black rooks from the lilac and elderberry bushes that surrounded the western tower of our "castle." We drove through the country yard of the estate, past the smithy and carpenter shop, the barn, the hayloft, the stable and the cowshed with its precious new attachment, the modern steam-powered dairy, which my mother had had built against the advice of my stepfather and the superintendent, who considered it an extravagance, despite its exceptional hygienic virtues of which my mother was justifiably proud.

The carriages reached "the Oakwoods" in file. We got out and were greeted by the butler and the other servants, who had been in the woods since early morning and had set and decorated a fifty-foot-long table under two of the oldest and tallest oaks that stood on the edge of the forest. The table was covered with a white cloth, decorated with garlands of fern and juniper and, between the plates and silver, bunches of lily of the valley stood in low, broad-mouthed pitchers. The meal began at once. It was long and copious and in no way different from the nonpicnic holiday meals at our house, except that here, in the woods, the festive veal roast was cooked on a spit over an open fire and the baked potatoes, or "potatoes in uniform" as they are called in Russia, gleamed with specks of salt crystals and white ash from baking on the ground in a heap of charcoal ashes. Champagne was served with dessert — an enormous ivory tower of vanilla ice cream with burnt-sugar hair falling down from its tip and a lacelike fence, also of burnt sugar, built around it. And with the champagne came toasts and speeches delivered by most of the mature males at the table, concluding each time with a loud, threefold "Hurrah." Finally, after the speech of the priest, whose thread wound itself in spirals around a number of supposedly happy marriages of the Old and the New Testament (Abraham and Sarah, Jacob and Rachel, Constantin and Helen), carefully avoiding the less fortunate ones (Mr. and Mrs. Lot, Samson and Delilah, Judith and Holofernes), the deacon, from the bottom of his bellows, began intoning a supplication for the "health, prosperity, and longevity" of Their Majesties the Emperor and Empress, their Imperial Children and their whole Imperial house, the Holy Synod of the Russian Orthodox Church, my mother, her husband, her children, her brothers, uncles, aunts, nephews, cousins, friends and well-wishers, absent or present, abroad or at home, traveling or resting, and our employees, our servants and fellow villagers, and so by gradual extension of the hoped-for Divine Blessing to an ever-growing and more inclusive circle he reached the pinnacle of his capacities and bugled out the last words of the prayer with such vehemence and intensity that the glassware on the table started shaking and Miss Slipcover muffled her ears against the onrush of the deacon's sonorous call:

> And to everyone and to a-a-all
> give, O Lo — o — o — ord, lo-o-ong
> yea — a — ars,

he howled, making a supreme glissando into the stratosphere of his range. Standing around the table, the champagne glasses in hand, all of us, family, friends, relatives and servants, picked up the topmost pitch of the deacon's last note and bellowed back to him, the familiar melody of the *Molyeben's* last prayer:

> Long years —
> Lo-o-o-ong years —
> L-o-o-o-o-ong ye — ars . . .

After all these exertions a rest was welcomed by even the most fidgety members of the company. We dispersed into the woods and, like the heroes of eighteenth-century nature-loving novels, reclined on the soft, fluffy moss under the shade of hazelnut bushes, soothed into slumber by the whisper of the oak trees and the soft twitter of the birds. We inhaled the fragrance of the early summer's forest, a compound of fern, heather, lily of the valley and last year's leaves, while our stomachs diligently assimilated the influx of fats and proteins which we had taken in such overabundant measure.

The digestive repose was soon interrupted by a general "call to arms," that is to the baskets, nets and insect boxes of our expedition. Presently, everyone for himself, we made our way through the underbrush trying to catch an exceptional specimen of a swallowtail (the *Papilio machaon* is a rare species in Northwest Russia) or a dreamy peacock's eye hiding under a hazel leaf, or to find a place where lilies of the valley swarmed, or else to pick a bunch of the rare wild hyacinths that hid in the marshiest ground of the forest and, because of their gentle scent, were called "night violets," although their tiny white flowers perching precariously on a thin hyacinth-like stem resembled more a species of orchid. Later in the season there would be strawberries to pick, and after, blueberries, cranberries, moss berries and wild raspberries, and finally, as the supreme and most exquisite gift of the summer season, those secret members of the forest family, its subtlest artists of concealment, the variegated species of Agaricales fungi, whose season in our part of Russia began in July and lasted until the first September frost. The search for them was our favorite, highly competitive sport. In fact, it has always been the favorite competitive sport of all Russian children and as such it is bound to outlast the noncompetitive enterprises of the collectivist state. To paraphrase a famous slogan: "Lenins and Stalins go, but competitive mushroom picking remains."

Aunt Carolina was usually the stationary pole and orientation center of our searching parties. Her volume and circumference precluded any form of crawling under fir or spruce branches, past prickly twigs of juniper and sweetbriar, or walking across moss-covered ground often concealing a dangerous swamp. Consequently, she would find a tree stump near a clearing and sit there with a volume of Baroness Orczy's latest "Pimpernel" adventures, giving bearings to anyone who wished to call her.

When the sun had slid far enough westward to reach teatime, Aunt Carolina would announce, "Come . . . come everyone . . . it's time for tea-a-a-a — " Immediately, like Professor Pavlov's conditioned dogs, we would converge upon her, each one anxious that his part of the loot should be judged the biggest, best and rarest.

It was at this moment, on one such occasion, that an incident took place which became famous in the annals of our family. Returning to Aunt Carolina's resting place in the forest, we found her, as usual, enthroned on a tree stump, her vast, white muslin skirt (and the many assumed underskirts) covering an imposing part of the ancient stump. When, after inspecting our baskets, boxes and bunches, she finally arose from her seat, there was a general gasp among us. There, on the ground that had been covered by her skirts, lay peacefully coiled a tiny black viper, that had probably crawled out of the old stump to catch a bit of sleep under Aunt Carolina's warm and well-sheltered expanse.

There was much excited comment and general jubilation at the lucky escape of Aunt Carolina, and a rule was passed at once prohibiting anyone, in particular the children, from using tree stumps as seats for fear of exposing the lower part of their bodies to viperous hazards. In vain did my brother and I point out that we did not wear any skirts and hence did not offer such inducements to snakes as did Aunt Carolina; the rules in our family were established by women and no discrimination was made between pants and skirts.

When we came back for tea the samovar was steaming and the table had been reset. Tea was a somewhat calmer and less formal affair. The "notables" had departed, having been driven home after their siesta, and we were reduced to our normal family circle. After tea we played games or wandered around the edge of the forest lazily picking a last night violet or lily of the valley, or else lingered at the tea table listening to the poems and tales of a little old peasant, a wandering minstrel and fortuneteller by the name of Moroz. No one knew his first name, nor where he came from, yet his fame as a native poet was widespread in our region. He would appear as if by magic out of the thick of the forest just in time to recite his latest poems and tales and inspect a half dozen of the company's palms, and he would be gone before anyone had noticed his departure, just as furtively as he had come.

Summer evenings were long in our part of the country and the change from day to night was slow and imperceptible. It took the sun many hours to make up its mind to disappear behind the horizon, and even then, after the edge of the burning disk had been swallowed by the Niemen, its scarlet, orange and pink memories still lingered fondly in the sky, and on the surface of the river, as if they were loath to forget our quiet land, and leave the penumbral plain and the silence of the forest.

Although tired by the day's events we always begged to be allowed to walk home instead of driving back with the grownups in the carriage. The boys walked back with Onia, Mlle. Vérrière and Tze-Tze, past heaps of freshly mowed hay, awakening as we went flocks of ducks that hid in the shrubbery and rushes near the low banks of the Niemen.

In front of us in the distance, silhouetted against the sky, shone the windows of our house. "I'm going out alone on the road," we sang in chorus, breaking the evening's silence, putting our whole heart into the languorous, sentimental song:

> Through the mi-ist,
> I see the rocky ro-o-oad . . .
> The night is quie-e-et, . . .
> The desert listens to Go-o-od
> And a star is talking to a star.

I I

The Open Window

OUR LIFE in Lubcza was by no means dedicated exclusively to the consumption of seven-course meals and the leisurely enjoyment of nature. Quite the contrary, we were provided with a balanced diet of organized study, exercise, and rest, constantly enforced by my Aunt Carolina (mild reproaches and peppermint rewards), Tze-Tze (kind, but stern orders), the governesses (inevitable scenes, often leading to the repetition, in our best calligraphy, of: *"Ich werde nie wieder Fräulein Abzieher ins Gesicht spucken"* — "Never again will I spit into Miss Slipcover's face"), and to a minor extent by the timid village priest, who came once a week and taught us the "Who's Who" of the Greek Orthodox faith. In fact all the elders of the household participated in the supervision of our daily activities including the hunchbacked housekeeper and the strawberry-scented butler.

Above all, in a halo of Paracletan infallibility stood the two benevolent monarchs of our lives: our strong-willed but warmhearted mother and our equally strong-willed stepfather.

(21)

Nicolas von Peucker, or Colo as we called him, was my mother's second husband, a friendly gentleman of conservative tastes and a somewhat haughty demeanor which, so we were told, he had inherited from both his imperial Byzantine and his Baltic ancestors. He had replaced my father when I was barely two years old. The full-length oil portrait of this obsolete parent, whose name was never mentioned in the presence of my mother and whose remembrance was generally taboo at our home, hung directly over my bed. He wore an imperial chamberlain's uniform and looked like a huge stuffed bird. His left hand disappeared in the rancid whipped cream of a beplumed three-cornered hat, his chest was covered with medals, fancy embroidery, and a large shining star whose diamonds (thick blotches of yellow paint) I tried in vain to pry off with my nails. From the golden collar of the bird arose a handsomely featured but quite banal face with a rosy tint, a wedge beard and a Prince Albert mustache. Absorbed by an obvious lack of thought he gazed abstractedly at the opposite wall of our bedroom.

Among the various occupations included in our diet I preferred the afternoon reading period sandwiched in between the midday siesta and teatime. During that period I was left entirely to myself, and since I had been a chain reader since the age of six, I needed no coaxing or supervision in this respect. Of all my books I loved best a novel on the life of Spartacus by Giovaniolli, which Tze-Tze had first read aloud to us at bedtime and which I must have reread several times for even now I remember the details of Spartacus's life from the escape from the gladiators' prison to his death in the battle of Petelia. It left me forever anti-Roman and permanently pro-gladiator and later, when I started writing music, it haunted me for many years as a heroic and revolutionary opera subject.

What I hated and dreaded most of all were my semi-weekly piano lessons and my daily hour of piano practice. During these hours Miss Slipcover would sit with a book in the corner of the drawing room, near one of the two large windows that overlooked the Niemen. She would interrupt her reading and bark at me: "Don't go so fast. . . . Why don't you keep time? . . . Why, your fingers are like jelly!" or, in a quite exasperated tone: "What in heaven's name *are* you doing? Can't you even hit the right notes?" Later on, as I grew older and was immersed in the dusty disciplines of harmony and counterpoint, my fear and hate automatically were transferred to these inevitable bugaboos. Only gradually did I realize that piano lessons and piano practice, the studies of harmony and counterpoint, and in fact most of the disciplinary activities devised to teach young aspirants to composition, are hateful to me because they are (and probably always have been) devoid of any relation to music. Unable to evoke pleasure, or even the remotest form of enjoyment, they are by that very fact contrary to the nature of music.

I am never surprised, when after two years of nibbling at meaningless fragments of Gregorian melodies and ensuing attempts to write emasculated motets in the so-called Palestrina style, and dissecting and atomizing the inventions and fugues of Bach, a young aspirant develops an indifference to, or even a dislike for, these pontiffs of the polyphonic craft. The living beauty of their art dies and is buried under the moss of awe-inspiring "canons," "inventions," "augmentations and diminutions," and all the other tricks of the polyphonic trade.

Similarly with piano practice: somehow or other, half-consciously or quite unconsciously, the student comes to equate the lovely sonatas of Haydn and Mozart, the magnificent fugues of Bach and preludes of Chopin (to name but a few of the victims of his daily practice routine), with those hideous rumblings and rummagings across the keyboard which go under the names of various "Gradi ad Parnassum" (the collections of "progressive" finger exercises prepared by such geniuses of anti-inspiration as Hanon or Czerny). All these pieces of music somehow lose their flavor and meaning, in their role as hurdles in his race for technical proficiency. Like the fugues of Bach and Palestrina's Masses, they have thus been despoiled of their innocence and their charm. It will take the student a long time to recover an untarnished sense of musical perception and rediscover their beauties and the perfection of their craft.

No, music finds other ways to get into a composer's life and into his bloodstream. Some of these ways are quite secret and unorthodox. Not in the bland study-room of conservatories, nor during the congealed Bach performances in Protestant churches (the "cold feet" Christmas oratorios and *St. Matthew Passions*, as Busoni used to call them), nor even during the recitals and concerts of the Pattons of the baton and the Rommels of the keyboard and the bow. As I reflect upon it now, after so many years of teaching in and out of schools and conservatories, hammering into other minds the devices of the classics, it seems to me that music came into my life in the way it came to the lives of most composers; through the illicit communication with that fertile subsoil, that vast underground of life where musical matter of all degrees of beauty and ugliness lives freely and abundantly and is constantly being reinvented, rearranged, transformed and infused with new meaning by a universe of memories and imaginations.

First of all music came to me through the large, open window of my early boyhood, the window of my bedroom on
the second floor of our house in Byelorussia. There, on its
broad window sill, I would sit through lingering summer sun-
sets watching the gradual recession of yellows, reds, and
purples from the glossy surface of the Niemen, breathing in
the gentle air, filled with the scent of linden and Nicotiana, and
listening to the resonant knock of an ax falling on the logs
of some distant timber raft and forming an ephemeral accompaniment to the "calling songs" of the lumberjacks, those
dirgelike evening conversations between the men who floated
the rafts down to the German border.

This curious dialogue, or rather antiphon, would fill the
shadowy stillness with solitude and desolation. It would rise
from afar, from the very edge of the northern horizon where
the darkening curves of the Niemen were being swallowed up
by the forest. It began with a question, intoned in the highest
range of a man's voice, plaintively sliding up and down the
narrow interval of a minor third, but otherwise remaining
quite dispassionate and expressionless. Then, at the end of the
question the voice, as if choking, would break off in a soblike
cadence and again there would be only the total silence of
the evening, interrupted by the knock of the hewing ax. A
moment, and then another voice, much nearer, quite close,
sometimes right down under my window, would answer,
tuning in to the last tone of the mournful sob. And from below in the same plaintive manner but with each word clearly
audible would come the awaited response.

> We're floating five ra-a-fts
> for Merchant Korneichoo-oo-ook . . .

would sing a silhouette standing on a raft near a small open fire.

> We will take off before dawn . . .
> . . . And you, when do you start?

After a moment's pause the faraway sorrowful vowels would again fill the air, prolonging this curious responsory far into the evening, until Venus had retired behind the last crimson streaks of the sunset and the farm dogs had begun their nightly roll call.

Or in the early summer mornings, the same open window would bring to my bed the voices of the peasant women, the haymakers, on their way out to the fields. I would slip out of bed and watch them from behind the blinds. They walked in rows, fast and lightly as if dancing, each one carrying a rake on her shoulder, and as they crossed the floating bridge their bare feet splashed in the water. They sang quick gay songs with short repetitive phrases. At the end of each stanza they paused. Two or three continued to sing alone and, as if reaching for an utterly unattainable object, their voices would rise in a shrill glissando to the topmost level of their range and there sustain a very loud and a very high tone. But soon the rest of the chorus broke in again with the next stanza of the song and with a savage and boisterous onrush toppled over the high note of the soloists. The voices of these women were harsh and strident and the songs they sang were strong and bright, as bright as the kerchiefs on their heads, as bright as the summer dawn whose first sharp rays were burning the mist over the plain.

In the evening the same haymakers returned to the village but they walked slowly and sang different songs. The evening songs, although sung much in the same manner as the morning ones, differed in mood and texture. They were slow and lazy. Their long wavy melodies lingered endlessly on sustained tones and their harmonies were so clear and so transparent that they gave the impression of constant unison. Here again it seemed as if the women haymakers, trudging homeward after a day's work, were obeying the eternal mimetic laws, fitting their songs into the mood of the evening, into its gentle, dying sunlight and its limpid, reposeful mellowness.

But the musical window of my bedroom did not limit its repertoire to the performance of folk songs by peasant women and the calls of lumberjacks. Other sounds, other particles of musical matter, came through my window and were avidly absorbed by my imagination. I do not speak of the calls and sounds of nature for to them I remained singularly indifferent. I never understood the addiction of musicians, particularly of the Romantic composers, to the sounds of nature. To me the twitter of birds (including the bothersome nightingale), the chirping of crickets, the gurgling of brooks and all such supposedly delectable phenomena were tolerable only when I had nothing to do. Even then, during the times of complete leisure they disconcerted me by their lack of any kind of order and pitch precision, and by a total absence of symmetry or any other intelligible structural principle. But when I played or improvised at the piano or when I was just brooding about music, then I shut my windows tight and forbade the cuckoo's false major third or the oriole's incorrect minor triad to disturb and distract me.

What I liked to listen to through my window were bits of music, bits of jagged dance tunes played by an accordion at a Saturday dance in the village, or snatches of sentimental trivia full of alcoholic loneliness bellowed by some despondent male on the riverside, or the gentle, more lyric songs of the girls who weeded the vegetable garden, hidden behind the moat that surrounded our house.

During the summer months the Jewish children of the village went bathing on the northern bank of the Niemen, opposite our house. I sat on my window sill and watched the gay, naked bathers run about on the riverbank and splash in the water. Through the laughter, the shouting and the loud gibberish of their talk I would hear the strains of quick Yiddish songs with their strange Oriental inflections and their catchy dancelike rhythms.

On the Day of Atonement the whole Jewish population of the village would go to the river and stand, knee-deep in water, for a whole day. In those early September days, the air was quiet and balmy and I could hear quite distinctly the low mournful murmur of the worshipers. They spat into the water, symbolically casting off their sins, bestowing them to the river which flowed them down to Germany and submerged them in the muddy waters of the Baltic Sea. Occasionally a sob or a wail would rise above the murmur of the praying crowd, or a restless child would start crying in the arms of his mother.

But the window was not the only ingress by which musical matter entered the awakening conscience of an eight-year-old boy, though it was perhaps the most intimate and the most cherished. I had other, more direct and more obvious contacts with music. First were the endless Greek Orthodox services in the village church; vespers on Saturday at 5:30 and Sunday Mass from 10:30 to 1 P.M., to which we drove in a *défilé* of three or four carriages and where a well-lubricated choir exhaled the totally giftless creations of nineteenth-century Russian Church composers, interlarding them with segments of traditional, or traditionally erroneous, singing of the liturgy.

Oh, what infinite boredom was evoked by those repetitive dialogues between the deacon and the choir, the so-called *Ektyenia* of the Greek Orthodox service in which the deacon implores God for His Divine blessings! Each new request is seconded by the choir repeating over and over again the same stuffy and utterly trite harmonies. Originally, in the Middle Ages, these responses were sung in unison and must have fitted into the serene progress of the liturgy, but after the late eighteenth century the practice of harmonizing these simple and unassuming melodic lines by means of stereotyped cadences (from a dominant seventh chord, with the seventh in the soprano part, back to the inevitable tonic triad) became and unfortunately remains the traditional practice of the Russian Church. And what masters of provincial taste were all those obscure composers who infested the Slavonic liturgy with imitations of the worst habits of Italian opera and the formulas of the German conservatory classroom!

Yet at the time of my childhood I did not discriminate between what music was suitable and what unsuitable for church worship. Nor did I know of the existence of the *Znamennoi Rospyev*, the Neumatic Chant, of the Russian branch of the Greek Orthodox Church, that extraordinary and completely neglected treasure of medieval devotional singing, equal in its beauty and grandeur to the *cantus planus* of the Roman Catholic Church. Quite to the contrary, I enjoyed most of the operatic excursions of our church choir. They were a relief from the dreary *Ektyenia* with its immoderate concern for blessings and its boring repetition of the same drab harmonies. What I liked most was a particularly suave setting of the *Gospodi Pomilui,* the *Kyrie Eleison* of the Slavonic liturgy. In it, a solo soprano roller-skated pleasantly up and down the tones of the tonic and dominant triads, to the accompaniment of a humming, or rather of a mumming choir. After a number of trills and frills at each repetition of the prayer's two words, she finally reunited herself with the rest of the choir and brought the prayer to its end in a velvety pianissimo, reminiscent of the last bars of the love aria from *Jocelyn* or of the polite death of Camille Saint-Saëns's Pavlovian Swan.

A more exciting and certainly a more valuable contact with Russian Church music came at Christmas time or, more precisely, on Christmas Eve. On that day a strict fast was imposed upon all of us until the appearance of the first star, the so-called "Star of Bethlehem." Then, as the darkness settled firmly upon the snow-covered countryside, we climbed into the sleighs and went to church, to attend the sumptuous candlelit Christmas vespers. The church was filled to capacity and we had to struggle to get through the crowd to the place reserved for our family on the left-hand side of the altar. This service differed from the usual Saturday vespers in that it contained a few traditional prayers sung in a purer, more medieval way, with but a few lapses into the trivial harmonies of Italian opera.

But it was not the Christmas vespers that excited me and inspired me with a lasting love for the ancient Russian Church chants. It was rather a ceremony that followed the service on our return home from church. The Christmas carolers, boys and girls of the village, making the rounds of the neighborhood, would appear at our front door singing their Christmas songs. They bore a large candlelit star which one of them held high above the crowd on a gilded stick. Twenty or thirty of them would enter our front parlor, and after a bit of stamp-

ing to shake off the snow from their winter felt boots, they
would arrange themselves in a circle around their star and
begin singing the carols and Christmas chants of Russia. They
sang them in parallel sixths and thirds with an occasional leap
into the octave, obeying the purest and most ancient tradition
of Russian Church singing. The words of these chants were
a curious mixture of church Slavonic and of the Byelorussian
dialect. Like most carols they spoke of the birth of a child
in a manger, of the kindly animals that kept him warm with
their breath in the "cold, cold Bethlehem night," of the shep-
herds that heard the angel's voice and saw a new star arise,
and of the Three Kings, "with their star that traveled
. . . traveled . . . traveled . . . through the days . . . and
through the nights." The melodies of most of these chants
were simple and childlike, yet profoundly jubilant.

Even more important than the Christmas carolers or the
peasant women in the fields was the lasting influence exercised
upon my musical imagination by a strange little old man, who
during the summer months worked as a night watchman in our
fruit garden. Trophim or Tróshka, as he was called, for no
one, including himself, remembered his last name, had only
one eye. According to his own story he had lost his left eye
in the Crimean campaign of 1855 or in the Balkan campaign
of 1878. He was never sure in which of the two, or else he
switched his story from Sebastopol to Adrianople and from
1855 to 1878 with the ease of a prestidigitator, confusing dates,
places, and enemies. To me both stories were convincing
enough but the villagers believed neither of them and said
that he was born one-eyed and hence was nothing but an old
chort odnoglazyi, a one-eyed devil. (The devil in the popular
legend of Russia has two horns, two tails and one eye.) He

(31)

denied it stanchly and as proof of his battle experiences exhibited scars on the back of his body, which, according to our butler, had more to do with the habits of the Imperial Gendarmes than with his exploits in the field. His other eye was covered with a dime-sized cataract which made him practically blind. Like so many blind people he had developed an extraordinary sense of hearing. He heard and knew the source of the slightest noise from the softest call of a newborn sparrow to the rustle of dry leaves made by a burrowing mole.

When I approached the tiny straw hut, which he erected every year under the same old pear tree, he would greet me from afar, recognizing me by the sound of my footsteps. Tróshka was a *Skazitel* of Russian folk tales — that is, both a narrator and a minstrel. I spent many afternoon hours with him, sitting on the ground in front of his hut, and listening to his goaty, quivering singsong. Tróshka told his tales in an artful and musical way. He enunciated his words distinctly and intoned pitches that lay much higher than the normal level of his speaking voice. Sometimes, at points of emphasis in the story, or when a word seemed to him particularly sonorous (like so many Russians he loved long, many-syllabled words with a dactylic ending), he considered the moment worthy of a special caress. He tilted his head backwards, and elongated vowels by singing in a tender vibrato, which made his crumpled beard tremble, his hands shake, and his lonely eye water. At the end of a sentence he would adorn his cadence with a few decorative notes. Yet in all of his musical narrative he would never exceed the interval range of a fourth.

Tróshka was a tiny shriveled-up man so mild and so friendly in manner that, when several years later I read Tolstoy's *War and Peace* for the first time, I was irresistibly drawn to compare Platon Karatayev, the gentle peasant philosopher, with his saintly reverence for life, with Tróshka. Tróshka never told the famous legends of the exploits of heroes and knights of Russian mythology, or any other well-known folk tales. Most of his stories were obscure and totally unknown to me. I never read or heard them, before or since. His stories were all about the loves, the nuptials, the deaths and the betrayals of princes and princesses, about great droughts and murderous plagues, about hungry wolves in the forest, mysterious, beautiful birds, the treacherous fox, the diligent beaver, the hard-working ox, and the worn-out work horse. Above all he sang about the abundance of God's gifts to men, and the continuance of man's seed. I have forgotten most of his stories but those few I still recall concern this Biblical theme, man's eternal fecundity, told in language so blunt and so forthright that only much later did I understand the meaning of the many words I had learned to repeat, and many of the symbols he described.

On name days and birthdays in the family, we usually hired a Jewish orchestra from our village, or from Novogrudok, the capital of our county. The orchestra consisted of a violin, a zither or guitar, or sometimes a small upright harp, an accordion and a contrabass. This combination played an extraordinary variety of music; potpourris of famous operas, military marches, Viennese waltzes, and the ooziest gypsy songs and Jewish dances, like the jumpy *Maiufess*, rampant with glissandos, tremolos, and tearful vibratos.

I particularly loved the violinists of these orchestras for I enjoyed their scratchy, edgy tone, their ability to slide all over the bridge of their instrument and their clumsy, harsh way of intoning double stops. I remember once after one of these teatime performances telling my stepfather how much I liked the violin and how much I would prefer to practice the violin than the piano or the cello, for which I was being secretly groomed by my mother. My stepfather, who had just returned from Vilna, our closest important town and the ancient capital of Lithuania, replied that to be a good violinist is very hard and if the playing isn't good the violin is just an awful nuisance. "And if you want to hear good playing," he added, "next time I go to Vilna I'll take you with me and you'll hear what I mean by good playing."

"Next time" came in either January or February of 1910, perhaps a year later. At any rate I know it was in the winter. I remember the two-day-long sleigh ride with several relays of horses and a night spent in the house of the famous Polish poet Mickiewicz in Novogrudok, a house my stepfather had rented in order to provide members of our family and our guests with a night's sleep on their way from the railroad station to our estate. I remember how bitterly cold it was and how clear the stars shone in the evening, when, lying on my back at the bottom of the flat sleigh, wrapped in heavy furs and mufflers, I tried to follow our course by keeping my eyes glued on the North Star and the Big Dipper. I also remember how that same evening one of the sleighs turned over and how we jumped out and waded through the crisp, fresh snow to rescue Aunt Carolina from a ten-foot snowdrift.

But I do not remember anything else about this journey, nor a single view of Vilna, nor the hotel we stayed in, nor even the room at the hospital where my mother was convalescing after an operation. Only one brief incident, one or two disjointed pictures, remain in my memory. But those I see clearly, as clearly as if they had been seen by a camera, and not by my reticent memory.

First snapshot. We enter a small store in the courtyard of a three-story house. I am with my stepfather and my sister. It is a music store, for there are stringed instruments hanging on the walls and the Jewish gentleman who opened the door and let us in is holding a violin in his hand. . . . We go to the end of the store to a counter. The gentleman, his round black cap bending over the counter, extracts various kinds of violin strings out of a long blue cardboard case. He coils them up and packs them up one by one in square, black envelopes.

Second snapshot. We are in a large, dark living room cluttered with unwieldy furniture. It is the living room behind the music store. The same Jewish gentleman in a black cap is with us. He and another man (his face is out of focus) are standing near my stepfather who is seated in a big, broad armchair with me on his lap.

In front of us, near the only window of the room, stands a boy in a dark velvet suit and a Lord Fauntleroy collar. He is taller than I am but much leaner and more fragile-looking. His gentle face has the pallor of indoor children. His eyes are blue and intense and two strands of his long blond hair curl neatly around his temple. Under his chin he is holding a violin which seems a bit too big for him. He tunes it up carefully and obeying a signal from the man in the black cap he begins playing. I cannot remember what he is playing, but with the first strokes of his bow I feel enraptured and overwhelmed. A big, mellow, round tone fills the room, penetrating the darkest corners of the stuffy apartment, shaking the windowpanes under its powerful impact. Its force, its warmth, the fullness of life which it represents are such that I feel as if an extraordinary, a miraculous gift were being received by my ears. It makes me tremble with sensuous pleasure and choke with delight.

The body of the boy sways back and forth to the rapid and ardent strokes of the bow. The fingers of his left hand run up and down the fingerboard with incredible deftness and precision. At moments of emphasis the neck of the violin flies up into the air and the boy tilts his head more sharply to his shoulder and his eyes close. Finally the miraculous tone comes to a stop. The room in its silence seems uglier, darker and stuffier, and my body is painfully aware of its ludicrous clumsiness. . . .

Suddenly a man's voice breaks the silence. One of the two men standing behind the armchair is saying something to my stepfather. I remember only part of a sentence: ". . . yes . . . yes, he is going to study at the Petersburg Conservatory . . ."

A few years later, in 1913 or 1914, my brother and I were taken to a concert at the St. Petersburg Conservatory. We were to hear a young prodigy, a violinist already acclaimed as one of the extraordinary instrumental phenomena of our time. My sister's violin teacher, the famous Leopold Auer, from whose classroom came so many of the best violinists of our time and whose method of violin teaching and playing was in great part responsible for the high standard of present-day violin performances, told my mother that he had never encountered a talent of such intensity and such instinctive power combined with a freaklike disposition for instrumental technique.

It was the first concert of my life, and everything seemed

(36)

strange, festive and beautiful to me. I remember the silvery organ pipes that formed the background for a large empty stage with a piano on it. I remember Tze-Tze pointing at a fat man with thin, drooping mustaches, who sat right in front of us in the second row and was talking lazily to a bearded, elderly general in the row behind him.

"That's Glazunov talking to Cui," said Tze-Tze in a respectful whisper. "And there — " he pointed at another pair of beards — "is the tenor Alchevsky with his friend Alexander Scriabin."

My eyes chased all around, excited, avid, and amazed by the crowd of people, by the brilliant lights, by the gilded ornateness of the hall. Suddenly from the left wing of the stage there appeared a young boy in a dark velvet suit, white collar and short knee breeches. He came down past the organ pipes, his violin under his arm, and as he approached the piano the applause, which had begun as soon as he appeared on the stage, reached its climax. He bowed several times and started tuning his A string to the A of the piano. It was only then that I recognized my young magician from the dark Vilna apartment of three or four years ago. I pulled Tze-Tze's sleeve and whispered in great excitement: "I saw him, I saw him before and I heard him play . . ."

But Tze-Tze did not respond to my excitement. "Yes, I know you've heard him," he replied calmly, "but now be quiet, sit still and listen."

But I did not need his admonition, for a moment later the same sensuous, round tone filled the hall of the Conservatory with all of its power and beauty and again I sat hypnotized by the perfection of the young boy's extraordinary art.

(37)

Thus for the second time in my life I heard Jascha Heifetz, one of the most accomplished artists of our time.

By 1911, the tedious piano lessons had borne fruit: I became proficient enough at the piano to enjoy playing it for my own private pleasure. When in the autumn of that year our family moved to St. Petersburg, I had developed the habit of spending most of my free time improvising and sight-reading at the splendid new Bekker piano my mother had bought to adorn the living room of our apartment. Soon I had a sizable repertoire of various kinds of music, mostly pieces I had gleaned from my mother's, my sister's and my brother's music racks. I had begun to develop my first set of critical judgments about the music I was deciphering, and to write down those particles of my own improvisations which stuck in my memory and which I was able to recover intact after a night's sleep.

My first original composition, a *berceuse* for piano, with bits of Caucasian orientalia in its melody, was written for my mother's birthday in 1911. I recall the long hours of constant erasing needed to put down that melancholy little piece of music on paper. This G-minor work was written in a curious mixture of B flat major and G major. The first half of the piece's melody contained two flats and one sharp, hence it seemed only natural to write them out at the head of each stave of the score.

The piece and my manuscript were received with enthusiasm and my new piano teacher, a quiet and timid Jewish lady (so different from the stern Miss Slipcover), was entrusted with teaching me the rudiments of music theory and harmony.

(38)

My earliest musical taste conformed with the musical tastes of my environment. In fact, it was probably quite similar to the tastes of most other Russian children of my time in whose households the art of music was being practiced. But soon I developed a succession of violent crushes on the music of certain composers, which greatly contributed to my emancipation from environmental influence. These crushes were reminiscent of the inevitable children's diseases, such as measles or scarlet fever. They came and left me with an appetite for new discoveries.

First I developed a tender affection for the Nordic spring rumblings of Edvard Grieg — the prickly heat of music, one of the most inoffensive and, so far as I know, now obsolescent children's diseases. I used to spend hours playing the polite love dance of Anitra from the *Peer Gynt Suite* and the sorrowful death of Ase, whom I imagined to be a fat, round lady not unlike Aunt Carolina. Grieg's rash came and went fairly quickly. Next came the measles of Frédéric Chopin, or rather of Chopin's preludes, a few nocturnes and one or two mazurkas. This second illness lasted much longer. For several years the living room of our apartment resounded as I scratched my way through such beloved pieces as the *Nocturne in C Sharp Minor* or the *E Major Prelude*.

Recently, in the last five or six years, the Chopin measles have struck me again. But this time the disease took a long time to incubate. My fresh understanding and my new love for Chopin's music came slowly, step by step. First I had to free myself from my reluctance to tackle Chopin anew because of the mushy legend that has been spun around his art. Clichés like "Chopin, the great suffering Pole," "Chopin, the composer of the most famous piano music in the world,"

"Chopin, the pearl of Romanticism," froze my potential sympathy for his music.

Next I had to overcome certain insipid characteristics of his music, such as his feline, neurotic sentimentality, Romantic bombast, excessive ornamentation, and many other trappings of the musical taste of his period. Having succeeded in overlooking these, I discovered in Chopin a composer much different from the Chopin I knew in childhood and adolescence. I know him now as a precise craftsman, an inventor of an original and imaginative style which at times is as clear and as accomplished as the styles of Bach and Mozart. Today I feel grateful to Chopin for being one of the very few composers of his time who did not give in completely to the debauches of unbridled Romanticism which have filled our concert repertoire with so much rubbish and balderdash. He kept his art within the mainstream of Western musical tradition and has produced masterpieces of stylistic and formal perfection.

Next after Chopin came a serious and protracted case of esoteric mumps: the music of Alexander Scriabin. It began mildly with the discovery of the Chopinesque preludes Opus 8 and the first three piano sonatas. Gradually it spread in area and intensity and I began to revel in the more "transcendental" sonatas of his later period until in my passionate *Flucht in die Krankheit* (flight into illness) I became addicted to the esoteric orgasms of such numbers as the *Poème de l'Extase*, *Vers la Flamme* and *Prometheus*. Scriabin's music kept me in total subservience for at least three years but then it left me abruptly. One morning I woke up with the realization that Scriabin's eroticism was good only for highstrung adolescents, that his orgasms were a fake, and that his musical craft was singularly old-fashioned, dusty, and academic.

Curiously enough all through these years I felt indifferent to the older Russian composers such as Tchaikovsky, or the bearded panoply of Russian nationalists (Rimsky-Korsakov, Borodin, Moussorgsky), nor was I moved by any one of the "classics," that is, by Bach, Mozart, Haydn or Beethoven. Their music seemed boring and stale because of what I felt to be sadly dated harmonies and dull, trivial melodies. Only after I started participating in our homespun string quartet did I begin to react to some of the early Beethoven quartets. Yet his symphonies, to which we were exposed from 1911 (when we began to attend the concerts of the Imperial Symphonic Court Orchestra and concerts of the Imperial Historic Music Society), not only left me indifferent but readily put me to sleep.

I suppose that I should be ashamed of such a tortuous development of musical taste. Yet I believe that it is more natural for children and adolescents to like the music of Grieg, Scriabin, Chopin and Wagner than to like the music of Mozart and Bach. A child loves primarily the outward symbols of art; he cannot comprehend and is totally unaware of its inward qualities. He likes the harmonic language of his time. Older music seems too simple and hence is boring to him. This is why most of the so-called "children's pieces" do not amuse children. They are too simple for them. In reality these pieces usually represent a sugar-coated image of what the grownups want children to be like, or in other words a grownup's wish-dream of a child's musical taste. A child rarely senses the depth and beauty hidden behind conventional musical language of past centuries. The outward simplicity of Mozart, the contrapuntal complications of Bach, are equally impenetrable to a child. In fact, the music of Bach, Mozart, Haydn, Scarlatti and Beethoven was not written, was not intended, for children; hence children have the right to be bored by it.

I am always suspicious when a youngster raves about Mozart or Bach. I sense that he does it only because he wants to behave like grownups, or that he is simply parroting what he has heard others say, or else that he is a freak, a precocious child with queer, unnatural tastes.

My last musical illness, the scarlet fever of Richard Wagner's music, came to me very late. It was intense, absorbing and, fortunately, shortlived. It did not strike in St. Petersburg but in Germany when, at the age of seventeen, as a Russian *émigré*, I was studying music at the Conservatory of Stuttgart. Perhaps the Wagnerian fever did not attack me earlier because the only performance of a Wagner opera that I ever saw in St. Petersburg was *Die Walküre*, to which I was taken sometime early in 1914. For since the outbreak of the war, Wagner's operas had stopped being performed in the Imperial Theaters of Russia. I remember only one incident of this armor-laden Teutonic drama; a forty-by-thirty-foot cloud painted on a large sheet of metal slowly creaked across the stage. It was cluttered with incredibly fat and incredibly blonde females in winged copper helmets. All of the females were angrily shouting something which did not seem to make sense in any of the four languages I knew, nor did it seem to have any relation to what I was accustomed to call music. Their red, round faces and their screaming created an image of such fury and indignation that I suspected that someone must have pinched them severely before letting them out on their ironclad cloud. Crossing the stage from right to left, the cloud disappeared in the left wing and a moment later it began creaking back in the opposite direction. The fierce mammoth goddesses swerved around and, their bosoms pointing at the right wing of the theater, drove their cloud once more across the full expanse of the stage.

Fortunately *Die Walküre* was not the first opera I saw on the stage of the Mariynski Opera House. My early contact with opera was, in fact, extremely propitious for an early development of a deep attachment to this greatest of all musical forms.

I I I
His Majesty's Gloves

THE YEAR 1913 was a jubilee year of the Romanov dynasty. The officialdom of tsarist Russia put on a nationwide show of festivals, military and popular parades or "manifestations," sumptuous official balls and other entertainments of various sizes and degrees of interest. They were all intended to commemorate the dubious benefactions accrued by the country from the 300-year rule of the Romanovs. In the light of the events of 1904–1905 (the unfortunate Japanese War and the revolution of 1905, quelled by the Tsar's government and its police) it seemed useful to the regime to offer special inducements to forgetting, at least for a while, "those mad dreams," as Tsar Nicolas termed the emancipatory efforts of the Russian people.

On and around May 9, 1913, Saint Nicholas's second holiday of the year (Saint Nicholas is one of those lucky saints who somehow succeeded in acquiring two holidays in one calendar year), St. Petersburg saw a week of many government-sponsored festivities. They ranged from resplendent services in the two main cathedrals of the city (the Cathedral of the Virgin of Kazan and the enormous St. Isaac Cathedral) to equally resplendent performances in the two Imperial Theaters (the Alexandrinski Theater of Drama and the Mariynski Opera House), attended (despite the fear of terrorist bombs) by the Tsar, the Empress and other members of the Imperial family, to "spontaneous" processions or parades of the populace led by priests in robes, bearing icons and crosses, carefully "protected" by a cordon of policemen and Cossacks on horseback. A decorative hysteria swept St. Petersburg. The Nevsky Prospect, St. Petersburg's main artery, and the adjacent streets looked ludicrously gaudy and unnatural. A wealth of flags and streamers hung over its normally gloomy façades, and the show windows of the stores were larded with plump garlands of evergreens and banners: red, white, and blue, yellow and black, the colors of Russia and of the Romanov dynasty.

On the ninth of May, a gala performance was to be held at the Mariynski Opera House in the presence of Their Majesties, Tsar Nicolas, the two Empresses, Mary and Alexandra, and other members of the Imperial family. The opera was, of course, Michail Glinka's *A Life for the Tsar*, now called *Ivan Soussanin*. Most of the greatest stars of the Imperial Opera and Ballet were to be in it. The list of performers was an impressive one when my brother and I first saw it in the *Bulletin of the Imperial Theaters* which our porter brought to the door once a week. Chaliapin was to sing the famous role of Soussanin, the hero of this patriotic opera, who had unquestionably the most beautiful bass part of Russian operatic literature. The superb lyric soprano Nyejdanova and the equally superlative contralto Zbruyeva and tenor Yershov were also listed. The veteran conductor, Napravnik, was to conduct the performance, preceded by the singing of the

National Anthem and another patriotic number, the *Kol Slaven*, by the full complement of singers and the entire chorus of the Mariynski. What attracted me even more than Chaliapin and Nyejdanova was the name of Marius Petipas — "Choreography by Marius Petipas," it said, "First Ballet Master of the Imperial Theater." Marius Petipas was one of the founding fathers of contemporary ballet, and it is chiefly to him that we owe the semantic origin of the American noun "balleyrusse."

Nicholas Legat, with the prima ballerina, Mathilda Kshessinskaya, the Emperor's former "friend," was to open the famous second-act Polonaise and lead all the great ballerinas and male dancers of the Mariynski — Karsavina, Yegorova, Lopokhova, Preobrajenskaya, Gerdt, Romanov, Vladimirov, Oboukhov, and many others — into the second act, which consists largely of a series of dances.

From January on, everyone in St. Petersburg knew about this gala performance. It was the central topic of conversation around town and in our house. Everyone we knew wanted to attend it and the telephone in my mother's room buzzed with conversations about who was going to be there, who was able to get tickets, and what could be done about getting another pair of tickets for Uncle Sasha and his wife, who were arriving in St. Petersburg for the festive week. We knew that my stepfather had been able to secure two tickets for my mother and himself through the offices of the Director of the Imperial Theaters, Telyakovsky, and we somehow hoped that "maybe . . . perhaps" our economical stepfather would do something about buying a few tickets from a *baryshnik* (speculator) and thus enable us to see the opera . . . and the Tsar.

For in our children's imagination the Tsar was the real show-piece of this rare festivity.

One night, returning from a boring subscription concert of the Imperial Orchestra, Tze-Tze, my brother and I were accosted by a strange-looking man in a long coat and a worn derby. He followed us, trying to persuade Tze-Tze to buy something at an exorbitant price. When the man pulled three large green tickets out of his pocket, I got so excited that I started shouting: "Please! Oh please! Buy them . . ." Soon I was seconded by my brother: "Please, dear Piotr Sigismun-dovich! Please buy them for us! . . . Please! . . . please! . . ." we yelled, until Tze-Tze angrily shook off the *baryshnik* and told us to shut up.

Exactly one week before May ninth my mother appeared one evening in the dining room, while my brother and I were having supper, and said, looking at me with a sly smile: "Do you still want to go and see the Tsar at the opera . . . be-cause I think I can get a box . . . ?" It appeared that some high-powered relatives had had an opportune case of death in the family and had offered my mother their box. From that day on, everything went topsy-turvy on the third floor of our apartment house. School was forgotten, music neglected, books unread, nights unslept. There was only one enormous all-embracing thought on our minds. It seemed as if someone had written a large, red, festive numeral 9 across all of our daily activities.

The lobby of the Mariynski Opera House was crowded and noisy. We made our way through the throng towards the stairway leading to the first-tier boxes. Guided by an impos-ing, richly liveried *Kapelldiener*, the prototype of present-day Salvation Army style ushers, we passed to the left of a broad semicircular corridor and entered the small but cosy anteroom of box number four. We took off our coats, smoothed our clothes, combed our hair, and, bursting with excitement, waited for my mother or my stepfather to open the door and lead us into the box. "Where does he usually sit?" I asked, suddenly remembering that I had promised my four-year-old sister, Lida, a detailed report about the Tsar. "Does he sit in the middle of the theater?" "Oh, no . . ." answered Onia in the tone of an habitué of the theater, "he sits on the right side, in the largest first-tier box." But my brother began arguing with her, saying that he had seen a plan of the Opera House and that Uncle Genia, "who after all is a general of the guard and should know," told him that the Emperor always occupies a large darkish box on the left side of the parterre floor quite near the orchestra pit. "Well children, are you ready?" interrupted my mother. "Let's go in . . ." and she opened the door of the box.

Oh, how often I have wished to relive those first moments at the Mariynski Opera House! What torrents of nostalgia it brings forth in me and what intense irritation at my ungrateful memory it arouses! Groaning under the burden of unimportant matters, my lazy memory is neglectful of all that is significant. It seems satisfied to preserve only hazy figments, imperfect and ever-deteriorating images. I often have to resort to an artificial, outward reconstruction of events in order to prod its mnemonic energies.

For example, I ask myself today: "What did you see, what did you feel, what startled you, when the door of the box opened and the inside of the Mariynski appeared before your eyes? Did you begin at once to look for the Tsar, in that sea of parade uniforms, diadems, bracelet-laden gloves, and sable or ermine draped décolletés? Or did you forget about the Tsar and the festive crowd and sit in your soft, ornate seat in the front row of the box, dazzled by the magnificent pale blue theater itself? Were your eyes wandering up and down the four glimmering crescents, the four stories of crowded boxes? Or were you unconsciously counting the heavy folds in the enormous curtain? Did you notice the play of light in the myriad crystals of the big central chandelier? Or were you keeping count of the musicians in the deep orchestra pit busily tuning up their instruments?" To all such questions my memory answers only that the moment was so complete in its excitement and its perfection that time seemed to stop, as if melted away by the luminous beauty surrounding me. I felt as if I had penetrated into the heart of a jewel, like a speck of coal caught in the blue waters of a diamond, dissolving in liquescent light.

Soon after we had come into the box the tuning had reached the intensity of an atonal concert program. Most of the ladies in the parterre and around us in the boxes were ostentatiously aiming their lorgnettes at the left side of the theater, at the largest parterre box, quite close to the orchestra pit. Suddenly there was a wave of loud murmuring and the aged conductor, Napravnik, mounted his stand. The tuning ceased and, except for the sedentary cello section, the whole orchestra rose to its feet. It was followed by the rise of the whole audience. The lights in the house remained bright while the curtain went up. The stage appeared, filled to capacity by the cast and the chorus of *A Life for the Tsar* in various costumes. The solo singers (I instantly recognized the leading ones from photographs I had seen) stood in two groups in front, the chorus arranged behind them in a semicircle. In the background was the set of the first scene of the opera, representing the inside of an enormous *izba*, a log cabin peasant house.

The conductor lifted his baton and . . . But at this moment I saw my mother's arm reach out and catch my brother by the collar. He was leaning precariously out of the box trying to see what was going on somewhere to the left near the orchestra pit. "Mitya, stop it . . . stand straight . . ." she whispered in a commanding tone. "Please . . . please," he whispered back, "let me see him . . . I *want* to, I *must* see him . . . Please let me . . ." Instinctively I followed my brother's example and bent forward outside the railing. But I could see nothing. Beyond the blue railing the orifice was dark and empty. The orchestra began to play and the audience sang the *Boje Tzarya Khrani*, the national anthem. Then they played and sang the anthem by Bortnyanski, the *Kol Slaven*. Standing near the railing in the front of the box, I could think of nothing else but the Tsar. "Will we get a glimpse of him?" I thought. "Will he and the Empress come forward and sit up front in their box? . . . Isn't it awful that our box is on the same side as theirs?" The curtain went down again on the last chord of the *Kol Slaven*. The audience sat down and resumed its excited chatter. But gradually and imperceptibly the lights of the central chandelier dimmed and finally went out completely. The glow of the footlights grew more intense so that the lower fringe of the curtain began to glow with purples, greens, and blues. Napravnik lifted his baton, and the first tender strains of the overture to *A Life for the Tsar* flowed into the theater.

Few people outside of Russia know Glinka's famous opera, *A Life for the Tsar* or *Ivan Soussanin*, as it has been renamed since the revolution. Yet *Ivan Soussanin* is undoubtedly one of the masterpieces of nineteenth-century opera. Modeled after the best examples of the Italian-Mozartian tradition, it reveals a powerful and abundant melodic invention coupled with impeccable craftsmanship. It is one of those splendid examples of Western music in which the national genius of a people molds itself freely into the universal and traditional patterns of European culture. It makes its contribution to the development of this culture by giving to it its own national memories, distilled, as in the case of Glinka, by a profound knowledge of the universality of culture. Composers like Glinka are singularly akin to the great explorers of the fifteenth and sixteenth centuries. By discovering new territories abundant with untapped resources, they act as cultural catalysts originating or causing important and fructifying changes in the slow evolution of Western culture. Although Glinka's official title is "father of Russian music" and *Ivan Soussanin* was called the "ancestor of all National Russian Opera" by Moussorgsky, a more important fact is that Glinka's music, like Chopin's, brilliantly solves the difficult problem of fusing a national heritage into a universal tradition. In doing so, Glinka set up certain rules, or rather patterns of "creative behavior," which, when they are *not* followed, result in an unfortunate ethnographic babble, like so much of the music of Russian composers of the Nationalist School, or of the present-day Soviet composers, and all of the pompous and hollow works of the "folksy" variety in America.

But aside from these essential considerations *Ivan Soussanin* is one of the best, if not the best, of the national Russian operas. At least the Russian public seems to think so, for since its first performance it has never left the program of Russian opera houses. The only other opera which rivals it in popularity is *Eugene Onegin* by Tchaikovsky. Together they have become the operatic ideal of the Russian people. Even now in the tortured absurdity of Soviet musical life, these two operas remain the most popular of the repertoire. Despite all pressure of propaganda, the Russian people still prefer the truly "cosmopolitan" arias and choruses of *Ivan Soussanin* and the universal lyricism of *Eugene Onegin* to the dull and meaningless contemporary Soviet opera, made to order by the music scribes of the communist fatherland.

Yet on May 9, 1913, it took Michail Ivanovitch Glinka at least one whole act to draw my attention to his opera. Throughout the first act, my sister, my brother, and I, and probably quite a few other youthful subjects of His Imperial Majesty, hung out of our boxes, avidly trying to get a glimpse of this awesome and elusive personage. But from our disadvantage point, all we could see were a pair of white gloves which, at the end of the two arias of the first act, and the ensuing sextet, politely led the enthusiastic applause of the audience. This sextet, or the *Cavatina* as it is called, is one of the most famous pieces in Russian operatic literature. It is certainly a brilliant example of Glinka's genius and skill. Its melodic lines are warm and generous. Its expressive power is simple and profoundly moving, yet its contrapuntal craftsmanship is precise and intricate. Sung by such superb artists as Chaliapin, Nyejdanova, Zbruyeva, Yershov, and two others of the same caliber, the canonic progress of its elegant polyphony was magnificent . . . yet . . . yet it did not bring me out of my Tsar-seeking trance. I kept watching the white gloves, hoping that their owner might move to the front of his box and, illuminated from inside, begin shining like a Hallowe'en pumpkin.

It was only with the first notes of the Polonaise in the Polish scene that I awoke to the realities of the music and the action, and forgot about His Majesty's gloves, in fact about the very presence of His Majesty in the Mariynski. As announced in the bulletin, Balletmaster Nicholas Legat opened the Polonaise leading Kshessinskaya in the first pair. Next came Gerdt and Yegorova; Karsavina led by Oboukhov, and then Preobrajenskaya and Romanov and others, others, others . . . It seemed as if the vast stage of the Mariynski had no space left, yet new pairs were emerging from the wings in an infinite procession, winding its way across the stage like a huge live ribbon. The dancing pairs formed repeated figures, then dissolved them, until, towards the end of the first part of the Polonaise, the dancers took up the traditional positions along both sides of the wings and in front of the backdrop. Thunderous applause greeted the arrival of a new troupe of dancers: the children of the Imperial Ballet School, appearing in time to dance the middle section of the Polonaise.

Soon after the Polonaise came the famous Mazurka. In those years the Mazurka from *A Life for the Tsar* was considered one of the greatest choreographic feats of the Imperial Ballet of St. Petersburg. It was certainly a unique and most polished example of superb character dancing. In all my association with ballet I have never seen anything approaching it in perfection. Nothing can compare to the enormous choreographic effect that can be achieved by a skillfully planned and brilliantly executed fast processional dance. At that time the Mazurka was danced by some twenty-four pairs of famous, first-rate dancers, most of whose names have since become legends of virtuosity and technical brilliance. They were supported by a *corps de ballet* of 100 to 120 male and female dancers in which even the last pair of "ladies at the fountain" (the plumpest and oldest ladies of the *corps de ballet* usually stood in the very back of the stage, concealed by the stereotyped fountain of the classical stage set, and hence acquired the nickname of "ladies at the fountain") danced with a technical proficiency superior to any *corps de ballet* I have ever seen.

But to us children, and to many other youngsters in the audience, the real *clou* of the evening was not the Mazurka, nor was it any one of the beautiful soprano and contralto arias of the opera. We all waited for the forest scene of the last act in which Ivan Soussanin (Feodor Chaliapin) sings his macabre ode to the rising sun just before he is killed by a band of "treacherous murderers, hirelings" of the Polish King Vladislav. This prayer is the most celebrated bass aria of Russian opera and Chaliapin was its most famous interpreter. No one else, before or after him, has been able to evoke its moving lyricism and at the same time show a great actor's perception of its dramatic meaning. The mellowness and the power of his voice in those years were supreme. The ease with which he mastered the technical problems of performing the long and broad vocal lines was unsurpassed.

Later on, when I learned to know the music of *A Life for the Tsar* better, I began to be irritated by the liberties Chaliapin took with the wishes of the composer, introducing here and there exaggerated rubatos, and holding the fermatas beyond any degree of musical need or tact. I also began to react against certain obvious failings in Chaliapin's musical taste which were not so apparent in 1913 and in his performance

(54)

of *Ivan Soussanin* but which, with the passage of years, increased and finally reached, it seemed to me, unbearable proportions. I came particularly to dislike his famous impersonation of Boris Godunov, wherein his liberties with the part made mincemeat of Moussorgsky's music, and his acting at moments was pure hamming, with a touch of the obnoxious "realist" method of the late Konstantin Stanislavsky. But during my first evening in the Mariynski, I joined my fervent applause to the ovation which greeted Chaliapin at the end of his scene, when, resurrected from the dead, he appeared before the curtain, his wig and beard still glittering with a few paper snowflakes. He was called to the proscenium over and over and each time bowed low in the direction of the Tsar's box. The white gloves reacted with increased and disembodied politeness.

A Life for the Tsar ends with a brilliant choral scene, an extraordinary feat consisting of some fifteen minutes of sustained, pure C major. This scene has inspired more choral opera scenes by Russian composers after Glinka than any other choral piece of Russian music. Its short, gay, and flamboyant theme has a marchlike quality and is directly related to the traditional finales of Rossini's operas. This choral piece had acquired a special "national anthem" flavor. In fact it was often suggested as a replacement for the suave national anthem which the nineteenth-century Russian composer, Lvov, transcribed from an Austrian military march. In the last scene of *A Life for the Tsar* the chorus repeats the same spirited melody in praise and commemoration of the election, or rather the "miraculous selection" of the founder of the Romanov dynasty, Tsar Michail, to the throne of Muscovy. Hence Glinka's patriotic choral piece became somewhat of a

Tsarist propaganda number, and on the evening of May 9, 1913, had naturally acquired added commemorative significance.

Throughout its performance the lights remained lit in the theater and the audience rose spontaneously to salute the invisible owner of the white gloves. Later I was told that Nicolas II, the last enthroned descendant of the dynasty, for the "selection" of whose progenitor, Ivan Soussanin had given his life (and the cast of the Imperial Opera and Ballet one of its best performances), was "profoundly moved" by the singing of the chorus and the salute of his "faithful subjects." He and his family, the two Empresses, the pretty Princesses and the sickly Tsarevitch, stood erect like church candles during the performance of the chorus.

It was past midnight when we returned home after our extraordinary evening. Tired, but still excited, we did not want to go to bed. But Tze-Tze had been waiting for us, and did not want to listen to our tales. "Morning is wiser than evening," he kept repeating. "Come, come, go to bed and tell me all about it tomorrow." Slowly and unwillingly we crept through the dark corridor to our rooms. As I passed in front of my little sister's bedroom I saw that the door was open. I stopped and in the moment's silence heard her whisper: "Nika, Nikoushka, come . . . tell me . . ." I approached her crib and in the shadowy flicker of the oil lamps saw her lying on her back, her big black eyes staring at me. "I heard your voices . . . I knew you were back . . ." she said quietly. "I couldn't wait till tomorrow . . . tell me . . . tell me now" . . . and her voice grew softer and dreamier. "Was he . . . all in crimson . . . and ermine . . . and did he wear a tall golden crown? Tell me . . ." I understood how much she needed confirmation, needed it for her sleep, for her dreams, and for the tiny smile which was about to break out at the corners of her mouth. "Yes . . . he was . . ." I whispered. "Yes, yes . . . all in red and ermine . . ." And I quickly left her room.

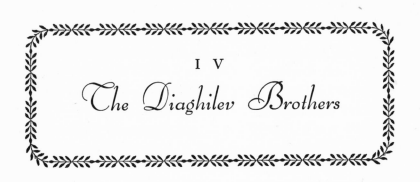

I V

The Diaghilev Brothers

I DO NOT KNOW how my mother came to devise the plan of transforming her children into a string quartet, but I remember that when I was eight and already sufficiently housebroken on the piano, I received on my saint's day (which, owing to the fortunate collusion of the Emperor's and my own first names, was a national holiday) a reddish, freshly lacquered, three-quarter-size cello.

I remember that on that same evening I took my cello to bed with me and fondled it with delight and curiosity until I fell asleep and was in my sleep bereft of it by my Aunt Carolina, who came in to cover me up and found me clutching the neck of the instrument much too fervently for my age and the cello's good health.

My older sister, Onia, who lost the *S* of her name with the loss of her front milk teeth (the *S* presumably escaped Onia's mouth through the gap formed by the absent teeth), had already been playing the violin for several years, and my brother Mitya (short for Dimitri) had recently added one hour a week of screeching on the viola to his former two

(58)

hours a day of piano and violin. Thus everyone was ready to receive me, the cello-playing brother, as the next step in the formation of the projected string quartet.

I started taking lessons with an elderly member of the Imperial Court Orchestra, whose name was Ossip Ossipovitch Piorkovsky or Oss' Oss'ch, as he was known to me. Despite his Polish name and exuberantly Polonized mustachios (which drooped over his mouth and which, because of frequent immersions in soups and sauces, had acquired a permanent ocher halo like the pollen-covered stamen of a lily), Oss' Oss'ch was a Russian patriot, a foe of things foreign (in particular, German), and a firm believer in the superiority of Russian music, Russian musicians, and Russian culture. He did not go so far as to ascribe the invention of the cello to Russian genius, but he did insist — with only barely perceptible hesitancy — that Davidov and Verjbelovitch, the two Russian cellists of the beginning of this century, were the first and finest in the world and that *his Russian method* of teaching me how to play the cello (its most important feature consisted in using Russian synonyms for such foreign terms as "position" or "vibrato") was superior to any other.

As a result of this method or of my own inadequacies, it took me two and a half years to graduate to a whining performance of Bach's *Aria for the A String*, which I gave on the occasion of my mother's birthday in 1914.

The reaction to my first public appearance was a mixed one: condescendingly warm in the parental age bracket, and openly adverse if not hostile among my contemporaries. Throughout my performance I caught glimpses of my brother and my two cousins Pavlik and Alyosha Diaghilev making faces at each other. It all ended, of course, in an eruption of tears and sobs which my mother, Oss' Oss'ch, and my Aunt Carolina tried to stem by telling me that I played like a real prodigy.

It had, however, one tangible result: soon after, I was taken into the family string ensemble as an alternate to Alyosha, equally a cellist and pupil of Oss' Oss'ch. He and his violinist brother Pavlik had been playing quartets with my own brother and sister for more than a year.

True enough, I was at first permitted to join the string ensemble only when it played easy transcriptions of Haydn or Mozart symphonies. My mother would then take over the piano part and I would play the part of the double bass. This consisted mainly in counting empty bars and entering at the up and down beats of loud passages. But even so, every time the piece was marked allegro or presto, I would get hopelessly lost, miscount empty measures, miss cues, and enter with great vigor and dubious intonation at the worst possible moment. Fortunately for me, my mother's presence prevented the irritation of my companions from growing into something more ominous than purely verbal recriminations.

"*La musique*," say the French, "*adoucit les moeurs*." I remember that sometime after I had finally graduated to real cello part playing and was tolerated by my sister and brother as a full-fledged member of the quartet, there occurred the following episode.

One late afternoon we had been practicing the *Second Quartet* by Borodin, in which the slow movement starts with an oozy, sentimental melody in the high register of the cello. After I had made several attempts to produce this melody, resulting each time in a kind of intestinal wail, my brother and sister became exasperated and decided to throw me and my cello out of the room into the long dark corridor which wormed its way all around our St. Petersburg apartment. I resisted and soon there was a scuffle in which the instruments began to play an unusually active role. I used the back of my cello to beat my sister over the head. Her head proved stronger than my cello, which flew to bits.

Several weeks after this incident (for which all three of us were duly punished), my mother and Oss' Oss'ch took me to the store of the lutenist Geissler and bought me a new instrument: a less crimson, larger, and far more expensive version of my first one.

By this time our family string ensemble had permanently absorbed the "Diaghilev brothers" outfit, and as a result of this merger we became an embryonic string orchestra. This was a case of the lean cows eating the fat ones without getting either fatter or better, for our own quartet could certainly not compare either in quality or in quantity with the Diaghilev ensemble to which, besides Pavlik, Alyosha, and their mother, belonged three other young men, cousins or friends of the Diaghilev family, and three of our mutual teachers.

Thus in the autumn of 1915 my sister, my brother, and I started to go every other Saturday afternoon to the Diaghilevs' for rehearsal. I remember how, instruments in hand, chaperoned by Miss Wiles, our English governess, the three of us would walk through the dark St. Petersburg dusk to the corner of Sadovaya and Karavannaya Street and there take the red and yellow streetcar marked Sennaya Ploshchad.

The streetcar was always hopelessly crowded and we would have to stand compressed among coats and furs for nearly an hour. We would get off at the far end of Sadovaya Street in a desolate neighborhood and trudge through the slush or snow for several blocks towards a barracklike compound of dun gray buildings. There, in the courtyard of one of those buildings in a small and crowded apartment, lived the Diaghilev family.

It consisted of Uncle Valya, or Valentin Pavlovitch Diaghilev, a short, stocky colonel with a large head and fleshy lips; his wife, the gentle and sickly Aunt Dasha; and their three sons: our confreres Pavlik and Alyosha and their ten-year-old brother Kolya, as yet untrained in the arts of chamber music.

The drawing room of the Diaghilev home was usually prepared in advance to receive us. The furniture had been moved against the walls; the chairs and stands were set up, and the music parts were arranged on the racks. We would unpack our instruments and tune up in the protracted, noisy way in which all amateurs, and especially children, prepare themselves for their instrumental battles. Then, after much sneezing, nose-blowing, and coughing, the practice would begin.

As I remember it now, our ensemble despite all its inadequacies was, on the whole, a hardworking and enthusiastic group of true music addicts, and I believe that much of my sustained love for chamber music stems from those early cello-beaten days of my adolescence.

Uncle Valya, although not a musician at all (he taught defensive engineering at the same military academy where the famous composer and less famous general, César Cui, taught the art of fortification), was our most fervent admirer. When we played, his round face glistened with pleasure. At times when we successfully overcame a particularly perilous passage (which to him must have been a kind of musical crossing of the Delaware) he would grunt and shout at us: "*Molodtzy rebyata!"* (Well done, boys!) as if we had finished scaling a mountain under heavy artillery fire.

At other times, usually before intermission, which consisted of tea, cherry jam, and anemic peppermint cookies — one of the driest and least delectable Russian specialties — he would turn to my mother and exclaim: "I don't see why Seryoja doesn't take them abroad. Even now, they aren't any worse than *his* famous artists. . . . Boys," he would add in a tone of a regimental commander addressing his troops, "just go on exercising and in a few years you'll be abroad. Seryoja will take you to play in Paris."

It must have been during this winter of rehearsals that I heard the name of Seryoja or Sergei Pavlovitch Diaghilev, the then already famous brother of Uncle Valya, for the first time.

Somewhere in the farthest recesses of my visual memory, where amidst penumbral silence live a few unconnected but brilliantly sunlit and strangely fascinating images of my childhood (as, for example, the oldest one: a child, a Me, squatting on a warm pebbled beach, supported by the soft arms of a synthetic nurse, part *nyanya*, part *Fräulein*, part *mademoiselle* — digging with a wormlike forefinger a tiny hole in the damp sand), I can observe a sequence of vivid events. I see myself, my cello in my left hand, pointing with my bow at a photograph which hung under an engraving of General Suvorov (an ancestral deity of the Diaghilevs) and asking a question (what question?).

The photograph represented a handsome young man in the uniform of the St. Petersburg University (in those days most Russian youths had to wear some kind of uniform). I distinctly remember the face of the young man (or did I learn to know it later when I saw this same — now famous — photograph in magazines and books?). It showed a pale and slightly puffy face, but its traits were so well designed (especially the high arches of the eyebrows) that it looked delicate and surprisingly tender. It had two striking features: slightly protruding and sensuous lips and a large head totally out of proportion to the rest of the body.

I could not say what led me to choose this particular photograph from among the varied portraits that lined the walls of the Diaghilev apartment, but I assume that someone must have told me that the pale-faced university student was Sergei Pavlovitch Diaghilev, the youthful patron and lover of the arts, who had been the aid to the Director of the Imperial Theaters and who after a short and tempestuous career had left Russia in a huff and was now in Paris presenting to the Western world, for the first time, examples of Russian achievements in music and painting, in opera and ballet.

From the earliest days of my childhood, until my mother succeeded in transforming at least one of her sons into a professional musician, the figure of Diaghilev fixed itself deeper and deeper in the realm of ambiguity. He seemed to me an impenetrable being, whose fame, a paradox in my child's conception of art, contained elements of princely splendor, the onus of sexual irregularities (of which I had, of course, no explicit suspicion at the time), and rumors of terrible irascibility and haughtiness. Every time his name was mentioned at his brother's house, or in the presence of my mother, which happened at least every other Saturday, such mixed feelings, part discomfort, part pride, were aroused among the ancestry, as we used to call our elders, that they were inevitably communicated to us, the children.

I remember asking Uncle Valya: "Does your brother Sergei compose?"

"Oh, just a little," he would answer, and add, "Rimsky-Korsakov, to whom he showed his compositions, told him that he should stop composing because he has no talent."

"Does he play an instrument?" I persisted.

"Yes, he plays the piano, but only a bit, and not at all well."

I also faintly remember an involved story about Diaghilev's unsuccessful attempts to become an opera singer. "He started to take lessons from Cotoni [the famous Italian voice teacher in St. Petersburg]," said Uncle Valya, "but after a few lessons he quarreled with the maestro and walked out in the middle of the lesson, and that was the end of that."

How difficult it was for me to understand how a man who did not compose, did not play, sing, paint or write, should become so famous. Organizing picture shows, directing a troupe of singers and dancers, and producing Russian ballet and opera abroad, hardly seemed enough to warrant such a dazzling reputation. I often asked myself, "What is his *real* relation to music, to painting, to the theater?" It took some fifteen years to understand, in part, the uniqueness and complexity of Diaghilev's genius.

"Look, look!" said my mother. "There he is." We were sitting in one of those middling Russian restaurants in Paris, which sprouted all over the world in the twenties, as a result of the "glorious" October Revolution. Opposite us, in another corner of the restaurant, a gloomy waiter in Russian haberdashery was serving a plate of extinct hors d'oeuvres to a big man with a monocle, and a flower in his buttonhole. A streak of white cut across his black hair from the right side

(65)

of his forehead, reaching the back of his large round head. He talked excitedly to the young man at his side.

I recognized him immediately. By 1924 I, as everyone else, knew the features of one of Europe's most famous men, and besides, I knew him instantly as the brother of Uncle Valya. Although the Colonel and Sergei Pavlovitch were only half brothers, the size and shape of their heads, the design of their eyebrows, and the form of their lips were so much alike that one could not miss the resemblance.

My mother, who had always been a parental field marshal, planning and shaping the destinies of her children, had been talking to me for some time about the usefulness and need of my meeting Diaghilev. Now she seemed elated at the sight of him sitting across the room. "Finish eating, and let's go to their table," she said. "I'll introduce you to him." But I prevailed upon her to wait until Diaghilev and his companion had finished their meal.

All through the rest of the lunch she kept looking at the Diaghilev table, trying to catch his eye, and when she finally succeeded, she beamed at him in such a pompous and obtrusive manner that he could not but smile back in that politely irritated way one smiles at people whose faces one has forgotten and who appear to be potential bores (later, I learned how terrified Diaghilev was of solicitous ballet mothers, who were constantly asking favors for their sons and daughters).

When they had finished eating and asked for their bill (which my mother duly observed), she pulled my sleeve and said, "Come, it's time now." While we struggled past the crowded tables, Diaghilev rose and started putting on an enormous fur-lined coat.

"*Sergei Pavlovitch, nye ouznayete?*" (Don't you recognize

me?), said my mother as we approached. He dropped his monocle and gazed at her with bewilderment, but before he could answer she introduced herself and, turning to me, added, "And this is my youngest son; the one who writes music."

"Ah, *chère amie*, so you are the mother of the second half of Valya's quartet," he said in a gay high-pitched voice. "Yes, of course I remember, we met in St. Petersburg." His face broke into a charming, benevolent smile. He put his monocle back in his eye and, taking my mother's hand, bent over and greeted her ceremoniously.

"What are you doing here?" he said. "Have you any news from Valya and Dasha? I haven't heard anything since 1921. You know, of course, that Pavlik and Alyosha have either been executed or were killed in the last months of the civil war. Valentin, I believe, is still in prison."

But my mother had no news and, seeing that he was about to leave, abruptly changed the subject. "Sergei Pavlovitch," she said, pointing at me, "I would like you to listen to his music. I want your opinion about it."

His face changed again and took on a bored expression and he mumbled hurriedly: "Yes, of course . . . sometime . . . gladly . . . but now I'm very busy . . . rehearsals . . . you know. Do give me a ring when you'll be back." And fixing me with an icy look, he added: "I'd love to listen to your music, *jeune homme*. I only regret it can't be now. *Au revoir, chère amie, je suis navré.*"

All this was said in such a cutting and final way that even my persistent mother did not dare pursue the matter or attempt to delay his exit.

Curiously enough this first, so painfully unsuccessful encounter gave me my most precise and vivid memory of the physical appearance of Diaghilev. I remember him as he stood near the exit flanked by his youthful companion (later I knew that it was Anton Dolin, the dancer), the fur-lined coat with its handsome beaver collar making his big, tall body and his tremendous head look even more majestic, more lordly, than it appeared in the pictures I had seen. I remember his tired, haughty look; his dark eyes and the even darker bags under them. I remember the sallow, wasted color of his heavy-set but well-kept face with the neatly trimmed mustache, the protruding lower jaw and the upturned upper lip revealing, when he smiled, a row of dubiously new teeth.

There was always a faint scent of violets around him (he used to chew tiny violet-scented candy) and it was during this meeting that I must have noticed it for the first time. But perhaps what my memory captured best that day was his voice, his unique manner of speaking. He spoke in a high-pitched, nasal, and capricious tone which seemed intended precisely for the phrase "*Au revoir, chère amie, je suis navré,*" and he dropped unaccented syllables of long Russian words as if he had chewed them up.

When I now recall this first meeting, and try to draw one whole from the many separate images, I see before me a Diaghilev unapproachable and haughty, imposing and slightly freakish in his appearance, charming and at the same time a little bit frightening, a little bit dangerous. And although successive years have modified much of this vision, a part remains; for, as often happens in first encounters, the intuitive powers of my mind, its perceptive antennae, were so sensitized that I was able to grasp certain traits of Diaghilev's character which later became the explicit basis of my understanding.

V

Diaghilev in Paris

B Y 1924 Diaghilev had been "in business" for about
twenty years with Paris as the center of his activity
since 1906. He had behind him a career of successes
which very few opera managers or ballet directors have ever
equaled.

Having come to France as a young Russian gentleman
whose name was totally unknown to the French public and
only barely heard of in Parisian art circles, he had taken upon
himself the task of acquainting Paris — and through Paris
Western Europe — with Russian achievements in the fields
of music, opera, and ballet.

At that time (as everybody knows but frequently neglects
to remember) Russian music and Russian art were practically
unknown in the Western world. Names that now populate
the musical Parnassus of the West and bring steady and sizable
dividends to the entertainment industry (from the New York
Philharmonic to the juke boxes), names like Rimsky-Korsakov, Borodin, Moussorgsky, and even Tchaikovsky, meant

very little to the average Parisian, Londoner, and New Yorker of 1900 or 1905.

True enough, a young Frenchman named Debussy brought back from Russia (where he had spent some time in the eighties as the tutor in the household of Tchaikovsky's "beloved friend," Mme. von Meck) a score he treasured more than any other in his life: *Boris Godunov* by Moussorgsky. True enough, Tchaikovsky traveled to the U.S.A. (much against his will) and conducted at the opening of Carnegie Hall. And Tchaikovsky's *Pathétique* was played by the New York Symphony Orchestra before it had even been played in Russia. But these were rare individual instances. They do not alter the fact in the slightest that before Diaghilev's arrival in Paris in 1906, Russian music, opera, and ballet were practically unknown in the West.

It is to Diaghilev and the signal success of the first three or four years of his artistic venture in Paris that we owe our first acquaintance, or rather our first real romance, with Russian art. Significantly enough right *after* Diaghilev's first seasons the first palatable translation of Russian classics appeared in French, English, and German.

In less than five years *Boris Godunov, Prince Igor,* and other Russian works, the singing of Chaliapin, the dancing of Pavlova, Karsavina, and Nijinsky, the playing and conducting of such men as Rimsky-Korsakov, Glazunov, Scriabin, and Rachmaninov, and above all the appearance of a first-rate young Russian composer, Igor Stravinsky, created such a sensation, aroused so much interest, that from then on Russian art became the fashion of the day for at least a decade, and its influence penetrated the whole artistic life of the Western world.

On the eve of the First World War the base of Diaghilev's enterprises had broadened considerably. Although primarily still concerned with the diffusion of Russian art, he had become a magnet for young musicians, painters, and poets of Western Europe. Starting with 1910–1911, names like Claude Debussy, Maurice Ravel, and Richard Strauss appeared on the programs of Diaghilev's Parisian seasons, and poets like Hugo von Hofmannsthal and Jean Cocteau wrote libretti for some of the new productions.

Diaghilev's Ballet and Opera Company in Paris rapidly evolved into a kind of workshop, a testing ground for new ideas, new techniques, and new styles. It maintained this position until Diaghilev's death in 1929. From 1917 on, it limited itself to the production of ballet and became the center of a very healthy and profoundly creative internationalism (or "rootless cosmopolitanism" as it is now termed on the other side of the Oder).

But Diaghilev's workshop also became the somewhat exotic meeting place for snobs from all over Europe and the fashionable set of Parisian society (as the society columnist of *Le Figaro* called it, *"ce bazar séduisant de sons et de couleurs éxotiques"*).

Diaghilev's attachment to and association with the snobbish elite has been a standing objection of his detractors. Even during his lifetime he was called a "lackey of fashion" and "an unscrupulous caterer to the corrupt tastes of a decadent uppercrust." On the surface these accusations appear valid. It is true that Diaghilev associated with and in a sense depended on the rich and fashionable in Parisian and other European society (which, by the way, has always included a few persons sincerely dedicated to the love of the arts). He *did* become a sort of "dictator of taste and fashion," and around his Ballet Company there existed an irritating kind of fashionable fervor.

For example, *every* work had to be stylish and startling, and a terrible fuss was made about what "should be done this year" and what "shouldn't," and about whose music one should like and whose one shouldn't. Besides, Diaghilev also sponsored the production of a few works whose slick appearance barely concealed an irretrievable lack of content; works that had no more meaning or value than the cover girl of last year's fashion magazine. (As a matter of fact he was the first to discard these works after their second or third performance.) But it is sufficient to glance at the long list of works of permanent value which were produced by the Ballet Russe, and at the quantity of serious and absolutely unfashionable experimentation which was carried on under Diaghilev's direction, to realize how partisan and unjust such accusations are.

It was Diaghilev and his collaborators that produced such masterpieces as Stravinsky's *Rites of Spring, Apollon,* Falla's *Three-cornered Hat,* Prokofiev's *Prodigal Son,* to mention but a few from the long list of first-class modern works. It was Diaghilev who first produced in Western Europe and adjusted to Western tastes most of the now famous classical ballets (*Les Sylphides, Le Spectre de la Rose, Swan Lake, Le Mariage d'Aurore*) which form the core of contemporary ballet companies, and on the artistic capital accumulated during the Diaghilev period exist the bleak Ballets Russes of today (those from over and around Monte Carlo).

Diaghilev's period created a truly novel style of classical dancing, now so often debased by a lack of new ideas and by the peripatetic wanderings of ballet companies on the leash of commercial managers.

But above all else, the profound and irreplaceable influence exercised by Diaghilev's Ballet Russe upon a whole artistic generation was dependent on the close association of his collaborators with the man himself, with his immense knowledge, his ability to inspire, to discriminate, to demand and expect the best of his artists. And more than this, the Ballet Russe was the center around which a great constellation of modern masters derived a precise if not easily definable direction. Such masters as Stravinsky, Satie, Ravel, Prokofiev, Falla, Picasso, Matisse, Derain, Braque, Fokine, Balanchine, Massine, and many, many others have given a distinct and brilliant visage to a great period in the history of Western art.

No, Diaghilev was never *at the mercy* of the fashionable set, and never really did he cater to their tastes. What he did was to *use* them; use their prestige, their money, their gossip, their vanity, their snobbishness, their elegance and depravity, for the benefit of his enterprise — which is to say, for the benefit of art.

He used them ably and subtly, often ruthlessly and cynically and at times quite unscrupulously. And they let themselves be done in gladly, for to them he was the *arbiter elegantiarum*, the great artistic leader, the focal point of fashion and good taste. They were led by his rough and somewhat erratic hand and liked it; and usually they accepted what he did without much question.

His real judges and critics always remained the artists themselves. They were his true friends and his true enemies, they were his collaborators and antagonists, and it is really to them and for them that he carried on his intense and exciting work.

It was for the artists of Paris and of all Europe, and ultimately for the artists of the whole world, that every spring (so often against the greatest financial odds) he offered a magnificent two or three weeks of what he believed was the best, the latest, the freshest, and the most daring in music, painting, and dancing. If sometimes he did not succeed, we must remember that we still thrive on and feed from the remains of his abundant and generous table.

When I finally succeeded in being presented to Diaghilev as a *composer* and not as Mama's son and an ephemeral relative (which as a matter of fact I have never been; my stepfather's first cousin married Diaghilev's half brother, as a result of which we called the Diaghilevs "uncle, aunt, and cousins") I was received with reserve, politeness, and marked skepticism.

This time the road that led me to Diaghilev was the usual road, the same one that composers have traveled for centuries. Mrs. B learned about me from Mr. A and passed me on to Mrs. C. Mrs. C (in my case a Mrs. D——, an active and kind lady, who for many years ran a music salon in Paris) invited me to a tea party and there introduced me to a Mr. D. Mr. D, who was about 25 per cent more influential than the original Mr. A, told Mr. E that I needed help (composers usually do, and I did rather sorely). Mr. E was an elderly gentleman, a hunchback and a relentless music lover. He had a niece, Mlle. F, a lady in her middle thirties, of Arab descent, who was endowed with an extraordinarily majestic bosom, a powerful voice, and a wooden leg. E bullied his niece into learning three of my songs. Several months later, in the winter of 1925–1926, she performed them at a hodgepodge concert of the SMI (Société Musicale Indépendante). This organization gave several concerts yearly, consisting of various first performances of unknown compositions.

The audience was bored and chatty, and applauded abstractedly the twenty-odd rubbery pieces of modern music which preceded my songs.

When the time came for Mlle. F and me to march on the stage, we got stuck in the narrow passage leading to the stage and I unwittingly tripped up my wooden-legged diva. Fortunately she did not fall on the floor, but once on the stage she turned to me and under her breath said that if it were not for the fact that we were *on* the stage, she would gladly break my neck. This naturally upset me at the very outset of our performance.

After the end of the first song, which was long and tedious, written to moldy words of the Persian poet Omar Khayyám (translated into the French from an English translation by FitzGerald), I saw Prokofiev, whom by that time (between A's and B's and C's), I had somewhere and somehow met, sitting right in the middle of the first row, smiling and quietly but insistently rubbing his chin, which in French means *Quelle barbe!* (What a bore!) I tried to look away, and in doing so caught a glimpse of another very familiar face, in the second row right behind Prokofiev. I recognized the bemonocled, bulldog countenance of Sergei Pavlovitch Diaghilev, who, as I later found out, was dragged in by Prokofiev to hear my music. This discovery made me so jittery that I lost control of myself and bungled the accompaniment to the remaining two songs.

Under those complex circumstances it was only natural that the concert ended as somewhat of a failure, but the reasons for the failure were not entirely musical. In those years I had been living in a small and cheap *pension de famille*, which was run by a Mme. de la Porte-Rose (Mrs. Pink Door). Naturally the inmates of the pension came in a body to the concert to listen to the first performance of their co-table-d'hôte-er's music. But what was worse: they put their funds together and sent me a large potted lilac bush with an enormous pink ribbon on each side of the pot. When the blooming bush arrived on the stage right after my last Oriental number, the inmates, occupying two middle rows of the tiny *Salle des Agriculteurs* (where chamber music was being dug up every night in the middle twenties), burst into thunderous applause.

Having, among other things, forgotten to send Mlle. F some flowers, and seeing that her temper was reaching a Vesuvian eruptive condition, I tore the card from one of the ribbons and lifting the bush from the ground sheepishly handed it to my Arab Polyhymnia. The cloudburst of applause ceased instantaneously. Mlle. F got "furiouser" than ever and the whole pension in a body stopped speaking to me for several weeks.

But after the concert, Prokofiev came backstage and said that Diaghilev was waiting in front in a taxi and wanted to see me.

When we came out I was surprised to find Diaghilev in a kind and considerate mood. He was sitting inside a red Renault taxicab, flanked by two of his minions, and he smiled at me as he said, "Your songs were not too bad, not as bad as you think, but tell me, where for heaven's sake did you find that female monster, and why don't you leave Omar Khayyám alone?"

He and Prokofiev laughed heartily at my story of the lilac

bush and before driving off Diaghilev said: "You must come
and show me your music. . . . I mean your *other* music, or
don't you have any?"

Thus I was spared any further wanderings through the
dreary alphabet of contacts which line the path of beginning
composers (some make it in four skips, others go twice from
A to Z before getting anywhere) and, at the insistence of
Prokofiev, went to see Diaghilev with my "other music" in
hand, at his residence in the Grand Hotel.

We were sitting around a broken-down upright piano in
what was probably one of the banquet rooms of the Grand
Hotel. Present besides Diaghilev and myself were Prokofiev;
Walter or Valichka Nouvel, Diaghilev's lifelong friend and
collaborator, a small wiry little man with glasses; Diaghilev's
secretary and official librettist, Boris Kochno; and the recently
"discovered" Serge Lifar. I had just finished playing my piano
sonata and followed it up by a few excerpts from a cantata
I had been working on for a year. After I had stopped, Diaghilev raised his eyebrows and said: *"Eh bien? . . . C'est
tout?"* I said yes, it was all I had to show.

Valichka, himself a composer of sorts, and Prokofiev started
to turn the pages of my score "fishing" for mistakes (which
is one of Prokofiev's favorite pastimes). While I was playing,
Diaghilev had been leaning on the silver top of his cane, but
as soon as I stopped he slumped back into his chair and sat
there with a bored and absent expression, saying absolutely
nothing.

After a while he turned to Boris Kochno and asked, "Boris,
when does the rehearsal start?"

"I think it is on already," answered Boris.

"Then let's go." He got up hurriedly and said to me, "Thank you, Nika, for playing your music . . . when you have written more, come and show it to me. *Au revoir*."

I felt discouraged and let down. "Oh, don't pay any attention," said Nouvel, after Diaghilev had left, "that is his usual manner. On the contrary, if he had disliked your music he would have been terribly polite to you and paid you all sorts of silly compliments" (which, of course, was an exaggeration). "Am I not right, Sergei Sergeiyevitch?" said he, turning to Prokofiev.

"Well . . . I think Nabokov should have waited to show him his cantata until he had finished it. This way it doesn't mean much," answered Prokofiev.

Curiously enough, it was this very same cantata which became my first and only Diaghilev commission. (It was produced in Paris and London as the ballet-oratorio *Ode* in 1928, barely a year before Diaghilev's death.) Thanks to it I finally learned to know Diaghilev, saw him at work, observed his ill and good humors, had long and unforgettable conversations with him, became for a while a part of his artistic enterprise, and grew to admire him as one of the few truly great men I have known in my life.

It is indeed very hard to describe the greatness of Diaghilev. What made him great? What was it that made him the center of attraction, the focal point and the symbol of a whole artistic movement?

His friends and admirers always had a hard time persuading outsiders of Diaghilev's greatness, while his detractors, both those who attacked his morals and those who repudiated him as an evil influence (as, for example, the wife of a famous dancer, or the present-day Soviet aestheticians), succeeded easily in depicting him as a kind of depraved monster totally lacking in any true value, residing in the "corruption of the tastes and ideas of his time" or abetting the "acceleration of the decadence of bourgeois art."

The reason for the attacks against him is simple: Diaghilev's faults and weaknesses were all too obvious and well publicized. His gifts, on the other hand, were not so easy to detect. They were of an intangible and a hybrid nature; only those who had known him well and had collaborated with him could appreciate the full measure of his extraordinary talents. To them, to his artist-collaborators, Diaghilev was primarily a shrewd and discerning critic, a friend and a patron. They knew that his faults were secondary and greatly overshadowed by his gifts. Very few of them were really concerned with the peculiarities of his private life — with the scandal attached to his over-public love affairs. Men like Stravinsky, Debussy, Falla, Prokofiev, Picasso, Balanchine, and many others regarded all this as none of their concern. They took Diaghilev as he was — a great man endowed with weaknesses and immense talents — and forgave him his fits of temper, his haughtiness, his intolerance to men and ideas, and his readiness to quarrel over a trifle at the slightest provocation. They knew that in him they had not only a friend but a unique judge and ally of their art. They knew that he was a fighter for the cause for which they stood. They gladly and enthusiastically worked for him, and to many of them this work at the Ballet Russe remains forever the most exciting adventure of their lives.

Diaghilev had never written a single piece of music, yet he knew more music, and in a way more *about* music, than many an erudite musician. Since his early youth he had developed a voracious appetite for all kinds of music — light and serious, old and new, romantic and classical. As a result of this profuse and polyglot diet he had accumulated a vast store of data (he knew a staggering number of compositions of various styles and historical periods) and had acquired a professional's grasp of musical techniques. What was quite exceptional in his knowledge was its intuitive, its immediate aspect; in other words, Diaghilev had the gift of detecting, after one incomplete and cursory hearing, the quality of a piece of music.

This gift, so simple and yet so infinitely rare, made it possible for him not only to determine the intrinsic value of a new work of art, but also to relate it to other works and thus to evaluate the extent and the quality of artistic discovery present in it. Diaghilev's personal taste (and he had a definite taste for the monumental works of late Romanticism) never interfered with his interest in music of all periods and styles. He was always on the lookout for something new — a new work, a new composer, a forgotten score by an eighteenth-century master dug up from some dusty French or Italian library. In this search it was his primary concern to determine right away whether the music was good or bad, and hence whether it was suitable for use by his company. The astonishing thing, of course, was not that he asked himself those obvious questions ("Is this good? Can I use it?") but that after hearing a new work only once he was able to make up his mind unhesitatingly and appraise the specific qualities or defects of the work with masterful precision.

I remember arguing with him about my own ballet after I had played it for him for the first time in the midsummer of 1927. The subject of the ballet was taken from a poem — an

(80)

"Ode to the Majesty of God on the Occasion of the Appearance of the Great Northern Lights" — by the eighteenth-century court poet and physicist Mikhail Lomonosov (referred to in Russia as the "father of Russian science"). It is a famous example of Russian didactic and "encyclopedist" court poetry inspired by French and German examples. Written in the flamboyant and archaic Russian of that period, it represents a thinly veiled allegory on the enthronement of Empress Elizabeth — the Aurora Borealis of the poem.

Diaghilev, of course, knew the poem and liked its oddly baroque metaphors and its resonant language (although normally he was quite indifferent to poetry); but chiefly what pleased him in it was its reference to Empress Elizabeth. According to a rumor (which he may well have started himself) Diaghilev was, on his mother's side, a descendant of Elizabeth — a great-great-grandson of one of the Empress's natural children. He was flattered by this illicit relationship to the Imperial house of Russia; it made him a direct descendant of Peter the Great, and gave him a kind of "morganatic" halo. There was, in effect, a slight physical resemblance between him and the puffy-faced daughter of Russia's first Emperor. As for Diaghilev's character, what could be more like that of the dynamic, quick-tempered, and despotic Peter?

But quite apart from this, Diaghilev liked the whole idea of a Russian "period piece." Boris Kochno and I concocted a two-act ballet libretto, the second act of which was supposed to represent the "Feast of the Northern Lights" — in other words, the coronation of Empress Elizabeth. I had written a short introduction to this second act; Diaghilev wanted a longer and more "ample" one. He objected to my introduction and called it a "meager pot of Conservatory porridge."

I felt hurt, and defended myself by saying that the way I had written it was right, that it was a good fugato in the style of the eighteenth-century French overtures. Diaghilev smiled mockingly and replied, "Maybe, *mon cher*, it *is* a fugato, maybe even a fugue, but it certainly isn't any good. You know I don't really care whether you write a fugue or a fugato, a French or a Brazilian overture; what matters is that you write good music." He concluded, "This goes equally for Richard Strauss and the waltz-Strauss, for Bach and Offenbach. It is a simple but a very golden rule."

On another occasion I remember him discussing a new ballet score by a young protégé of Prokofiev. Prokofiev, Diaghilev, and I had just finished listening to it in the rehearsal room of the Monte Carlo Theater. Diaghilev was in one of his most explosive moods; he ranted and shouted at Prokofiev, "How can you like this, Seryoja? Don't you see that it's drivel? It's stupid, it's dull; worse than that, it's eely and slimy; it sounds like Arensky. There is only one page of it that seems acceptable. Here, give it to me." He took the score out of Prokofiev's hands and started to turn the pages angrily. "Here it is. You see . . . this melody. It's the only piece of light in this dusty piece; but unfortunately it only lasts five measures."

Many years later Prokofiev and I played that piece over again; it was utterly inept and dull. When we came to the page which Diaghilev had pointed out, Prokofiev muttered, "Damn it, Diaghilev was right. This is certainly very 'dusty' stuff."

His knowledge of music of the past was both broad and detailed. One would ask him a question about a composer, say for example about Méhul, a forgotten French opera composer and contemporary of Beethoven. "Oh yes," he would answer, "Méhul was a first-rate opera composer, but he did not know how to handle big scenes (as did Mozart). Nevertheless he had an excellent melodic gift and his operas are full of attractive arias." And then he would quote an aria from a totally obsolete opera by Méhul and maybe even sing a tune from it. "You know," he would say, "Méhul wrote at least twenty operas; one of them, *The Epicure*, was, I believe, written in collaboration with Cherubini. He also wrote several ballets which contain superb examples of classical dance music." He would conclude sententiously, "Why don't you look at Méhul's music? Some of it is in music stores but most of it is at the Bibliothèque de l'Opéra."

I remember the way he listened to a new work, always earnest and respectful. If he liked it, he would discuss it page by page and point by point, and make you play sections of it over and over again. If, on the contrary, he did not like the piece, his face would immediately take on a sour and worn expression; he would look bored and sleepy. As soon as the composer had finished playing Diaghilev would thank him with that icy, exaggerated politeness with which French courtiers brushed off importune commoners, and leave the room without saying another word. Sometimes he would interrupt in the middle of the performance and shout, "Wait, wait! Play that over again!" And having heard it once more, he would say, "This comes straight from the tenor aria of X's opera." If you disagreed, or said that you did not know the opera or the particular passage, he would order one of his minions to get the score, and then he would make you play the aria. He was usually correct; the measures he had pointed out and the aria would bear a noticeable resemblance.

His remarks about music were always clever and penetrating and revealed a profound understanding of the particular characteristics of certain composers. I once arrived unnoticed in the apartment of Missia Sert (the wife of the Spanish painter) and found Diaghilev at the piano, with his glasses on, painstakingly deciphering the *Davidsbuendler* by Schumann. When I asked him why he was playing this particular piece, he said, "I always wonder what makes Schumann's music hold together. Look how he repeats and repeats the same phrase," and he started playing the third part of the piece very slowly and clumsily. "And yet, you see, it is never dull. It is filled with a peculiar kind of lyric nervousness. Of course, I am only talking about his piano music; his symphonies are at times terribly dull and boringly repetitious." He looked at the music again and added pensively, "Schumann's music is best when it is played in a very small room with no people in it at all, when it is just between you and him."

It sometimes seemed to outsiders (and even to some of his collaborators) that Diaghilev's taste for music was too eclectic, too lacking the indispensable "positive partisanship" to make a real dent in the annals of music history. It is true that the musical inventory of his ballet company for the twenty-five years of its existence represents a remarkable mélange. It is a hodgepodge of styles, of musical traditions, and of aesthetic attitudes. In it, you jump from the musical perfection of Stravinsky's *Les Noces* or his *Apollon Musagète* down to the grotesque inanities of a score like *Cleopatra* (an Egyptian extravaganza of about 1909–1910 made up of stale tidbits from the music of eight-odd Russian composers) and from the admirable pages of Prokofiev's moving and lyrical *Prodigal Son* (a work so unjustly forgotten by present-day ballet companies) to the banalities of Georges Auric's *Pastorale*, probably the silliest ballet produced in the twenties by the Diaghilev company.

This lack of a specific line in the choice of music was quite disconcerting at times and made one think of Diaghilev as a kind of director of a musical zoo, as someone who wanted to own every species of animal under the sun from the platypuses to the pandas. Yet Diaghilev had a very definite personal musical taste, different from, if not contrary to, those of some of his younger contemporaries.

During one of my last conversations with him in the winter of 1928, he vituperated against the light and easy *musiquette* of young Parisian composers. "All this fake little music," he shouted, "doesn't mean anything at all. I've had enough of it. *Merci!* I can have a ballet by X every year, and next year it will be as stale as an old *blin* [Russian pancake]. Only the snobs and *les limités* [a favorite expression of his] like that. No, no. There is no one now who has *le souffle*, *l'élan* of Wagner, of Tchaikovsky, or of Verdi — those were real, full-blooded, great men."

"But Sergei Pavlovitch," I asked, "what about Stravinsky and Prokofiev? And what about your new 'discovery' Paul Hindemith?" (He had just commissioned Hindemith to write him a ballet.) "Hindemith . . . yes, probably he is good . . . perhaps very good . . . but we'll hear him and judge him next year."

To Diaghilev a contemporary composer existed only by virtue of his having written music for the Ballet Russe. His peculiar egocentricity and megalomania made it seem that a composer who had not written for his ballet company was a composer whom he did not want, either because he considered his music bad or because the composer had not come around to be given a commission. Even if this were not the case, he wanted it always to appear as if he had "discovered" his composer, which in the case of Hindemith (who by then was already a famous man) seemed particularly comical.

"And Stravinsky?" I asked again.

"Stravinsky is a great composer . . . the greatest of our time; even the stupid British critics have learned their lesson and know that Stravinsky's greatness is a settled issue. To me, however, his best works are those of the beginning, those which he wrote before *Pulcinella;* I mean *Petroushka, Le Sacre, Les Noces.* This does not imply that I don't admire *Oedipus Rex* and adore *Apollon;* both are classically beautiful and technically perfect. Who else can write like that nowadays? But you see — " He stopped abruptly and changed the subject. "You were speaking about Prokofiev?" he said in the tone of a man who is answering his own question. "Yes, of course, his *Prodigal Son* is in its way a masterpiece; it has a lyrical quality new to Prokofiev, and what is particularly good about it is that it is his own and no one else's." He underscored each word by knocking the floor with his cane. "Have you heard it?" he continued. "Did he play it for you?" And without waiting for an answer he said, "You know, Prokofiev is furious at me for wanting to cut a few pages. Did he talk to you about it?"

Few things seemed to give Diaghilev more pleasure than to make cuts in a new score; it was a kind of delightful ritual with him, and he surrounded the "operation" with exquisite politeness and princely formalities. Usually he would invite the composer to lunch; then, using all his charms, he would tell the story of how he cut eighteen pages of Rimsky-Korsakov's *Schéhérazade* and *x* pages of Richard Strauss's *Joseph's Legend*. After reciting a list of equally famous musical appendectomies, he would finally come to the point. "Don't you think," he would say, "that the second act of your ballet is too long? Don't you think it should be cut?" And before you could say yes or no, one of his helpers would hand him the score and he would point to the spot he wanted cut, saying, "I looked at it carefully yesterday and I think the cuts should be made here and here . . . don't you agree?" All the questions in this speech were purely rhetorical and, together with the unusually sumptuous lunch, provided the preparatory anesthetic before the inevitable operation.

"Few composers today," Diaghilev went on, "have Prokofiev's gift of inventing personal melodies, and even fewer have a genuine flair for a fresh use of simple tonal harmonies. You know, Prokofiev has never fallen prey to all such rubbish as atonality, polytonality, and '*tout ce fatras de l'Europe Centrale*.' He is much too talented and much too genuine for that. He doesn't need to hide behind inane theories and absurd noises. His nostrils are big and open; he is not afraid of breathing fresh air wherever he finds it. He does not have to sit in cluttered rooms and invent theories. But even in Prokofiev's music there is a lack. I don't know what it is, but something is incomplete . . . some measure of greatness is absent."

Yet it appears that during the last days of Diaghilev's life, in a hotel room on the Lido, he returned completely to the musical passions of his adolescence. He spoke with excitement and fervor of the greatness of Wagner's *Parsifal* and *Tristan* and the majestic splendor of Beethoven's *Ninth Symphony*, and he hummed the familiar tunes of his beloved *Pathétique* of Tchaikovsky.

(87)

These, then, were the true musical loves of Diaghilev throughout his life. He certainly admired and loved classical music, but his unswerving devotion went to the massive works of the masters of the Romantic period; it was their art which had formed his taste and in many ways molded his approach to music.

The Gare de Lyon was crowded and noisy when in the early days of April, 1928, I boarded a second-class car of the 21.30 o'clock *rapide* — "Paris, Lyon, Marseille, Vintimille." I always enjoyed the immutable ritual of French departures. The bustle and confusion, the fight for porters and window seats, the squeeze through the narrow corridors of railroad cars, and the little game of deception (in which I always participated) which most French travelers play when they try to prevent a late-comer from getting a seat by covering all the available space with their own bags, bundles, coats, and lunch boxes. Russians and Frenchmen have at least these things in common: both are addicts of the *pagaille* (mess and bustle) of departures, and both travel with thousands of pieces of the most eccentric-looking luggage.

But on that damp and foggy April evening of 1928 the whole ritual of departure seemed doubly pleasant to me. I was traveling second class (instead of third), I was going to Monte Carlo at Diaghilev's invitation and expense, and I was going to work there on the production of my ballet — my first commission, my first important work. "Tomorrow," I said to myself, "I shall be walking on the warm, crackling gravel of the *jetée du Casino,* the promontory behind the Casino, looking at the gentle carpet of the Mediterranean and the equally gentle silky sky. Tomorrow will begin my collaboration with the most famous artistic enterprise of Europe."

I felt exhilarated and proud. I thought of the talks and discussions I would have with Diaghilev and his associates, with the many composers, painters, poets, and choreographers who would be in Monte Carlo at the time Diaghilev was preparing his new productions for the coming Parisian season. I thought of working with Léonide Massine and Pavel Tchelitchev, whom Diaghilev had selected to do the choreography and the *décor* for my ballet; I imagined the excitement of rehearsals, the pleasure of seeing my composition take shape and form.

Valichka Nouvel had come to the station to see me off. He gave me the name of the hotel I was to go to in Monte Carlo and handed me a check — the second installment of my ballet commission. "Don't you get in a row with him," he said with a smile, "and come back in despair. It has happened, you know." But I was not going to let it happen; I was sure that everything was going to work out well and that by the time I returned to Paris the ballet would be spick-and-span for its Parisian *première*.

V I
Ode

NIGHT TRIPS in French coaches both soft and hard are
a delight to those who love comedy; there is always
a funny face or a comic scene in store for you. But
to those whose legs are long, whose nostrils are sensitive, and
who believe in the use of soap and water they represent an
acute and intense discomfort. The average Gallic stature is
no more than five and a half feet; hence the benches in French
railroad cars are painfully low and narrow. As soon as the
train pulls out of the station, one of your seven-odd companions — so often a determined-looking mother of a brood
of fidgety children — is sure to shut the door and close the
window (leaving a tiny crack to let in the soot). Next, everyone settles down to a highly odoriferous meal: hard-boiled
eggs halved with a penknife (sulphur); tough, granite-
textured sausages (garlic); vicious Roquefort cheese (feet).
Red wine spills on the floor, and oranges squirt in your eye.
Occasionally a Vichy bottle of lukewarm coffee is passed
down the line (to all except the one-year-old). This adds the
chicory touch to the intense and aggressive bouquet. In the

early hours of the morning, when the priest starts mumbling his prayers (there is always a priest in a second-class French compartment), the ladies, obeying ancient custom, take out small bottles of Eau de Cologne, pour a few drops of it on a piece of cotton, and rub their necks, foreheads, ears, cheeks, and chins with it until the cotton gets black and the faces start to glisten like Wagnerian armor; *la toilette* is completed.

These night-long ordeals in French trains have always had a peculiar kind of charm and attraction for me. Is it because all things in France — things you sense, you perceive and observe — are so infinitely human that being together for one night with seven strangers in a compartment is enough to establish a secret, an unconscious and yet an intensely personal bond between you? I have never felt this way in German, Polish or even Austrian compartments.

Or is it because one can go out of the stuffy compartment and be alone, and smoke, and open the window and stare into the dark nothingness and daydream, and remember, and give oneself completely to that peculiar longing, that melancholy reverie that comes to one in the midst of a lonely night, on top of mountains or in the emptiness of the steppe? Or is it perhaps the strange companionship of sleepers? By midnight the compartment is silent, dimly lit by the shaded blue light bulb. The faces of the sleepers become like early cubist paintings: trembling, fragile rhomboids of gray and brown, deep-shaded triangles of mauve and ocher. Some of the heads bend backwards, their mouths half-open, their skin drawn like parchment. Others nod and sway to the rhythm of the tracks, their heads like ripe fruit ready to fall from the stem of their necks.

There was always a deathlike fascination in those silent night scenes between Paris and Marseille.

But this time my thoughts were far from melancholic. I was not observant, nor was I amused by my companions; in fact, I was oblivious of their presence. Standing at the open window in the corridor, I thought about my *Ode* and what would happen to it in the immediate future. I was happy that my part of the work was done. I had written and orchestrated all the music, and now, I thought, I should be able to sit back and watch how Massine's choreography would grow from my music, and see what kind of visual interpretation Tchelitchev would give to the somewhat stilted, old-fashioned ballet story.

There had been a considerable amount of internecine argument about the whole project. Boris Kochno, the librettist, was eager to have Balanchine do the choreography of *Ode;* I myself was inclined in favor of Balanchine. But I had little to say about these matters; I was a newcomer to the Ballet — one of Diaghilev's perennial "foundlings" — and I knew that Balanchine had already been engaged to do the choreography of Stravinsky's new ballet, *Apollon Musagète.* Thus, very much against the wishes of Kochno, *Ode* was delegated to Léonide Massine. Fortunately Massine liked my music at once and seemed to understand its somewhat sentimental, lyrical spirit.

As for Diaghilev, although he liked the whole pageant side of *Ode,* he seemed at first not entirely convinced by my music. He was also worried about the excessive expense of its production; my score required not only a very large orchestra but also an equally large choir and two solo singers besides. When, during the previous summer, I had played him

(92)

the piece in its entirety, Diaghilev had seemed enthusiastic about most of it. But certain sections he did not like at all; he found them weak and incompatible with the rest of the music, and wanted me to change them by writing three new dance movements which would be incorporated into the second act.

It goes without saying that I made all the changes and wrote the new pieces as quickly as possible; they were ready by October 1927. Still, Diaghilev would not commit himself definitely to the production of *Ode* and would not sign a contract with me.

I have the impression that it was Stravinsky's liking my music that decided Diaghilev in favor of *Ode*, for it was shortly after my first encounter with Stravinsky, when I played him my piece, that Diaghilev told Valichka Nouvel to draw up a contract. The meeting with Stravinsky was of course arranged by Diaghilev and was part of a carefully planned and slightly feudal ritual. I felt that I was following in the footprints of many a young composer whom Diaghilev had "discovered" before me. First the "foundling" was tested for several months by the closest members of His Majesty's Household; these included Roger Desormière, the eminent French conductor, Boris Kochno, Valichka Nouvel. Then, after he had passed the preliminary "household test," he was to meet the great ones: Stravinsky, Picasso. Next came the influential friends and patrons of Diaghilev: Princess de Polignac (Singer sewing machines), Lord Rothermere (*Daily Mail*), Coco Chanel (*haute couture*), and Missia Sert, the clever, warm, and attractive friend of Diaghilev and of two generations of famous painters and musicians. The ritual also included drawing up a list of people the foundling was advised not to see. At my time this list was headed by Jean

(93)

Cocteau, with whom Diaghilev had quarreled, and Ida Rubinstein, the dancer who with the help of Mr. Guinness's money
(stout) was starting a rival ballet season at the Paris Opera.

Only after these preliminaries had taken place would the
foundling's name be announced to the outer world. He would
be presented as a new Diaghilev find, a young man who
merited extraordinary attention by virtue of the great future
Diaghilev held in store for him. And then the ballyhoo would
begin; the foundling would immediately become the object of
everybody's attention, he would have five lunches and three
dinners per day to choose from, his name and photographs
would appear in magazines and newspapers. He would be
asked on every possible and impossible occasion to play his
ballet music, and Parisian artistic circles would heatedly discuss the merits and defects of his score.

A further element complicated the plans for *Ode's* production. For many years Diaghilev wanted to have a ballet by the
painter Pavel Tchelitchev, then still a very young man, who
was having an extraordinarily brilliant success. Diaghilev had
seen his work in the early twenties in the Berlin theaters and
admired it very much. He urged him to come to Paris and
work for him. But Tchelitchev, one of the few authentic
geniuses of the theater, had at that time turned his back on it
and was deeply involved in painting pictures. Like many imaginative and highly gifted artists, he believed that the theater
only detracted the painter from the real problems of his art.
He preferred to abandon the more lucrative and successful
career of a theatrical designer and give himself completely to
his own painting.

Finally, in the fall of 1927, Diaghilev and Kochno persuaded
Tchelitchev to design the sets and costumes for my *Ode*. In

the meantime, through pictorial experimentation, Tchelitchev had discovered a completely new approach to the problem of stage design — an approach in which light and motion played an unusually important part; moreover, he was preoccupied by such problems as the relation between pragmatic experience (with its crude and clumsy logic perceived and transmitted to the mind by the senses) and the experience of the unreal (or suprareal) with all its hidden, illogical laws and its "journey to the end of the night."

Tchelitchev was engaged in the surrealist experimentation of the period and, although he did not belong to the official group of surrealist painters (Dali, Max Ernst, Tanguy, and the others), by 1927–1928 he was regarded, for all intents and purposes, as one of the founders of that broad and fashionable trend. On the other hand, he was one of the first to express in his art that new lyricism of the late twenties, a lyricism restrained in its mode of expression and untarnished by grandiloquence. Later this became broadly popularized by the work of the late Christian Bérard and a few other European and American painters, but Tchelitchev was one of its initiators.

But all these pictorial experiments of Tchelitchev and all his new ideas about stage design had little in common with the whole project of the ballet *Ode*, with my music, and with the didactic-allegorical ballet story cooked up by Boris Kochno. Tchelitchev seemed to like my music, but not the story; or at least he did not like the allegorical allusions to Diaghilev's "Imperial great-great-grandmother." He thought that the story had nothing to do with what my music was "really" expressing and that the whole piece should be treated as a surrealist vision of a mysterious phenomenon of nature,

(95)

the Aurora Borealis. Thus from the outset there were three different and in a way irreconcilable points of view involved in the *Ode* project. First there was Diaghilev's notion about a grand Elizabethan period piece, a tribute to the epoch of the great Russian court-poet Lomonosov; second there was Tchelitchev's view of *Ode* as a modern surrealist experiment; and third there was my music, which did not fit into either of the first two categories.

The music of *Ode* was essentially tender, gentle, and lyrical, and in its lyricism it was kin to the music of Russian composers like Glinka, Dargomijsky, and Tchaikovsky, especially to their songs. To me those composers were always particularly attractive when they wrote their charming little vocal pieces, mixtures of the nineteenth-century German lied and the Franco-Italian *romance sentimentale*. In these pieces they blended in a superb way the native Russian melodic inflections (those tiny melismata by which one can recognize any piece of nineteenth-century Russian music) with the warm and suave beauty of the Italian vocal line.

Few people abroad know these pieces, the songs of Gurilev, Alyabiev, Glinka, Dargomijsky, all of them nineteenth-century composers of the Russo-Italian school. Even Tchaikovsky's songs are little known abroad, with the exception of *None but the Lonely Heart*. Yet to me these Russian songs were a treasure of intimate lyrical invention which reflected so well the moods and longings of that period — one to which I felt myself closely attached and which I have never ceased to admire. During my childhood many of these lieder became daily companions of my life; we hummed them in the woods and in the streets, we sang them alone and in chorus, we played them on our instruments and listened to them in concert recitals. By the time I left Russia in 1920 I knew hundreds of them and cherished them with the nostalgic devotion with which one cherishes tender memories and lost hopes. They became somehow like human beings, like those lost companions of my Russian adolescence whose features remain fixed and vivid in my memory and who have become the inexorable symbols of exile.

In *Ode* I attempted to evolve a larger choral piece from these small lieder forms and to write a full-scale oratorio based on a series of such pieces bound together by a common idea and a common lyrical mood. Thus what excited me in composing *Ode* was the attempt to produce a first Russian oratorio, formally and stylistically tied to the grand tradition of the Russo-Italian school. Few of these Russian composers had written oratorios, and those they did write were usually *des pièces d'occasion* patterned after the Western oratorio form and of little musical value. Before the Soviet composers embarked on their series of moth-eaten "Songs to Stalin," Russian music had few examples of aboriginal oratorios.

But besides this "Russian nostalgia," *Ode* had of course a French, a Parisian side (at least I hoped it had). In 1923 I got acquainted and quickly fell in love with the music of Erik Satie and what Erik Satie represented (and still represents) to many modern composers. His "pupils" and ardent admirers, Henri Sauguet (one of the leading French composers), Roger Desormière, and later his great friend Darius Milhaud, led me into the orbit of the extraordinary halo of new ideas, actions and reactions, agonisms and antagonisms, which had emanated from Satie during his lifetime and which were still burning bright in 1927, two years after his death. In another place I will give my due to Satie, I will speak more fully of what he taught me and, I believe, several generations of Western composers (some of them are only now "discovering" Satie; others are in dire need of such a discovery). Here I will only say that it is Satie's art and his ideas that taught me how to exercise a restraint and an economy of means in my own music, to prefer brevity and conciseness of musical discourse to the ramblings and rumblings of impressionism; how to limit myself to the absolutely indispensable, the minimum needed for an adequate formulation of a musical sentence and reject the camouflage of floridity and grandiloquence. Above all, Satie's art taught me that one should not be ashamed of being simple, intimate, "puerile," and even naïve to the point of appearing childish (provided one remains sincere), and to regard all these qualities as virtues rather than as vices.

Some of these virtues, I hopefully believed, I had incorporated into my *Ode*, and as a result the music of *Ode* had indeed very little to do with an Imperial Russian pageant or with the presentation of "nature's mysteries" expressed in modern surrealist terms.

On the train from Paris to Monte Carlo the city of Lyon usually appears out of the darkness at the deadest spot of the night. As soon as the train stops at the Lyon station the corridors are crowded with scores of Moroccan and Algerian soldiers carrying large sacks and with metal flasks and cups hanging low on their leather belts. When the train starts moving, this metal dishware provides a rattling accompaniment to the guttural and rapid conversations maintained in an Arabic dialect. From Vienne on, the train starts playing hide-and-seek with the Rhone River, whose bed gets shallower and shallower as the train moves southward. Dawn overtakes the *rapide* somewhere between Valence and Montélimar (at the latter point the travelers are awakened by the strident shouts of the vendors of "*Nougat de Montélimar! Nougat de Montélimar!*"). By the time the train reaches Avignon and is ready to descend into the delta of the Rhone, the sky is all blue, the sun is all gold and the naked and wintry landscape has changed to a sea of white and mauve, dusty green and bright, bright yellow. The sweet fragrance of the Provençal spring bursts through the cracks of the windows into the tired train and chases away the last remnants of yesterday's cheese, wine, garlic and sulphurous eggs.

That time, in April 1928, standing in the corridor of the time-worn French car amidst the African *poilus,* most of whom had dosed off in limp poses, I again felt this fragrance pressing against me, invading me from inside, choking me with irrepressible laughter and making the tears come to my eyes; I felt the intense joy that comes from the sight, the feel, the smell of all this mellowness, this beautiful sunlit abandon, this miracle of color and shape which the Provence has always been to me and will always be to all men of the North.

As the train puffed along the Mediterranean and from Cannes on started making its brief courtesy calls at every little resort town on the "azured coast," my excitement mounted. "Who is going to meet me at the station?" I was asking myself. "Boris Kochno, Massine, Lifar? Or maybe even . . . Diaghilev himself? Will there be a rehearsal today? Will I have supper with Diaghilev?"

Approaching Monte Carlo from Nice, the train started to worm its way past Cap Ferrat and around the Bay of Villefranche. Then, after one last smoke-filled tunnel, it slowed down, and suddenly on the south side of the tracks appeared the life-size version of the famed colored "scenic" postcard — the Monaco peninsula topped by its medieval castle, with a cluster of quaint houses descending to the marcelled, lapis lazuli harbor.

We pulled into the Gare de Monaco et Monte Carlo, and leaning out the window I looked anxiously for a familiar face. But among the gay crowd of welcomers in exaggerated resort-type clothes there was no one I knew. I pushed to the exit — my good humor somewhat impaired by the absence of a welcoming committee — and the story of Erik Satie's arrival at Monte Carlo came to my mind.

Satie, who hated all forms of travel (he used to walk back and forth to Paris from the suburbs of Argenteuil, where he lived, rather than take the streetcar), was persuaded by his disciples, the composers Darius Milhaud, Georges Auric, and Francis Poulenc, to come and see the *premières* of their first ballets in Monte Carlo in the spring of 1924. Auric and Poulenc were supposed to meet Satie at the station, but something went wrong; when his train pulled in, there was no one on the platform. Infuriated, Satie went to the other side of the tracks and took the next train back to Paris.

But I did not follow in Satie's footsteps. Instead, I took a cab and went to the Hotel Excelsior; there another disappointment awaited me — no reservations, no rooms. The hotel was full. Feeling hurt and neglected, I telephoned Diaghilev's hotel. No one there. "*Monsieur de Diaghilev est sorti. . . . Il est au Théâtre du Casino.*"

"*Et Kochno?*"

"*Sorti aussi.*"

"*Lifar . . . ?*"

"*. . . avec Monsieur de Diaghilev.*"

I called the theater and tried to get Grigoriev, the company's stage manager, on the telephone. Finally, after a great deal of waiting, Grigoriev's assistant came to the phone, yawned, and said in a surly voice, "They are all on the *plateau* . . . rehearsing. I can't disturb them." When I told him who I was, and what I wanted, he woke up a bit and mumbled, "Oh yes, I heard something about it from Grigoriev . . . they couldn't get you a room at the Excelsior. . . . He said something about another hotel, but I've forgotten the name." Just as I was on the point of hanging up, he suddenly turned cheerful and shouted into the receiver, "Wait a minute! I remember . . . it is the Hôtel de la Côte d'Azur. Go there and ask for a room reserved by Grigoriev."

The cab drove uphill through the hotel-infested area of central Monte Carlo and stopped in front of an old-fashioned, pinkish building. Yes, there was a room for me, even with a *salle de bain*. There was also a garbled message from Grigoriev — "parts of Mr. N. have arrived, would he come and collect them . . ." I climbed five stories to the room and found it of strange oblong proportions, but bright, large, and clean. The floor was covered with the familiar brown tiling of old Southern French houses, and its tiny balcony faced south, disclosing a panorama of Monte Carlo, Monaco, and the blue, blue sea. But what grafted itself most strongly on my memory was the budding wisteria vine on the ramp of the balcony, which later, a week before I left Monte Carlo, fell into rich violet bloom and scented the room day and night, bringing back tender memories of other Southern springs — springs in the Crimea, in Sebastopol, in Yalta, and all along the northern shores of the black Scythian sea.

I washed, ate a sandwich at the corner *buvette*, and walked down to the Casino. The Théâtre du Casino, or rather "His Princely Highness's Opera and Ballet Theater of Monaco and Monte Carlo," is conveniently located in the same building as the Casino, behind the gambling rooms of this gambling citadel of Europe. It is an exemplary monument of Edwardian tastes and habits; gilded, plushed and cherubed, it has the same coziness and comfort as the *salons privés* of certain Parisian restaurants (those where the French senators of the Third Republic took their lady friends for intense gastronomic exercises) or as the luxurious house of pleasure on the rue Chabannais — the recreation center of so much nineteenth-century royalty. By the time I and a group of American friends visited its exquisite salons and bedrooms after a lunch in a celebrated bistro next door, it was still working on a twenty-four-hour schedule and had acquired international fame as a showplace of illicit nineteenth-century love habits and had thus become a unique *Monument Historique* of France.

"Ces dames du Chabannais" who showed us around the place drew our attention to a number of peculiar objects and apparatus used by certain famous customers of the two last centuries. Two of them seemed particularly attractive; one was a grandiose and terribly complicated love chair allegedly built (or, as the ladies said, "prepared") in the 1880's for the Prince of Wales. "But," they said, "it was used mostly by the robust and impatient Russian Grand Dukes." The other was a daintily carved bed in the form of a swan which, with its inlay of silk-covered, Valencienne fringed eiderdowns, had been "prepared" for Louis the Second, the mad King of Bavaria (a token of highly refined *délicatesse de sentiment* on the part of the management, revealing its profound appre-

ciation of the King's taste for Wagner's swan-ridden *Lohen-grin*). I do not know what happened to the Chabannais since the "new love" laws of the Fourth Republic have prohibited all houses of pleasure but I sincerely hope that these two objects will take (if they have not already taken) their place of honor near the chastity belt and the flagellants' whip in the penumbral silence of the Cluny Museum.

Behind the Théâtre, with its well-proportioned stage, its large and deep orchestra pit seating about eighty musicians, its rows of broad damask-covered armchairs encased in a semicircle of parterre boxes (the theater has no balcony, and seats only about 250 to 300 people) are several large rehearsal rooms and storage halls for scenery and costumes. Still further lies *la jetée du Casino* overlooking the Bay of Monaco. From it, the desperate losers of the Casino put a stop to their ill luck (at the rate of two or three a year) by leaping several hundred feet down to the tracks of the Paris–Lyon–Méditerranée railroad.

After a little questioning and searching I made my way through the labyrinth of gambling rooms, corridors, and rehearsal halls and stepped onto the stage. Diaghilev was sitting on the left side near an upright piano, his back turned to the empty theater. On a chair next to him sat a funny-looking man with thick glasses, in disorderly dress and endowed with a crooked goatee. Behind him, leaning against the piano, stood the massive figure of André Derain, who, hearing me creep up, turned his head, smiled, and signaled me to come and stand near him. So did Rika, the dark-haired, beaked lady at the piano, whom I had met before in Paris and who inevitably reminded me of an ingrown toenail. But she beckoned me with her head, her hands being occupied with the wide, difficult

(103)

chords of a piece unfamiliar to me but which I easily guessed to be Stravinsky's *Apollon*.

Diaghilev couldn't see me; his back was turned, and he seemed absorbed by what was going on on the stage. There, in the center of it, a group of three ballerinas were clustered around and over a male dancer. The ballerinas were Tchernicheva, Doubrovskaya, and Nikitina, three of the best prima ballerinas of the company. The male dancer was Serge Lifar. That group's pose had since become famous in the annals of choreographic classicism: Lifar knelt between the three ballerinas, who were in an arabesque figure; each had one leg up in the air; their bodies dipped forward and their necks stretched upward so that they looked like three drinking swans whose precarious balance was maintained by a trembling hand firmly clutching Lifar's shoulder. In front of the group stood its inventor, the slight and incredibly young-looking George Balanchine, Diaghilev's recent discovery, his new choreographic genius.

"Did you see Boris and Alexandrina?" whispered Derain in my ear. "They went to meet you just half an hour ago."

I said that I had not, and was about to ask the identity of the man who was sitting next to the *patron*, when Diaghilev turned around, evidently to say something to Derain. He saw me, and an ironic smile came over his face. He said in a teasing voice, "Ah, Nika, why are you so late? Where have you been all these weeks? Everybody has been waiting for you to start working," and without waiting for an answer he pointed at Balanchine and said to Derain, "What he is doing is magnificent. It is pure classicism, such as we have not seen since Petipas." Then he turned his back on us again and continued watching the dancers on the stage.

While Diaghilev was talking to me the little man with the beard had also turned around and was examining me intently. Then, without apparent reason, he let out a bleating giggle. I was startled, and felt abused at Diaghilev's rude reception. It was unfair and unjust; no one had told me that "everybody" was waiting for me in Monte Carlo to start working. On the contrary, I had been waiting for more than two weeks to hear from Diaghilev. But no news had come. Finally it had been Valichka Nouvel who decided to send me off, to get the tickets and put me on the train. As I stood there getting madder every minute and somehow centering my anger on the silly-looking giggler, Derain bent over and murmured, "*Ne vous en faites pas*, he is in a bad humor. Something went wrong between him and this man," and he nodded in the direction of the giggler. "Besides, he has been very ill-tempered lately."

"Who is that man?" I finally asked Derain.

"Oh, he's quite a character. He's Bauchant, the painter. He's doing the sets for Stravinsky's *Apollon*."

Soon the rehearsal came to an end. Diaghilev got up and told me to come along with him to the hotel. "Ah, haven't you met?" he said, as Bauchant was trying to introduce himself. "This is the young composer of *Ode*, Nicolas Nabokov, and this is Monsieur Bauchant."

"Bauchant-*jeune*," corrected the odd little man. "I am pleased to meet you, and please forgive me for laughing at you a moment ago," he continued in a jolly patter, "but you see, your face . . . it looked so funny when he" — he pointed at Diaghilev — "greeted you. Besides, you know, his annoyance was really addressed to me. I irritate him. . . . Isn't it funny?" And the man bleated again. Diaghilev chuckled, but I didn't find it funny at all; I wanted to shake off the importune gabbler.

As we came out into the sunshine of the *jetée* and started walking towards the Hôtel de Paris, Diaghilev said, "Come on, Nika, I have to talk to you." He began by telling me that *Ode* was getting to be a problem, that no one really cared about it, and that everything was being mishandled from the very start. "Boris doesn't know what he wants to do with it and Massine knows even less. As for Tchelitchev, I can't make head or tail of his experiments, but I do know one thing: they have nothing to do with the original conception of *Ode*." He reproached me for showing no interest in my own work: "You should be here all the time and you shouldn't think that once the music is written your task is over." He said that the only reason he decided to do *Ode* against his better judgment was that Seryoja Lifar liked the music and wanted to have a second ballet for the coming season — "to satisfy his enormous vanity. . . . You know Seryoja hasn't a brain in his head, and the fact that he likes your music is therefore nothing to boast about."

While he was talking he got consistently more irritated and the adjectives he used became more abusive and unprintable. Finally, as we reached the doors of the Hôtel de Paris, he said in his most exasperated tone, "If all of you continue to be indolent and lazy nothing will come of your *Ode*. I can't do anything for you. I simply *won't*. I will wash my hands of the whole business like *Pontius Pilatus*. You had better go and find *ces coureurs*, Boris and Seryoja, and start working at once." Then, abruptly, he turned his back on me and went to the door. But before he started revolving he shouted at me once more, "If all of you finally decide to start working, don't pull the cart in three different directions. It will get stuck and *I'm* not going to help you pull it out of *your* mud!" And with a curt "*Au revoir*, I'll see you tomorrow," he disappeared in the door.

It was only natural that, as a result of this monologue (it was the first time I had seen Diaghilev in a tantrum), my first evening in Monte Carlo, in the bosom of the "greatest artistic enterprise in Europe," was a melancholic flop. If it had not been for the warmth of Alexandrina's and Boris's welcome (I met them in front of the Casino right after my encounter with the vituperative *patron*, as they were returning from their abortive attempt to meet me) and the charm of Derain's conversation, I would perhaps have taken Satie's way out of what appeared to be a hopeless mess.

Alexandrina, Boris, and I dined at the tiny restaurant of the Hôtel Belli, which lay beyond and below the *jetée du Casino* on the other side of the railroad tracks. Hôtel Belli was Alexandrina's residence; hence it was the center of all ballet gossip, for Alexandrina, Diaghilev's female secretary, was an incessant collector of gossip, rumor, and love lore about everyone connected with the ballet. She was a warm-hearted, gentle, and unattractive Russian girl in her early thirties, who had at one time aspired to become a ballerina. Several years after Diaghilev's death she went on a pilgrimage to Jerusalem and remained there as a sister in the Russian Orthodox nunnery. Alexandrina was as completely muddleheaded as she was devoted to "the cause" of the Ballet Russe, and she lived in constant dread of Diaghilev, who teased her at every opportunity.

Boris and Derain tried to cheer me up. They said that Diaghilev's *sortie* was just another one of those flurries of ill-temper which had become routine that spring. Boris assured me that everything was working out well, that Tchelitchev had invented marvelous sets for *Ode*, that Massine liked them and was anxiously waiting for me to start working. "Of course," he said, "all will be ready by the time we leave Monte Carlo. Diaghilev is angry because he doesn't seem to grasp *our* ideas about the ballet. He isn't sore at you or at me but really at himself."

And Derain explained that Diaghilev had had a bad cold, "and you know how he reacts to diseases. A sniffle to him is like pneumonia."

"Besides," said Derain, "this morning he had a run-in with *ce drôle de type* — Bauchant. Alexandrina will tell you all about it. You know, Bauchant walks around the place with his pockets bulging with photographs of his own work. If someone says something in his presence about a cucumber, Bauchant immediately pulls out a photo and says, 'Here's a still life of mine with a cucumber. Won't you buy it?' If someone says that he's going to America on the *Lafayette* Bauchant pulls out of his pocket a 'Lafayette meets Washington.' "

I had heard very little about Bauchant before coming to Monte Carlo; I knew that he was one of the several "modern primitives" whom the Parisian picture dealers had been tracking down after Vollard had made so much money with Henri Rousseau's pictures. I was amused to hear Derain's and Alexandrina's story about the bleating giggler who had made me so mad.

It appeared that on the morning of my arrival Diaghilev walked into the studio where Bauchant was supposed to be painting the sets for *Apollon*. He found Bauchant putting the last touches on a still life of his own. Looking about, Diaghilev saw a few other "contraband" still lifes. There wasn't a trace of *Apollon* around. Bauchant proudly acknowledged having painted the pictures since his arrival two weeks previously in Monte Carlo. Diaghilev got furious; he informed M. Bauchant-*jeune* that he had not been invited to Monte Carlo to paint pictures but to prepare sets; that he, Diaghilev, was not a provider of free studios for M. Bauchant-*jeune* and that M. Bauchant-*jeune* had better stop painting his silly pictures immediately. Bauchant listened carefully to this diatribe and riposted with indignation. He said that his pictures weren't silly at all and that if M. de Diaghilev did not understand them it was the fault of that "*saltimbanque*" Picasso and all the Russian barbarians around M. de Diaghilev in his ballet troupe. Naturally *they* could not like his pictures, because one had to understand the whole tradition of French painting to understand what he, Bauchant, did. But the *real* public enjoyed his pictures and they sold very well. . . .

We laughed at the story and at many similar stories and gossip of which Alexandrina's memory was a storehouse. By the time the dinner was over I felt happy and gay. But I was sleepy after my night in the train and the inhospitable reception in Monte Carlo; yet it was long past midnight when Derain finally walked me to my hotel, past the last open cafés near the Casino and through the silent, steep streets of the upper reaches of the town. "Cheer up," he said as we parted, "*ça va marcher.*"

The routine took shape the day after my arrival and for the rest of the four weeks I spent in Monte Carlo my life was regulated and my time "normalized." I worked with Massine from ten to one and sometimes again from three to six. I thumped out over and over again parts of my ballet on the horrible little upright pianos which populated all the rehearsal halls of the Monte Carlo Theater. Massine was composing the choreography while I played and in the intervals between parts and sections he would ask me to explain the construction of the music. "Where does this melody end? What instruments hold this chord? Is it correct for me to assume that this is one long phrase?" Then he would take profuse notes in an imposing leather-bound scrapbook which he carried around.

Contrary to what I expected, Massine, who in those years was unusually stern and taciturn, was voluble with me and at moments even gay and smiling. On the whole our work progressed without a hitch. There was, however, an inherent anomaly in our collaboration. It came from the fact that I had no experience whatsoever in working with a choreographer. To judge choreography "in the rough" under the drab conditions of a rehearsal hall requires experience and imagination. I felt unable to make any valid judgment about what Massine was doing, for what I saw were disconnected bits of a whole which my imagination could not put together. Besides this, there was something disconcerting in having to repeat the same measures at the piano hundreds of times and see the same steps accompany them. At times I felt so completely dulled at the end of a rehearsal that I did not know whether I liked it or not. How could I know whether it was good or bad? I did what many young composers do with their first stage works — I acquiesced to almost everything Massine did with my music. After all, he was a famous choreographer who had been "in the business" for more than a decade while I was a complete newcomer. When he would ask me, "Do you like this?" or "Do you think this fits your music?" I would usually reply in the affirmative.

Not until the broad outlines of the choreographic whole began to be recognizable (which happened about the third week of my stay at Monte Carlo) did it dawn on me that with the exception of two or three lovely lyrical dances, Massine's choreography, although probably very good in itself, had very little to do with my music and with the whole eminently romantic mood of *Ode*. Naturally enough it was Diaghilev who made me aware of it. He came one day to a morning rehearsal to watch Massine compose a dance for Serge Lifar. He sat through half of it, his eyes closed, his head drooping. Then, without saying a word, he got up and left. Astonished, Massine and I looked at each other. Massine laughed and said, "I don't see the point of his coming to rehearsals when he does nothing but sleep through them."

But Diaghilev had not slept. Quite the contrary, he was very much awake and equally upset. At eleven o'clock that evening I was hauled out of bed by a messenger who told me that Diaghilev was waiting for me in the rehearsal room, that he wanted to see Lifar's dance again, and that several messengers had been dispatched all over Monte Carlo to search for Lifar and the librettist Kochno, who were both somewhere at a party.

When I arrived at the theater Diaghilev was all alone in the tiny office next to the rehearsal room. In the hall I found his old "uncle" Pavel Iegórovitch Koribút-Koubítovitch, who really was his cousin and whose face was as funny as his name. He was sitting in a large club chair, his fat body slumped, his bearded, Pan-like features contorted with worry. "Be careful," he whispered, "he is in a rage."

But Diaghilev, though angry, was calm with me and looked genuinely concerned. He said that what he had seen that morning was "utter rubbish," that Massine did not understand anything at all — "not the first thing" — about *Ode*. He said that he wanted to see it *now*, again, without Massine's presence (Diaghilev and Massine had been at odds since the early twenties), but that the *coureurs* (meaning Lifar and Kochno) could not be found at that hour. He then gave me a long instructive talk about how he imagined the choreography of my ballet. He saw it as romantic, lyrical, with rich, suave, and soft movements, "rather of a Fokinesque" character. "At moments it should be pure pageantry — festive, glittering and brilliant. At other moments it should be tender, mysterious and gentle. What Massine is doing is modern cold angular stuff that has nothing to do with your music."

We waited for more than an hour, but neither Lifar nor Kochno appeared. Finally he said in a sad, tired way, "Nika, you had better go back to bed. I'm sorry about your ballet, but what can I do? Nobody seems willing to co-operate."

The evenings at Monte Carlo were usually spent at the Ballet or at the Opera and it was there that I had the opportunity to see much of Diaghilev's repertoire that was not always played during the ballet seasons of the company in the capital cities. Some of this repertoire was totally obsolete — when Diaghilev revived it, he himself could not look at it without laughing; but some of it, on the other hand, was as fresh as when it had been first produced. Thus by seeing his old productions anew Diaghilev was able to choose a few of them, freshen them up, and prepare them for an eventual revival in Paris.

This was one of the unique advantages which Diaghilev's contract with the Casino gave him over the many "latter-day" itinerant ballet companies in America. Monte Carlo was for Diaghilev and his ballet company a workshop, a storehouse, a resort; it was endowed with one of the most perfect theaters to work in and, besides, it was placed in one of the most beautiful spots in the world. The American ballet companies suffer in many ways from the absence of such places as Monte Carlo (and the generous contract with the Casino authorities). They have never had such convenient conditions and opportunities for the creation of new works as had the Diaghilev Company during the ten-odd years of its existence.

April 1928 was not the first time I had visited Monte Carlo. I had been there quite often before on short visits from Nice, where my mother used to live in the middle twenties. Yet it is only when one stays in Monte Carlo for some time that the unreality, the grotesqueness, the absurdity of this "jewel of the French Riviera," as the proud Monegasques call their native city, become apparent.

Monte Carlo is a set of clichés. It is the happy ending of Hollywood movies, the night clubs' hula-hula and the enticing language of American bra advertising translated into all levels of life. The scenery: a colored postal card (or as Virgil Thomson once remarked, "expensive real estate"). The houses: an anticipation of juke boxes. The lawns: Italian opera (the outdoor Swiss or Scotch peasant scene). The people: character extras from Warner Brothers.

There is always a creature in white lace and organdy, bedecked like a Christmas tree with all the tinsel of Victorian jewelry. Her worn, spaniel face is covered with many coats of powder and rouge while the blue under her eyes, the pencil marks on her brows, and the mascara on her remaining ten and a half eyelashes are hopelessly asymmetrical. She is led on a leash by a microscopic ball of fuzzy wool, and she clutches in her hand a twenty-franc note which the bored croupier has slipped under the table into the palm of her hand.

These women are known as the *rentières du Casino* and next to the professional pickpockets they are the management's worst pests. When one of them gets a seat at the roulette table she begins by watching her neighbors' games. Only after long delay, prodded by fairly brutal hints of bystanders and sometimes even by the croupier, she starts playing her "system." The game for her is a passionless ritual which she performs with the calm of a mortician embalming a body. Her face never changes, her eyes are fixed on her green square (her "dozen") of the gambling carpet. She starts with the smallest stake (two francs, in my time), then she doubles it and continues her geometric progression to the second power, always returning her bet to the same square, the same dozen. If after three or four bets her dozen turns up, she wins, and having collected her sixteen or thirty-two francs she goes home as deliberately as she came. If after three bets the little black ball does not fall upon one of the numbers of her dozen, she plays the system once more, but never more than twice the same day.

The whole procedure takes up a full afternoon. This is why the croupiers of Monte Carlo prefer to pay the *rentières* twenty francs in advance (many *rentières* settle for ten, provided it is on a regular "salary" basis) to prevent them from hogging a seat at the roulette table.

Then there are the *desperados*, those "addicts of gambling," straight from the Musée Grévin or Madame Tussaud's collection of wax vices. They sun themselves on the benches in front of the Casino and look like villains from an 1880 melodrama. Their faces under their worn boaters are sanguine and apoplectic, their eyes embedded in deep blue-green caverns, their chapped lips and false teeth scarcely concealed by tarblack mustachios. At any moment they appear ready to rush into the gambling room, unscrew their right arms, squeeze out their glass eyes, and hand them to the croupier for a last two bits' worth of chips.

In all this unreality, this smörgåsbord of clichés and monstrosities, only two things seemed real to me: first, the lovely old city of Monaco, the hinterland of the principality, where in dignified Mediterranean poverty and apparent happiness lived some 20,000 Monegasques — loyal subjects of His Highness Prince Louis of Monaco and Monte Carlo; and second, the Ballet Russe of Diaghilev. It is significant that Diaghilev never went into the gambling rooms and that gambling rarely attracted the members of the company. When I told Diaghilev that I wanted to see the gambling, he tried to discourage me: "Why? It's boring and flat. I hate it," and he added with a satisfied smile, "Mine is a different kind of gambling."

Somehow the hothouse atmosphere of the gambling rooms never reached Diaghilev's hard-working organization, and this is perhaps why even an old, stuffy ballet like the *Russian Fairy Tales*, when performed by Diaghilev's troupe in Monte Carlo, seemed real and fresh in comparison with the activities in the rest of the Casino.

The troupe at that time was a splendid, well-functioning organization. Most of its dancers, including its *corps de ballet*, were young, competent, and devoted. It had two permanent choreographers, Léonide Massine and George Balanchine. It also contained in its repertoire the best inventions of Michel Fokine and Bronislava Nijinska, composed over a period of some twenty to twenty-four years. Some of the first dancers and guest dancers of the ballet, notably Tamara Karsavina and Olga Spessivtzeva, were certainly the best dancers of the period, and the younger dancers like Doubrovskaya, Nem-chinova, Nikitina, Danilova, and Markova (who then was only in her teens) were, I believe, of a class far superior to the average prima ballerinas of the present-day Monte Carlist Russian ballets. The male complement was equally good. Of course, it did not have Nijinsky, but there were old-timers like Massine, Voizikovsky, Idzikovsky, and the younger men like George Balanchine and Lifar.

But besides all this, what made the Diaghilev workshop at Monte Carlo such a creative, lively enterprise was the many artists around Diaghilev and his company, working at new productions or helping revive old ones. In the month that I was in Monte Carlo, Diaghilev and the ballet company received a stream of visitors from all over Europe, from Paris, from London, from Italy and Germany.

Prokofiev drove up one day with Vladimir Dukelsky (Vernon Duke) on the last leg of a gastronomic tour of France. Prokofiev stayed a few days and discussed with Diaghilev plans for a new ballet (which was to become *The Prodigal Son* — Diaghilev's last production during the season of 1929). Matisse came from his Provençal villa to look over his sets for Stravinsky's *The Song of the Nightingale*, which had been revived with a magnificent new choreography by Balanchine. Vittorio Rieti came to visit us all from his family's home at San Remo and also to talk to Diaghilev about a new ballet. Stravinsky's sons came from Nice, where the family lived at that time. Fedya and Svyetik Stravinsky visited the rehearsals of *Apollon* and we went for long walks around Monte Carlo. (One of the walks I loved best was through the hanging gardens high above the city, a masterpiece of unreal landscaping full of fantasy and of the strangest botanical freaks.)

Then, too, there were the "rich" visitors, Diaghilev's financial patron saints (or as the composer Henri Sauguet called them, *les poires de Diaghilev* — Diaghilev's suckers): the Otto Kahns and the Aga Khans, the Rothermeres and the Rothschilds, the Poliakovs and the Polignacs.

Diaghilev's mood was not always so harsh and unmanageable as it was the day I arrived in Monte Carlo. Quite the contrary, his fits of bad temper were brief. Normally he was gay and pleasant. The day following my arrival I met him on the street in his elegant black coat and white silk scarf (he was always well dressed and his clothes looked fresh and neat). He greeted me with smiles, as if nothing had happened the day before, and scolded me paternally for not wearing a coat.

"This climate is treacherous, you know. It only looks warm."

He invited me for a cup of chocolate at a *confiserie*. We had chocolate and pastries and talked about dieting.

"This is my way to treat diabetes," he said laughingly and pointed to the empty plate in front of him.

Balanchine, Kochno, Derain, and a number of dancers patronized a small Italian restaurant, Giardino's, on top of the hill in the upper reaches of Monte Carlo. There we used to have noisy, gay lunch parties. Diaghilev liked to join us and bring his visitors from outside. When he came, the bill was paid for all of us. Lunch then became a sumptuous two-hour affair with many courses and much wine, although Diaghilev himself never drank either wine or liquor. Only the funny "uncle" Koribút-Koubítovitch, the perennial butt of Diaghilev's teasing, would not be permitted to choose his own meal.

"You better bring him a small portion of . . . *boeuf bouilli*," Diaghilev would say to the waiter. "That's the best thing for him, he is too fat anyhow."

The "uncle," both a gourmand and a gourmet, would shiver with indignation and shout, "I don't want *boeuf bouilli*. I won't eat *boeuf bouilli*," his voice trembling and tearful.

Diaghilev would roar back, "Pavka! Eat your *boeuf bouilli*. The doctor says it's good for you."

Finally he would give in and meekly eat his boiled beef.

As I had hoped before coming to Monte Carlo, I saw Diaghilev almost every day. Between rehearsals and during meals I often had long, exciting conversations with him. Egged on by my questions, he would reminisce about his early years in Paris, about the first performances of *Boris Godunov*, *The Rites of Spring*, or the first concerts of Russian music which he organized in Paris in 1906. He would talk about the great dancers of that period — Nijinsky, Bolm, Fokine, Karsavina, Pavlova, and Trefilova.

In the excited voice of someone who remembers something particularly dear to him, he would speak of his work in Russia, of the foundation of the art magazine *Mir Iskousstva* in 1903, with a group of friends, chiefly Alexander Benois and Léon Bakst, and of the famous art exhibitions organized by this group, which were like a breath of air in the stale atmosphere of St. Petersburg.

He spoke of his work in the Imperial Theaters and described the stuffy, intrigue-ridden atmosphere of its management. ("I couldn't stand it. It was like living in a morgue.") But chiefly he liked to speak about the great exhibition of Russian portraits which he organized in 1904 in St. Petersburg, for which he collected some 3000 masterpieces of Russian portraiture of the eighteenth and nineteenth centuries. It was a tremendous job of artistic research which involved thousands of miles of travel. Diaghilev was a pioneer in this research and did it almost singlehanded. His stories about how he discovered lost treasures of Russian art in palaces and country estates of Imperial Russia were full of adventure and were told with an explorer's sense of observation.

"I would get a hint," he would say, "by reading in somebody's memoirs or letters that the painter Borovikovsky [one of the two finest Russian portrait painters of the eighteenth century] spent a month at the Volga estate of Prince O. That would start me on one of my hunting trips. First I would visit the direct heirs of the eighteenth-century seigneur, who were so often half-witted in matters of art, and I would try to find out from them whether there was a Borovikovsky portrait in the family. If no one knew, I would take a trip to the Volga estate of Prince O. There I would turn the place upside down until I found what I was looking for.

"You can't imagine how many of these palatial estates, these jewels of eighteenth-century architecture, were falling in ruins at that time. Their gardens were unkept forests, the floors of their empty salons and ballrooms were littered with fallen plaster. The pigeons and swallows had made their nests in the galleries. Everything was death, decay, the collapse of a lost civilization. It was there that I felt how inevitable the revolution was, how the pygmy heirs of a great period were not able to keep the past alive or cope with the ideas of the present, the new trends, the new desires and the new needs of our time. Sometimes in an obscure and dilapidated country estate in a remote government beyond the Volga I would be greeted by a whole row of superb portraits painted by some anonymous serf. They would be hanging, cracked, dirty, their varnish gone, in the drab office of the administration building. No one would know or care who painted the pictures, when they were painted, and whom they represented."

But of course the main topic of conversation was music. I asked Diaghilev a thousand questions about composers he had known, operas he had heard, and music he had liked most during his life. His answers were whole stories, amusing anecdotes full of charm and witty details.

He told me how one day on the streets of Paris he met Gounod, who had just become rich after the success of his *Faust*. Diaghilev asked him about his plans for the coming season.

"I'm preparing my old opera *Adam and Eve* for production," said Gounod.

"And may I ask, *cher Maître*, in what costumes the opera will be played?" asked Diaghilev. "In . . . fig leaves?"

"*Tiens, je n'ai pas pensé à ce détail*," said the embarrassed composer.

Or how he saw Debussy emerge from the train at the Moscow station with enormous mittens on his hands despite pleasantly warm fall weather ("That barbarous climate of Russia!") and how he took Debussy to a Moscow night club to listen to the singing of gypsies and how Debussy could not tear himself away from the songs, "those languorous gypsy melodies," and how, in his last letter to Diaghilev, in the spring of 1917, he spoke of them with tenderness and longing.

Diaghilev spoke of Rimsky-Korsakov and Tchaikovsky, of Richard Strauss and Scriabin, of the musical taste of the late Pope Leo XIII (who loved Viennese waltzes and would dance them in his private salons with the Cardinal Secretary of State to the accompaniment at the piano of Abbé Liszt) and of the lack of musical taste of the whole Romanov dynasty, and of course of his contemporaries, his collaborators, Stravinsky, Ravel, Prokofiev, Satie, and many, many others.

After the night of crisis when he had wanted Lifar to show him Massine's utter rubbish again, Diaghilev never brought up the subject of Ode, nor did he ever seem interested in Massine's choreography. He stopped coming to the rehearsals to see what Massine was doing and when I would mention my ballet in his presence he would keep silent or change the subject.

Only once did he acknowledge the fact that the project of Ode still existed, when he asked me to bring over the score and the orchestra parts and told me that the orchestra had twenty minutes of free time and could read it through. I tried to dissuade him by saying that Ode was forty minutes long and that, besides, the parts were still full of mistakes. He replied that Scotto, the conductor, would read it through in a fast tempo, and as for the mistakes, they were not his concern but my "funeral."

That orchestral "reading" became one of the worst musical tortures of my life. Scotto had never seen the score before and was beating the beat in double time as best he could.

The parts, because of my inexperience and the copyist's carelessness, were a sea of mistakes. Diaghilev and I sat in the front row in the dark hall. Every time I wanted to jump up from my seat, the heavy hand of Diaghilev kept me back.

"Don't disturb them. They haven't much time."

The piece we heard was a mass of inchoate rumblings and noises reminiscent of the tuning-up period of a school orchestra. At the end, I felt limp and beaten. Diaghilev turned to me and said, "You like *that?*" and without waiting for an answer got up and went out of the theater.

At the same time I began to realize that Diaghilev's earlier prediction was coming true: the "cart" named *Ode*, or what there was of the cart, was definitely being pulled in several directions. I did not know, nor did I see, what Tchelitchev was doing (he was guarding his work from any intrusions on my part), nor did I quite like or understand what Massine was doing with the choreography.

Only once was I permitted to attend the ritual of Tchelitchev's experiments — he needed me to time some film shots he had made for *Ode*. I saw some extraordinary pictures of young men wearing fencing masks and tights, diving in slow motion through what seemed to me to be water. I could not understand what this had to do with my ballet but I was told by Kochno (Tchelitchev wouldn't speak to me), who had, in default of Diaghilev, somehow assumed the responsibilities for the production of *Ode*, that this represented "the element of water."

Much as I respected the "element," I still could not understand what connection it had with my music and the whole conception of the ballet. All in all, when I left Monte Carlo the prospects of a successful production of *Ode* seemed hopelessly remote. Massine's choreography was only half finished, Tchelitchev's *décor* was a total mystery to me, but I knew that it was largely still in an experimental state and that Diaghilev had had several tantrums about it. Worst of all, so far as I was concerned, was my own orchestration (my first attempt at writing for a large orchestra), which in part did not "sound" at all and needed intense overhauling. I left Monte Carlo filled with apprehension and dark forebodings.

I arrived in Paris only a few weeks before the ballet season was to open. The press had already begun to print anticipatory articles about the new productions. I was pestered by so many social calls, interviews, and dinner engagements that my friends Sauguet and Desormière decided to hide me in the apartment of a musical friend, where I could quietly re-orchestrate certain sections of *Ode* and correct its shamelessly incorrect orchestral parts.

Finally, ten days before the start of the season, Diaghilev and the ballet troupe arrived in Paris and the rehearsals began again. Massine and I renewed our long morning sessions and in a few days he completed the choreography. But the Tchelitchev side of the project, so far as I knew, remained on the same equivocal plane as ever. This time I was shown some of the drawings of Tchelitchev for the sets and costumes. Kochno even showed me a complete little model of the stage, the opening scene of the ballet. Here, for the first time, I began to realize what Tchelitchev wanted to achieve.

The model was all in blue tulle which when lit with a tiny flashlight became strangely alive and acquired an extraordinary mysterious and ephemeral beauty. I understood also that Tchelitchev's whole project depended on many intangibles.

It required mechanical perfection and virtuosity in the use of lighting equipment (then still in its infancy), perfect coordination between light and movement, between camera (for many of the "light sets" were achieved by means of motion-picture projections) and music, between choreography and the changes of scenic effects.

To all this, up to the last two or three days before the first performance of *Ode*, Diaghilev remained completely indifferent. It seemed as though he had abandoned all of us to disaster.

On the morning of the second of June, 1928, the telephone rang very early despite the warning I had left the night before at the hotel desk not to disturb me until 10 A.M. I had returned late that night after a full day of rehearsals, an orchestral reading of *Ode*, and a grueling choral rehearsal. Diaghilev had come to the latter with Prokofiev but had left brusquely long before it ended.

At first I thought of letting the telephone exhaust itself, but the ringing persisted. I picked up the receiver and was about to bark a curse into it when to my utter surprise I heard the voice of Diaghilev barking at me.

"Why don't you answer your phone? Why are you sleeping when you should be in the theater? Get up and get dressed right away and come to the theater. This mess can't go on any longer. I have ordered a full stage rehearsal at ten, a full orchestra rehearsal at two, a full chorus rehearsal at five, and all evening we will rehearse the lights." He hung up on me just as abruptly as he had started shouting.

From that moment on and for the next three days, until the

last curtain had fallen on a highly successful performance of *Ode*, I lived in a state of frenzy. Like everyone else connected with the production, I worked day and night, in an agony of sleeplessness and exhilaration the like of which I never experienced before or since.

Diaghilev had taken over in the fullest sense. From then on *he* gave the orders, *he* made the decisions and assumed the responsibilities. He was everywhere, his energy was limitless. He ran to the prefect of police to have him overrule the fire department's decision forbidding the use of neon lights on stage, which Tchelitchev wanted to use in the last scene of the ballet (neon lights were a novelty at the time and were considered unsafe). He supervised the dyeing, cutting, and sewing of costumes. He was present at every orchestra and choral rehearsal and made the conductor, Desormière, the soloists, and the chorus repeat sections of the music over and over again until they blended well with the choreographic motions and the light-play of Tchelitchev's scenery. He encouraged the leisurely and sluggish stagehands of the Théâtre Sarah Bernhardt by bribes and flattery. He helped all of us paint the props and the scenery.

But above all else he spent two whole nights directing the complicated lighting rehearsals, shouting at Tchelitchev and at his technical aids when the delicate lighting machinery went wrong, at me when my piano playing slackened and became uneven, and at Lifar when his steps ceased following the rhythm of the music and the changes of lighting.

On June 6, the day of the opening, I was exhausted, stunned and shaking with the kind of precarious excitement which comes after long exertion and sleepless travel. But when, fifteen minutes before the curtain went up, I saw Diaghilev come in through the backstage door, in full dress, bemonocled, his famous rose pearl shining on a snow-white shirt, I knew that it had been only thanks to this man's incredible drive and energy that *Ode* had been pieced together and that the curtain would be able to rise at all.

Until the last minute I had been painting the scenery, and had seen Diaghilev leave the theater an hour before the performance was to begin. He had looked worn, gray, and sallow as he crossed the stage; his face was covered with a two-day beard. Now he was his usual self again, calm, confident, and resplendent.

He stopped in front of me and told me to go into the theater. I mumbled something to the effect that I hoped all would go well and that the performance would be a success.

"Well . . ." answered Diaghilev nonchalantly, his face changing to a charming affectionate smile, "it's up to you," and he opened his arms and moved them backwards in the suave and deliberate gesture of virtuoso conductors, by which in apparent modesty they raise the orchestra musicians to their feet and make them acknowledge the public's applause.

I saw Diaghilev for the last time in July 1929, a little more than a year after *Ode's* first performance. We met briefly at the Baden-Baden music festival. He was in the company of his old friend the Princesse de Polignac (Paris's greatest music patron of the time) and his new youthful "composer-foundling," the birdlike and brittle Igor Markevitch.

Diaghilev did not look well; his face was puffy with the glazed, yellow quality of diabetics, during or after an attack. He had come to Baden-Baden to hear a new work of Hindemith, "his" new composer-collaborator. After the performance of this work I walked him back to his hotel. Despite his appearance his mood seemed happy. He talked gaily about his plans for the rest of the summer and for his autumn season. "I am going to take Markevitch for a visit to Richard Strauss and also to a few Wagner performances at the Munich Opera," he said; "then I'm going as usual to the Lido. Why don't you come with us and visit the funny old German in his villa in Garmisch?"

But much as I would have liked to go, I was bound for Berlin on the morning train.

I asked Diaghilev how Hindemith's ballet was progressing. He answered that he had spent a day with Hindemith in Berlin and that very little of the ballet music was actually on paper. "But I'm not worrying," he said, "I know what an extraordinary craftsman he is and how fast he works."

He asked me what I was writing and when I told him that I was in the middle of my first symphony he grew interested and wanted to know all about it — what it was like, whether it was going to be as lyrical and romantic as *Ode*, how many movements there would be, and how soon it was going to be ready. "Splendid!" he exclaimed. "As soon as I'm back in Paris you will play it for me, won't you? I also want you to look carefully at the music of young Markevitch. It's very exceptional stuff — still very green, but enormously gifted."

The next morning to my surprise Diaghilev met me at the tiny suburban station of Baden-Ost, where the through trains from Switzerland to Berlin stop.

"You see, I've come to see you off," he said, coming towards me, "or rather partly you, partly those people," and he pointed at a foreign-looking couple surrounded by many pieces of elegant luggage.

(127)

It was then that I took my last photograph of Diaghilev. Although taken against the light, it clearly shows Diaghilev's big, black figure standing against the low picket fence, and the field surrounding the railroad station of Baden-Ost.

Three weeks later I was returning from Berlin to my summer home in Alsace. As usual I took the night train, which left Berlin at 6 or 7 P.M. Around ten o'clock the train stopped at Halle. I went out and bought the Halle evening paper. I couldn't read in the compartment, the lights were down and the five-odd Germans were asleep. I went to the men's room. There in the dim light of its 25-watt bulb I glanced at the front page of the paper. At the top, in the right-hand corner I saw a two-line message from Venice. It was dated August 19 and read: —

"This morning at 5 A.M. the famous Russian dancer Diaghilev died here."

From then on at every stop of the train I was on the lookout for fresh papers. But either the newspaper booths were closed or the papers carried the same garbled message. Yet because it was garbled a glimmer of hope remained. Maybe it wasn't he who had died? Maybe it was a dancer of his company and the German press had made a message like "a dancer of the famous Diaghilev Company" read "the famous dancer Diaghilev."

Even the early morning edition of the *Frankfurter Zeitung* carried the same message, this time with an old 1906 photograph of Diaghilev. Once the train had crossed the Rhine and stopped at the rainy platform of the Strasbourg station there could be no doubt. Here were the Paris papers, his face looking at me from every one.

The shock, the loss, the feeling of emptiness and profound

désarroi were overwhelming. How did it happen? Why did he have to die? What will happen now to his work? And what will happen to all of us, his friends, his young artist collaborators, his troupe of dancers? I went to the post office and sent incoherent telegrams to Kochno, to Missia Sert, to George Balanchine, to Prokofiev.

Several days later a letter from Prokofiev arrived. He was in the Savoy, near the Annecy Lake, not far from the place where Stravinsky was spending the summer. Prokofiev wrote: "First when I read the news I couldn't believe it. It sounded unreal and absurd. It is an awful blow. I went to visit Stravinsky and he too was profoundly shocked. What will happen now? What will happen to his company?"

These questions were on everybody's lips, in everybody's mind. Rarely had so many artists of so many nationalities, cultures, and ages felt a loss that united them in a mutual sense of profound impoverishment.

Gradually the circumstances of his death became known to me. He died from an attack of diabetes, his old neglected illness. He suffered a great deal, physically and morally. All his life he had been afraid of sickness, of loss of power and of consciousness. Since the attack had begun he must have known, although he would never have admitted it, that his days, his hours, were counted. Near him were two close friends, Lifar and Kochno. Later, during the last few days of his life, two other faithful friends arrived, Missia Sert and the Baroness d'Erlanger.

He died at dawn on August 19 at the age of fifty-seven after a long, tormented agony. He died as he had lived all his life, in a modest hotel room, a homeless adventurer, a great exile and a prince of the arts. And just as his life had been a strange and exotic pageant, so was his death. On the morning of the twenty-first of August a procession of four gondolas took his body to the Russian cemetery on the tiny S. Marco Island. The coffin was covered with tuberoses, tea roses, and carnations. A Russian priest and the small choir of S. Giorgio dei Greci sang in ill-accorded voices the doleful chant of the Slavic funeral service while the procession moved to the cemetery through the still waters of the Venetian lagoon.

VII
The Specter of Nijinsky

OUTSIDE the New York City Center mosque a line of genteel pickets strolled among the late-comers in evening clothes. I took a leaflet from a pleasant-looking young girl — "It's shocking . . . It's appalling . . . Serge Lifar . . . to Russia in Goering's private plane . . ." — and pushed my way past the Chevaliers de la Légion d'Honneur and the French Cultural Relations staff, with all their cultured relations, who efficiently blocked the narrow entrance. Seated inside the darkening theater, I could still see the Moorish delights which walled me in. Less Moorish really, I thought, than Caucasian: a monstrous specimen of one of those intricately worked enamel snuffboxes to be found in secondhand stores on Sixth Avenue. I felt shut up in such a box, fixed before a red curtain, with French flags on either side of the stage, when the footlights harshly thrust my attention toward that land of medieval extravaganza so popular in France during the occupation, when ladies' hats appeared to be *châteaux forts*, and playwrights had the King Arthur rash. Two knights dueled for fifteen minutes with a whole category of fighting

(131)

utensils, beginning with halberds, and ending with five-and-ten-cent-store kitchen knives. One of the knights fell down and was carried away. An otherwise exquisite ballerina turned into a green goat, inspiring several knights to be alternately in flora, and in fauna.

The applause was sufficient to elicit several curtain calls from the two stars, Kalyujny and Chauviré, who bowed, bowed again, vanished behind the red curtain, and reappeared, thrusting Lifar firmly on the stage. In the orchestra, the applause remained polite, and a few people stood in order to see better, but the balcony audience, evidently more affected by Lifar's reputation as an airman, made noises menacing enough to cut short his intrusion. But in that moment I saw the miraculously well-proportioned body; the luminous white teeth; the hair, rooted in a semicircle low on his forehead, that still looked as unctuously combed as that of an Argentine gigolo! Only his Greeky nose — an invention of Diaghilev, who once took Lifar to a plastic surgeon — looked different, more artificial, like a marble relic set in an aging human face. And the sight of that gaunt, dark Tartar, almost unchanged, gave me my first instant of crystal-clear consciousness, and sent me stumbling over memories and half-forgotten associations.

When I first knew Seryoja Lifar, he had no such aviatorial or choreographic pretensions. Sergei Pavlovitch Diaghilev, who then ruled the original of the original Ballets Russes de Monte Carlo like an eighteenth-century Russian potentate, would never have permitted him to misbehave. In fact, in 1928, when Lifar danced in my first ballet *Ode*, he was the obliging, smiling, and somewhat childish young man who acted as the obedient show dog of Balanchine and Massine, the choreographers, Grigoriev, stage director, Boris Kochno, Diaghilev's secretary, Valichka Nouvel, Diaghilev's friend and factotum, and, of course, Diaghilev himself. Lifar trotted in awe after all the ballet old-timers, and loved to listen to their wonderful myth-making stories — especially stories about Nijinsky, for Lifar, having acquired a splendid technical skill as a *corps de ballet* dancer, had quickly risen to the position of a star, and thus had become a *faute de mieux* successor of Nijinsky. I suspect that from Lifar's earliest days he thought of himself as a kind of Adonisian re-embodiment of Nijinsky. There was no greater pleasure for him than to dance *L'Après-midi d'un Faune* and *Le Spectre de la Rose*, ballets which, as the critic Levinson suggested, could just as well be called *L'Après-midi de Nijinsky*, and *Le Spectre de Nijinsky*. After Diaghilev's death, Lifar danced them wherever and whenever he could, going so far as to wear bathing trunks under his evening clothes at private parties. After a little coaxing, he would strip off his clothes and lie down on the piano with his thumb in his mouth, fingers upraised in the drinking gesture that begins that erotic little number, *L'Après-midi d'un Faune*.

In fairness to Lifar, one should say that to most of the younger collaborators of Diaghilev's enterprise, like Balanchine, Rieti, Tchelitchev, and myself, Nijinsky was also a kind of "Golden Age of Ballet" myth. Most of us had never seen him dance except on photographic stills. Nijinsky had left Diaghilev's company long before I came to France, and in 1916 he was stricken with an illness which made him a melancholy and mute wanderer from one Swiss sanatorium to another, and thus the most famous and the most romantic insane person of his time. We young men of the twenties had to be content with the Nijinsky stories, with which the older men of the company would treat us at every possible occasion. The most voluble of them all was Diaghilev's long-time servant and bodyguard, Vassily Ivanovitch Zuikin, a stocky copper-bearded Mongoloid whose behavior and appearance combined the features of an Al Capone minion and an NKVD colonel. Always hovering backstage and sneaking up from behind a prop at the most inopportune moment, during, say, a ballet-omanic flirtation, Vassily performed the role of His Majesty's gossip collector, and protector of his personal and bodily interests. Vassily, by virtue of his long connection with the ballet, had not only acquired a unique collection of lurid stories (concerned for the most part with the amorous feats and defeats of the subjects of Diaghilev's empire), but he was also informed, with the most astonishing exactitude, of the whereabouts and activities of everyone who had even the remotest connection with the ballet.

One day early in October, 1928, I went out to lunch with a friend, between rehearsals, in one of those tiny bistros with four round tables growing out of a frieze of boxwood, which cluster around the Place St. Lazare. When I arrived, I spotted Vassily sitting in the bistro's darkest corner, obviously absorbed in a conversation with a "ballet mother," one of those embittered and protectively jealous matrons who always follow ballet troupes, peddling gossip about their daughters' closest rivals. As soon as we sat down, Vassily came to our table, bent over as if he were communicating a state secret, and whispered, "Do you know that Nijinsky is coming tonight to the ballet to see Lifar dance? Diaghilev wants him to say something about Lifar's dancing, and has persuaded the doctors to let him come." He shrugged his shoulders. "But what can he say? He's mute, isn't he?"

I knew that Nijinsky was in a sanatorium somewhere in the suburbs of Paris, and I had heard that morning that Diaghilev was bragging, "I'll make him speak . . . you'll see!" The elderly Russian painter, Korovin, with whom I was lunching, was appalled at the notion. "Why be so cruel?" he said. "Why disturb a poor insane man? Only to satisfy Diaghilev's colossal ego and his proprietary instincts? He likes people to admire *his* musicians, *his* painters, and particularly, his boys and girls of the ballet company. And he doesn't really care if the admirer is the Bey of Tunis or an insane genius." Korovin paused a bit and added, "Of course, this case is rather special. After all, both Nijinsky and Lifar were more or less his finds."

After lunch I returned to the opera and found Diaghilev sitting on the stage watching a rehearsal. The whole company, in tights and tutus, was spinning around in a circle to the shotlike clapping of Grigoriev's hands, "*Raz, dva, tri, tchetyre* . . ." (one, two, three, four). A little lady at the piano was turbulently banging out the Russian dances from Rimsky-Korsakov's *May Night*. Diaghilev looked angry and bored. He leaned with both hands on the silver knob of his cane, his eyes half closed, the monocle in his right eye in perilous position. After about a half hour of this choreographic *salade russe*, Diaghilev suddenly stamped his feet, knocked on the floor with his cane, and shouted angrily in his babyish voice, "Enough of that! *C'est de la merde, pure et simple!*" He turned around and yelled for Boris Kochno. "Where is Valichka?" he whined, not noticing that Nouvel was standing at his side. "Where is Karsavina? Where is Seryoja Lifar? I can't sit around for hours waiting for Their Majesties to arrive. I must see their *pas de deux* before tonight. Tell them to come immediately." He continued to rant until Karsavina and Lifar finally appeared in costume ready to dance. Meanwhile he shouted at Nouvel, Grigoriev, and Kochno, and even at the pianist, who begged to be excused after a day's rehearsal. "I also want to go home, my dear Madame. I also am tired. Do not blame me, blame the prima donnas." As soon as the pair began rehearsing he quieted, his eyes glued to the movements of their miraculously precise and agile feet. "Boris, what time is it?" he asked in the midst of the rehearsal. "Six? My God, it's time for you to go! I told the doctors you would be there at seven." Vassily winked at me, and beckoned me to follow. "Don't you want to come with us?" he whispered. I followed them to the backstage exit.

Boris, Vassily, and I caught a taxi on the rue Auber and drove through the gentle autumnal evening light of Paris, across the rue de Rivoli, and past the Tuileries. Having reached the left bank of the Seine, the taxi turned northwards, and by the time we reached the Bois de Vincennes, the twilight had settled down and the pinkish lanterns along the road began to shine on the background of a mauve-colored sky. As we drove through the Bois, past the stone walls and bric-a-brac villas of the northern Parisian suburbs, I could not help thinking of what I knew and remembered of Nijinsky. I was a child in St. Petersburg when I first saw his photographs. The Director of the Imperial Theater, the foxy-looking Prince Sergei Volkonsky, with his sixteenth-century beard and mustachios, brought them to show to my mother soon after he had returned from Paris. He also brought a series of postal cards representing Diaghilev's famous dancers, Pavlova, Karsavina, Bolm, Nijinsky, and others. I was particularly struck by two of them: Nijinsky in the costume of the blackamoor in *Schéhérazade*, his face brown, his eyes and teeth gleaming with a virile, sensual smile. He was in a pantherlike pose, about to jump. And the other: Nijinsky all covered with rose petals, his beautiful body stretched out in a languorously effete pose of an androgynal-looking youth. (I take it that in the hothouse atmosphere of Paris in 1910, this "spirit of the rose" with its absurd rose-petaled costume and suave choreography was the perfectly justified dream of a pre-Freudian ballet-soxer.)

It was perhaps because of these images that the shock of seeing Nijinsky that October night at the gate of a sanatorium in a dingy Parisian *banlieu* was more acute than I anticipated. The taxi stopped in front of the sanatorium compound, which was closed in by a quadrangle of high stone walls. Boris jumped out and asked Vassily and me to wait in the taxi. After about a quarter of an hour we heard footsteps on the pavement outside the compound, then an attendant in a long white smock and Boris appeared leading Nijinsky to the taxi. I cannot say that I did not *recognize* Nijinsky, but it was difficult to *identify* that baldheaded grayish little man (one always forgets how small dancers are) with expressionless eyes, and a sallow, sick look on his face that was accentuated by the white lights of the sanatorium lanterns. He looked more like a commercial traveler out of a job, or a schoolteacher in a small Polish mining town, than the embodiment of a terpsichorean legend. He was dressed in an oversized dark wool overcoat with a neat white scarf tied around his neck. He did not greet us, nor utter a sound.

Driving back to the Opera I felt uneasy, as if all of us, Boris, Vassily, the male nurse, myself and even the taxi driver, were accomplices in a strangely unsavory crime. I was glad to sit near the driver, not to face the victim with his empty eyes and sick face. When we drove into the semicircular courtyard which surrounds the back entrance to the Paris Opera, I saw that a crowd of company members were gathered near the stage door. Vassily got out and began shoving people out of the way. Grigoriev came running up to the taxi, leaped inside, and embraced Nijinsky. "Vaslav Fomitch, what happiness! *Kakaya radost*, what joy!" The whole group started for the taxi and hauled Nijinsky out. There was no response from the sick man. He remained mute, and his eyes retained their dead look. Only once did his expression change, when he stood at the foot of the staircase, and his nurse urged him to walk up. He shook his head in a curiously vehement way, and his face twitched nervously. I think that it was Boris and Vassily who carried him in a hand-chair, up the narrow stairs leading to the director's box. The theater was dark and the performance of Stravinsky's *Firebird* had begun. Only a few people in the audience could have seen the Ulyssean return of the famous dancer to his master's box.

In the box were Alexander Benois, the painter, Nouvel, a few ladies, and myself. Diaghilev stood behind Nijinsky's seat, and leaned over to whisper in his ear. It seemed to me that a barely perceptible animation appeared on Nijinsky's face. For the first time, at least, his eyes were focused in a definite direction, and he seemed to see the dancing. Throughout the performance Diaghilev continued to talk to Nijinsky in a nagging, insistent whisper, and once or twice I heard him say, "*Skaji, skaji*, tell me, tell me, how do you like Lifar? Isn't he magnificent?" He tweaked Nijinsky's ear, poked him in the shoulder, chuckling in the tone with which elderly men, unaccustomed to infants, usually bring about a prolonged tantrum. To all of it, Nijinsky remained silent, but when the poking turned into actual pinching he mumbled something like, "*Aie, ostav,* stop it!"

I lost Nijinsky from sight immediately after the performance. He was surrounded by a crowd of old-timers, elderly Russian painters, designers, dressmakers, stagehands, ballet mothers, and aging ballerinas — all moved to tears by the sight of their idol. They whisked him on the stage where cameras began clicking, and where a group was organized around him for the now famous photograph. It consists of Diaghilev, looking at Nijinsky with an oily smile, Benois, Grigoriev, Nouvel, Karsavina, and, as an exception to the rule of seniority, as special recognition of the princely heritage that had become his lot, Serge Lifar was added to the group.

I was unable to observe Nijinsky's reaction at that moment, but a few days later, looking at the photographs, I noticed that a vague and helplessly benevolent smile lighted his face.

A short while later, Diaghilev vanished, the crowd dispersed, and I found myself struggling through a group of dancers who were rushing out the backstage exit. Nijinsky had been carried downstairs, this time by two men in tights, and was waiting outside alone with Boris and the male nurse. On my way out I met Vassily, whose Oriental face was beaming with the pleasure of a prison warden who has just thwarted an escape. He whispered, "You see, I told you Diaghilev wouldn't get a word out of him. Serves him right."

This time we drove back in a large funereal limousine, and again I sat in the front seat but squeezed in between the driver and Vassily, whose bulging left thigh prevented me from leaning back. Vassily tried to start a conversation with the bearded chauffeur. "*Vous savez* who is inside the car? Nijinsky!" he said, obviously expecting an excited response. "*No hablo francés*," mumbled the driver into his beard. "*Ach, on ispan-yetz*," said Vassily sententiously, and dropped into silence. I was grateful for that silence, glad to be outside again, even in that damp, opaque night which enveloped us as soon as we crossed the narrow avenues of the Bois de Vincennes and drove into the surburb of Villejuif. It was past midnight when the limousine stopped at the sanatorium gate, and the ceremony of extracting Nijinsky from his seat began again. He looked paler than before, and because his body had become as limp as an oyster, it took some time to put him on his feet. Finally, a mere shadow of a prisoner between two jailers, he walked past me toward the gate. I watched him from the car, saw him stop, turn around, and although the car's motor was on I heard him say in a gentle, halting, and somewhat tearful voice, "*Skajite yemou chto Lifar horosho prygayet.*" (Tell him that Lifar jumps well.)

VIII

Srg Srgvtch Prkfv

"NOT AT ALL like Paris," I thought as I came out of the doorway of No. 2 rue Valentin Haüy, into the sharp sunny light and turned left. The frost tickled my nostrils; a bell chimed in the distance. I counted the chimes: twelve.

"What are you doing here on my beat?" said a jovial Russian voice behind my back. "Don't you know that this is my own private terrain?" I turned around and saw Sergei Sergeiyevitch Prokofiev. He was in a huge gray overcoat of flashy herringbone tweed and a flat tweed cap. He had just emerged from the doorway. I explained that I had left my new songs with the concierge. His wife, Lina Ivanovna, had asked me to bring them and now I was going home. "Oh, no," he said in the same jovial baritone, "you aren't going home, you're going with me. We're going to circumscribe a circle around that thing there," and he pointed at the squat yellow dome of Napoleon's Tomb. He put his cream-colored gloves on my shoulders, turned me around and said: "Forward, march!"

"How healthy he looks," I thought as I watched the steam

come out of his nostrils in rhythmical puffs — as out of a toy locomotive. His face was pinkish, round and shiny, his eyes cheerful, and his heavy protruding lips which often looked so sulky held a happy smile.

"You know," he said, "this is a ritual with me. I started it a year ago. And now I do it every day. I leave the house before lunch and march up the Avenue de Breteuil. At the end of it I turn right and left and by the time I'm in front of the Invalides, I begin to get ravenous. I can think of nothing else but food. I'm ready to eat five lunches. You'll see, you'll feel the same way in a moment," he grinned, as we strutted through the empty street. "I've got it down," he added, "to precise timing. It takes me exactly twenty-six minutes seventeen seconds to twenty-six minutes thirty-five seconds — from door to door. But," he looked at his wrist watch, "now you've made me lose time. One minute and four seconds . . . I always pass this house here, four minutes and ten seconds after I've left the door. Let's walk faster. Don't be lazy. Come on!" He accelerated his step. I followed him and soon we were crossing the square behind the Invalides. For a while we marched in concentrated silence like soldiers on parade, Prokofiev counting his seconds, I listening to the hollow sound of our steps. He looked again at his watch and exclaimed: "Ah, you see, we've made it up. We've passed the halfway mark. There," and he pointed at a lamppost, "now we can go slower and talk. We have plenty of time."

The night before we had gone together to a concert of modern music, one of the season's first concerts of a society of modern composers called *La Sérénade* which had been organized the year before, in 1930, and which gave a series of concerts in the Salle Gaveau. The Sérénade had wealthy and

fashionable patrons and its concerts were elegant society affairs with a touch of the same kind of snobbishness that surrounded Diaghilev's ballet season. Both Prokofiev and I were
members of the Sérénade (it only had some eight composer-
members) but Prokofiev did not like the atmosphere of the
concerts. The night before, he had vanished during the intermission, before the *clou*, the main piece of the program,
had been performed. "Why did you leave so early last
night," I began, "even before Markevitch's piece had been
played?"

"Because," he answered, and his face took on a surly expression, "I had enough of that phony concert. Besides I had heard
part of Markevitch's piece in rehearsal and . . ." He paused
for a moment, but before I could say anything he went on
again, as if following a special trend of thought. "You know
Markevitch's music surprises me." (Markevitch, a young
composer of Russian origin, had suddenly blossomed into
fame.) "It all sounds terribly clever but in reality it doesn't
make any sense. It's as if someone were engaged in acoustical
experiments with the instruments of the orchestra." And he
turned to me looking eager and ironic. "But . . . did *you* like
it? Did you?"

"Well," I started, "the man is still very young. He is
very . . . gifted you know, but . . . but . . ."

"But what?" interrupted Prokofiev, falling back into a
surly tone. "Why don't you ever say what you feel? All of
you are this way. Why don't you come out and say: 'Yes,
I like it,' and then explain why, or else, 'No, I don't like it'?
Instead you find excuses. 'The man is very gifted' . . . 'He is
young.' What does that mean? Absolutely nothing. It sounds
like the jargon of society ladies who really don't know *what*

to say" — and he added in a calmer tone: "I told Markevitch that I don't like his stuff and told him why." He stopped and again we walked in silence until he took one more glance at his wrist watch and brightened up. "Good!" he said, "now we can creep. We're way ahead of schedule."

We passed in front of the old cannons that stand in front of the Place des Invalides. Prokofiev stopped and pointed at one of them. "See how angry it looks," he remarked. "This is the way I feel when I go to one of these Parisian concerts. All these countesses, princesses and silly snobs make me angry. They act as if everything in the world was invented to amuse *them*. And . . ." his voice got harsh and irritable, "look what all their *salonarisme* has done to French music. There hasn't been a first-rate French composer since the time of . . . Chabrier and Bizet. Because the French composers have been busy entertaining and 'tickling the ears' of their princesses, countesses and marquises."

"But Sergei Sergeiyevitch," I tried to interject.

"I know, I know," he cut me off, "you like everything French. You even like that old crank Satie. And I know what you think about his followers. You think they are important. Well they're not. They're pure mush. The only one in France who knows what he's doing is Ravel. All the rest are hopeless."

"But what about . . . Debussy?" I said timidly, as we were turning into the rue Valentin Haüy.

"Debussy!" he smirked. "Debussy! You know what Debussy is: it's *stouden* [calf's head or feet in aspic] . . . it's jelly . . . it's absolutely spineless music." His voice grew excited and loud: "No I can't share anyone's admiration for Debussy. Except perhaps," and he grinned again, "it's very 'personal' jelly and the jellymaker knows what he's doing.

(144)

You know — " But he interrupted himself abruptly and raised the glove-covered index finger of his right hand. We had stopped in front of his house. He looked at his watch and beamed: "Wonderful!" he said. "Twenty-six minutes and twenty seconds. Excellent time. Won't you come up and have lunch with us, Nika?"

When I think of Prokofiev and try to recall how he looked, it is always this brisk morning walk around the Invalides that I remember first. I see him standing in front of his doorway, jovial, virile, and full of a kind of uncouth, rugged optimism. The image is so clear and at the same time so like him, so typical of the kind of man he is (or at least *was* in those years I knew him in Paris), that I select it instinctively before the many other images I had collected during the five or six years of our friendship.

The first time I saw Prokofiev was a long, long time ago. I was a boy of twelve or thirteen living with my family in St. Petersburg. In 1915 or 1916, after Alexander Scriabin's death, Sergei Rachmaninov came to St. Petersburg and gave a concert for the benefit of Scriabin's widow. The concert took place in the hall of the St. Petersburg Conservatory, and I was taken to it by my tutor, Tze-Tze. It was, of course, a very exciting occasion, my first concert of Rachmaninov, a famous pianist and composer of whom I had heard talk since I was a baby. It was particularly exciting because Rachmaninov was performing an entire program of works by Scriabin, under the spell of whose music I was at that time. My memory of the concert remains hazy and about the only incident I can muster is that, sitting in one of the front rows of the hall, not far from our seats, a group of oddly assorted people chattered and whispered throughout Rachmaninov's performance. Among them was a thin young man with fleshy, protruding lips and an extraordinarily large blond head precariously fitted to a thin stem. I asked Tze-Tze about these people, and in particular about the young man. "I don't know who they are," answered Tze-Tze, "but the man is . . . I think that's the young composer Sergei Prokofiev."

Many years later in Paris, Prokofiev told me a story about this concert. Rachmaninov at that time was the idol of Moscow, while Scriabin was ardently admired by a small group of aesthetes and music lovers, pseudo-mystics and pseudo-philosophers, in St. Petersburg. This latter group regarded Rachmaninov with a certain amount of disdain, and considered him the chief representative of that decadent salon romanticism of which the post-Tchaikovskian school of Moscow was the center. Thus Rachmaninov's appearance in St. Petersburg to play a whole concert of Scriabin's music and to dedicate the concert to his memory was quite an unexpected event. After Rachmaninov had performed the esoteric pieces by Scriabin with his usual precision, thoroughness, and matter-of-factness, the little group of St. Petersburg melomanes burst forth with scathing remarks and criticism of Rachmaninov's failure to grasp the meaning of Scriabin's music. But Prokofiev thought that Rachmaninov had done a good job in his performance. He went directly to the artist's room, and in his usual straightforward and rough manner told the Moscow idol, the great and famous man, that his performance "was not bad, not bad at all."

"What do you mean — not bad?" asked Rachmaninov, and furious and indignant he turned his back on Prokofiev.

It took many years and their chance meeting over a chessboard on an ocean liner to patch up that early St. Petersburg incident.

The next time I saw Prokofiev was during a chess tournament in St. Petersburg to which Tze-Tze, a passionate chess-player, and I went as "observers." I noticed Prokofiev sitting in front of his table, his big blond head bent over the chessboard, looking solemn, concentrated and angry. The champion Alekhin, then still a young man in the uniform of a university student but already a famous chess star, was walking from table to table; he stopped at each one for an instant, made a move and went on to the next. Prokofiev sat immobile, always with the same stern and intense expression on his face. He did not even lift his eyes when Alekhin came up to his table. I watched the game for several hours until most of the players had been beaten and had dropped out of the tournament. Prokofiev and one or two others remained. As we were leaving the crowded hall, the final score was announced. Alekhin won twenty-eight *parties;* one had been a draw; one had been lost to young Prokofiev. The Rachmaninov concert and the chess tournament marked the only two times I saw Prokofiev in Russia. I did not see him again until much later, in 1923 or 1924 in Paris, when as a young man of twenty I moved from Germany to France and entered the University of Paris. But in the meantime, between the chess match and Paris, I grew to know Prokofiev's music and began to like it.

The first time I laid my eyes on a piece by Prokofiev was in Yalta in 1919 where a strange and grotesque incident brought it to my attention. By a chain of unreconstructible events I obtained two scores of Prokofiev's pieces for the piano. Perhaps it was the little old organist of the Yalta Catholic Church, knowing my yearning for new music, who brought them to me as a Christmas present. New music was scarce in those early post-revolutionary civil war years. Since Lenin's government had nationalized the publishing houses, nothing or near to nothing was being printed. Our Yalta music store was empty and the only new piece that I had seen since 1917 was a piece by Arthur Lourié called *Our March* (Lourié was then the vice-commissar for music in Lenin's government) which had been printed in millions of copies and was distributed throughout all the music stores of Russia. The pieces of Prokofiev contained his tender, lyrical *Grandmother's Tales* and I threw myself on them with the avidity and eagerness of someone who has been deprived of new musical food for too long. I played them over and over again, interested by their curiously twisted and at the same time naïve and sincere simplicity. Naturally I wanted to show my new acquisitions to my harmony teacher, the composer Vladimir Ivanovich Rebikov.

Rebikov was a cranky, elderly gentleman — what one used to call in Russia an *original* (an eccentric). He had a frightful temper and a totally unpredictable mood. Besides he looked like a freak. He was big and flabby. His face, a large, flat, pink oval, was divided into two halves by a purple gourdlike nose. He had a triple-decker chin, a pair of small, shortsighted and hopelessly crossed eyes, hidden behind thick lenses, and a tiny mouth full of disorderly teeth that peered out from under an ill-trimmed greenish mustache. His bulky cranium, which hung low over his narrow forehead, was covered by a thin layer of capillary vegetation. This last grew, or what remained of it grew, on the back of his head, in a semicircle from ear to ear, all carefully combed in the same direction as if it were attracted by a magnetic field somewhere in the middle of the forehead. Of his eccentricities, the most marked was his method of obtaining a wig for himself. Rebikov used to keep two squares of cardboard, one white, one black, on his piano. During my harmony lesson he would suddenly stop and start a shortsighted search of the keyboard. Having spotted a hair, he would pick it up with his big clumsy fingers and after careful inspection deposit it, if gray, on the black square, if brown, on the white one. "You see," he would explain each time this incident took place, "when I grow old I'll have a wig made of my own hair."

Rebikov was what one would call a "composer of note." He had written a pleasant little waltz in his opera *The Christmas Tree* which had gained great popularity in Russia and abroad. Even today it comes at you occasionally from such places as the muffled orifice of a Muzak loud-speaker. Some of the music he had written was surprisingly dissonant and in its harmonic texture resembled the advanced works of Scriabin and Debussy. According to him his discovery and his use of these "advanced" harmonies always preceded his illustrious contemporaries by some ten years. "They have copied, plagiarized me and robbed me of my inventions," he would proclaim, pointing at a date of publication of one of his pieces, thus reminding you that it was published long before Debussy's "this" or Scriabin's "that." "But the worst thing of all is that they distorted them!" he would add in a grandiloquent tone.

When I came for my lesson with the Prokofiev pieces in my hands, he made a sour face at once. Yes, he said he had heard about the young man, but what he had heard was not encouraging; in fact it was "rather unfortunate." The man was "rude," "barbaric" in his musical tastes and "terribly arrogant." As soon as he opened the score and started playing Prokofiev's pieces, he got angry. At the end of the first piece he asked mockingly: "What am I supposed to do? Am I supposed to tell you that this . . . nonsense *here*," and he slapped the music in front of him, "is good?" Then he played a few more pieces, muttering words like "absurd," "idiotic," "senseless," "disgusting." Suddenly in the middle of one of the prettiest and most lyrical pieces from the *Grandmother's Tales*, he picked up the music from the piano rack, got up, went to the window and without saying a word threw it out. I rushed to stop him, but the music was already floating down to the street. Rebikov went to the door, opened it ceremoniously and said in a solemn, theatrical manner: "Young man, leave this room at once. By bringing that — " and his right hand pointed at the window in a monumental Napoleonic gesture — "that trash to me you have heaped insult and indignity upon your master." Seething with fury I ran down to the street and started gathering the loose, mud-stained pages of the music. Having collected them and put them together I went home determined never to show any new piece to the old maniac. Such was my first baptism in Prokofiev's music.

My friendship with Prokofiev began in the years 1926 and 1927, when Diaghilev produced Prokofiev's *The Steel Leap*, the first and only ballet of post-revolutionary life in Russia ever produced abroad. This was the beginning of an intense relation between us on a level of mutual musical interest, the kind of friendship of which there were so many in Paris during the twenties, and which gradually died out under the impact of the changing world of the thirties. For four or five years in succession our relationship consisted in playing to one another our new music and that of others, and of bitterly criticizing and violently reacting to all the things we liked and disliked. There were long telephone conversations about nothing and everything, about the most recent concerts, and Meyerhold's *Inspector-General*, about Stravinsky's *Apollon*, and about the best restaurants in Paris, and all this was in the particular atmosphere of suspense and gaiety of which the Ballet Russe at that time was a symbol.

Sergei Prokofiev came from a middle-class Russian family. His father was an employee of a rich landowner in southern Russia where he exercised very efficiently the office of overseer of the large estate. His mother belonged to the intelligentsia and was reared in the oppositional revolutionary ideals of the late nineteenth century. It was she, I believe, who taught him to play the piano, and I saw a photograph of Prokofiev as a boy sitting near an upright piano with the score of his first opera, *The Giant*, written at the age of eight or nine.

Two or three years later the boy wrote an overture called *On the Desert Islands*. S. I. Taneiev, the famous Moscow composer and teacher of counterpoint at the Moscow Conservatory, to whom he had had the chance of playing his overture, suggested that he take up the study of composition and theory with Pomerantzev and Glière, both teachers at the Moscow Conservatory. Glière was a friend of the Prokofiev family and had spent two summers (in 1902 and 1903) in Sontzovka, the estate of which Prokofiev's father was the superintendent. Thus it is from Glière that Prokofiev received his first theoretical instruction. Later, in 1904, Prokofiev was taken to St. Petersburg and introduced to Glazunov. Glazunov, who became his protector and best defender in the years to come, suggested his entering the Conservatory in St. Petersburg. Prokofiev did so in the fall of that same year. There his teachers were Liadov, Vitol, Rimsky-Korsakov, and Tcherepnin in theory, composition, and conducting, and Winkler and Yessipova in piano.

These names are those of a pleiad of brilliant craftsmen, first-rate teachers in their particular fields, from under whose wings rose a whole generation of famous instrumentalists, composers, teachers, and critics. The Moscow and St. Petersburg Conservatories, founded by the two Rubinstein brothers, were always great centers of musical ideological activity, and also centers of cliques and aesthetically-minded groups. An old traditional feud had ideologically separated the two conservatories since the days of Tchaikovsky and the "big five." The big five (Balakirev, Borodin, Moussorgsky, Rimsky-Korsakov, Cui) represented the nationalistic tradition of St. Petersburg, while Tchaikovsky followed the Western European leanings of progressively-minded Moscow. To us this ideological war now seems like a storm in a teacup, but in Prokofiev's youth the antagonism between the two institutions and their followers was still acute. Moscow was then permeated with a salon style of late post-Chopin, Tchaikovskian emotionalism, of which Rachmaninov and Arensky were such good examples. This decadent salon romanticism was not being redeemed by the earnest scholastic efforts of Taneiev or by the drab formalism of Medtner. St. Petersburg, on the other hand, after having gone through the big hullabaloo of the musical nationalism of the big five, had settled down to a dusty renaissance of academic technique under the leadership of Rimsky-Korsakov and Glazunov. Quite apart from all this stood the lone figure of Scriabin plowing heavily, with the help of all the nineteenth century's technical paraphernalia, through the esoteric clouds of a confused mysticism. Around Scriabin was a flock of faithful admirers who regarded him as something between a prophet and a messiah.

This was the atmosphere into which young Prokofiev was suddenly projected. I can well imagine him, with his open, healthy, peasant grin — Prokofiev for whom all such things as the esoteric, aesthetic dreams of Scriabin were sheer nonsense — laughing to his heart's delight at the St. Petersburg of 1904 to 1908. Fortunately for Prokofiev, besides all the dust and mysteries there were those excellent craftsmen, those great technicians and teachers, and foremost among them was Rimsky-Korsakov himself, the greatest teacher in orchestration since the time of Berlioz. It was from them that young Prokofiev would soon learn his admirable instrumental skill, his impeccable technique of writing, and his flawless though somewhat academic style in orchestration.

St. Petersburg just before and during the First World War was a congealed city. Everybody knew that the old world of Imperial Russia was coming to an end. Everybody was aware that the end would bring with it a turmoil of immeasurable changes. The air was full of frozen neuroses, frozen hysteria. At the same time there was a great deal of intense expectation among the intelligentsia of the city, but again it was that kind of rigid, passive expectation which comes from disillusionment and the recognition of the inevitability of the approaching storm.

However, in order to produce this storm a generation of hardheaded, realistic, ruthless and optimistic men appeared and took over the responsibilities for the future. In a certain sense Prokofiev was one of those young men destined to play a part in that future, and his presence in the corroded artistic society of St. Petersburg around 1910 was one of those anomalies which always precede revolutions.

By his enemies (and in his early years he had many) he was soon called "the football composer." He was accused of breaking all the sacred conventions of the nineteenth-century tradition; of writing "stupid, square, marching music that does not signify anything," as a St. Petersburg critic expressed it at that time. Among his elder contemporaries, Prokofiev was a sore thumb. His coarse sarcasm, his jokes, his hearty laugh, the frank, savage, blunt orderliness of his music, did not fit into the mists of St. Petersburg of 1910 to 1915.

Prokofiev's studies at the Conservatory took up some thirteen years. This seems an incredibly long time today when one year or even six weeks of courses include harmony, counterpoint, composition, orchestration, some "appreciation," and perhaps even a bit of training in musical inventory — otherwise called musicology. This does not mean that Prokofiev spent all of his thirteen years in the Conservatory. He took regular undergraduate training at the same time. Long before his graduation from the Conservatory, he became fairly well known among a group of advanced music lovers and in the circles around the Conservatory. As early as 1911, Jurgenson in Moscow started publishing his music (at that time Prokofiev had already a dozen orchestral pieces, one opera, and about one hundred piano pieces to his credit). It was in 1909 that the unconventional young man appeared for the first time in a public performance, and about this same time his music was performed at the Society for

Contemporary Music, organized by a group of enterprising music lovers, some of whom belonged to the Diaghilev circle. Very soon he began to be known as one who attacked every form of convention, who tried to destroy traditions, and who was so arrogant as to express with cutting words his opinion about people and values long considered unassailable.

His music of that period does not seem to warrant the acute animosity he aroused. Granted it was out of the ordinary academic run; granted also that most of it was out of tune with his elder contemporaries and had none of those neurotic, soul-searching qualities which filled post-romanticism, post-impressionism, and later post-expressionism, still, up to his *Scythian Suite*, his music was tame and intimate in comparison with some of the feverish late works of Scriabin or the noisy excursions of Richard Strauss. Surely such music could not have warranted that particular hatred which Prokofiev earned in his youth from the older generation of his colleagues. It was due rather to Prokofiev's rough and gruff manners coupled with an incorrigible frankness in his public and personal relations. Yet these same qualities of his character have endeared Prokofiev to many others.

Prokofiev has always seemed to me to be a kind of big baby who must tell the truth on all occasions, and for whom to conceal his personal opinions is the most difficult thing in the world. If he does not like someone, he says so to that person's face; and even when he manages to control himself and does not say it, one does not need much imagination and sensitivity to discover what is happening inside him. How often have I seen him puff and grumble when someone was present whom he considered a bore! Once in a concert hall in Paris a fairly well-known composer came up to him and introduced himself. This man in the usual superlative manner of French bores started his "my deep and inexpressible admiration for your work, dear master . . . what an infinite pleasure to meet you." Prokofiev stared at the man with cross bull eyes and grumbled: "On my part there is *no* pleasure," and turned away.

Another time after a concert he told a famous singer, who had just performed a few of his songs, that she did not understand anything about his music and had better stop singing it. He said it in the presence of a large group of startled onlookers and in such a boorish way that he brought the poor fat lady to tears. "You see," he continued reprimanding her, "all of you women take refuge in tears instead of listening to what one has to say and learning how to correct your faults." In the touchy milieu of professional musicians, critics, and composers behavior like this hardly produces a friendly reputation. As a result few composers had so many quarrels, feuds and lawsuits and made so many enemies as Prokofiev.

But this irascible behavior was not reserved for backstage encounters with prima donnas and the brushing off of what he considered importune bores. He could be just as boorish and disagreeable with his wife and with his friends. Normally jovial and friendly, Prokofiev was inflammable. He would blow up suddenly at the slightest provocation. His face would grow crimson and he would begin ranting and being abusive. Fortunately his outbursts would not last long, but after they had worn off he would sulk for a long while, like a child, and during his sulking period he would have to be left alone, otherwise the rage might begin all over again.

Once in the summer of 1930 or 1931 I went with him and his wife on what is called in France *le tour gastronomique.*

The last leg of the tour was a drive from Strasbourg across the Vosges Mountains to Nancy and from there to Paris. I was eager to get back and start nursing my ruined digestion. The tour had been long and tiring, partly because most of the day was spent in first ordering meals, then eating them and then attempting to digest them; but also because the Prokofiev ménage had hourly squabbles (often ending with tears) about what to do next. While Lina Ivanovna wanted to stop in every village, visit every cathedral, château and museum, her husband wanted to go from one three-star restaurant to the next one in the town he had scheduled as our next stop. While his wife looked for "cozy" inns with "lovely" views, hidden in "green valleys" or on the slopes of a "charming" mountain, he wanted to stay in town in the best hotel advertised in the *Guide Michelin*. He was not a bit interested in museums, châteaus and cathedrals and when compelled to join us in what he called our "phony gravedigging ritual" he looked bored and gloomy. The only thing he could find to say looking at Chartres Cathedral was: "I wonder how they got those statues up so high without dropping them." But when he had a large, fancy menu in his hand his mien would change, he would brighten up and start ordering for each one of us the *plat du jour* or the *spécialité de la maison* with the concomitant *vin du pays*.

My exhaustion from the trip was further enhanced by Prokofiev's abominable driving. It was, I think, his first prolonged driving experience and he drove slowly, overcautiously, and shook us up whenever he had to shift gears or stop. Consequently we crept along the roads of France in his tiny new four-seater at the rate of twenty miles per hour. He had computed every particle of our time at this average rate of speed and planned all our stops in advance. Everywhere we went we had to arrive on the dot of x o'clock and leave the same way.

It was 9:30 A.M. the morning we started for Nancy. The day was gray and foggy but we succeeded in keeping up with "our schedule" and arrived exactly at 1 P.M. at the top of the Vosges Mountains in front of a famous restaurant where tourists stop for two hours of crayfish, trout, partridge, goose liver and tarts. Having barely finished eating the crayfish we were told by Prokofiev that due to the fog we should leave right away in order to be on time for dinner in Nancy. Lina Ivanovna began protesting and made a feeble attempt to change our itinerary, suggesting that instead of going to Nancy we drive to Domremy, the birthplace of Joan of Arc. Prokofiev blew up, of course. "Nonsense," he said, "it has been decided long ago that we spend the night in Nancy. Furthermore Domremy would be a big detour." But I backed up Lina Ivanovna and to my surprise, without much argument, he gave in.

Unfortunately the visit to Domremy was a complete flop. The village inn was uncomfortable and ugly. The dinner was monastically meager. The weather had turned rainy and everything was closed when we arrived. Prokofiev got sulky and blamed us for the ridiculous "detour" and the ensuing "loss of time." He grumbled all through the meal, was rude to the waitress when she brought the bill and then to the porter when he did not appear to appreciate Prokofiev's tipping habits; and after we said good night, and went to our respective adjoining rooms, I heard him grumbling at Lina Ivanovna until he put out the light.

The next morning we were told that we would leave

Domremy at 9:30 A.M. ("and not a minute later"). But Lina
Ivanovna and I wanted to visit Joan's birthplace, the Domremy Museum and the Basilica. We met at 8:30 and started
our tour while Prokofiev was still shaving. We went from one
hideous memorial of Joan of Arc to the next until we reached
the monstrous Basilica which was built after Joan's beatifica-
tion. Here, in the crypt of the gaudy Basilica surrounded by
all sorts of patriotic and devotional emblems, we found the
only attractive object of our inspection tour. It was a collection of coins given to the Jeanne d'Arc Museum by Madame
la Maréchale Foch and although it had no relation to Joan
of Arc (not even a coin of the period) it contained a few large
silver Russian coins of the time of Peter the Great and his
daughter Elizabeth. When we left the crypt of the Basilica it
was 9:35 A.M. Anticipating a scene we ran back to the inn.
Prokofiev stood in front, his face blue with rage. At his first
angry bark Lina Ivanovna burst into tears. This made him
madder and the ensuing barks grew louder and more intense.
He turned the heat on me. "What kind of behavior is this?"
he shouted. "Who do you think I am? I'm not your lackey
to wait on you. You can damn well get your bag and go by
train." The outburst lasted for at least a quarter of an hour
while the porter went on calmly packing our bags into the
car.

When we finally drove off, Prokofiev and I sat in total
silence in the front seat. His lips pouted. They were thicker
and sulkier than ever. He looked positively grim, and from
the back seat of the car came the ill-controlled sobs of his
spouse. After about an hour of this business I turned to Prokofiev and said: "Sergei Sergeiyevitch, either we stop this
scene at once or let me out in the next village and I'll go by

train." At first he did not answer. Then in about five minutes he smiled awkwardly and said quietly:

"Yes, it does look funny, doesn't it? Two grown-up people sit in front with sour faces and a third is bleating away in the back."

But Prokofiev's boorishness, his roughness, the rudeness of his temper had also another side — and that side contributed to constant, true friendship. Prokofiev, by nature, cannot tell a lie. He cannot say even the most conventional lie, such as "This is a charming piece," when he believes that the piece has no charm. Nor would he, when one showed him a new piece of one's music, shirk the responsibility of critical judgment and remain silent. On the contrary he would say exactly what he thought of it and discuss at great length its faults and its qualities and give valuable suggestions as to how to improve the piece. Thus to those who were ready to take his occasionally gruff manner and accept the frankness of his opinion he became an invaluable friend.

There never was a misunderstanding between Prokofiev and me in all the time of our friendship, nor was there ever an iota of falsity in it. To me, when I first knew him and until he went back to Russia, he was always kind and understanding and extremely helpful. I admired his frank, gay and optimistic personality, his enormous appetite for life, and (as I had also discovered) his childlike gentleness. The same man who in public life was often unbearably arrogant and even impudent could be a thoughtful, amusing and charming companion, a sincerely concerned and helpful friend. The same man who sued the Chicago Opera Company in the most tenacious and ungraceful way for not having produced his opera on time, or who refused to play his program at a concert in

Berlin and let his audience wait for several hours, because the impresario would not pay him his fee in advance, this same man would be unsparing with his time and incredibly patient when he was discussing the music of a friend-composer, giving him all the advice he could think of.

Prokofiev always liked practical systems. He planned his day according to a schedule and loved method in everything. Consequently he had a passion for such games of systematic calculation as chess and bridge. He used to play chess by correspondence with his Parisian publisher during the summer months. As for bridge, I remember two May weeks in Paris during the thirties when a group of twelve of us would sit down and play every day from three in the afternoon until two in the morning in Prokofiev's crowded and smoky apartment near the Invalides. Prokofiev had devised a system of graphs for this tournament. Those graphs showed the relative position of every player at every phase of the game.

In the purely grammatical writing of his music Prokofiev was always more meticulous than any other composer I knew. The calligraphy of his manuscript is not so astonishing in its perfection as that of Stravinsky (Stravinsky's scores look like illuminated manuscripts), but when his manuscript reaches his publisher it is completely free of mistakes. Prokofiev is very precise about his metronome markings, the opus number, and the dates of his compositions. All the little systems which he has devised are generated by the same kind of practical-mindedness which one finds in his music. The Russian alphabet used to have two i's, one which is like the Latin i, and one derived from the Church Slavonic, which resembles the Latin u. Long before the reform of the Russian alphabet went into effect, Prokofiev had dropped the old Slavonic *u*, employing only the Latin *i*, which is chiefly used in the Ukrainian dialect, and which gave a Ukrainian appearance to Prokofiev's Russian script. Strangely enough, when the alphabet reform went into effect, it was the Slavonic *u* which was retained. However, Prokofiev continued to write with his Ukrainian *i*. When he wrote postal cards, he often adopted a space-saving device. He dropped all vowels. Thus his Russian began to look like one of the many consonant-ridden Balkan dialects. A postal card of his would start "Dr frnd," and would end, "Yrs, Srg Srgvtch Prkfv."

Since his earliest years Prokofiev has been a hard-working composer. When I knew him he worked mostly at the piano and his hours were always carefully scheduled. To my knowledge, the only piece Prokofiev has not composed at the piano is his famous *Classical Symphony*. He used to laugh at all the complicated discussions among critics about his "neoclassical style" of which the *Classical Symphony* was supposed to be such a striking example. He told me that the reasons for writing that kind of symphony were of a purely practical nature; he wanted to prove to himself the extent of self-control he could exercise over his hearing. He therefore decided to write a piece without the help of any instrument, but in order to hear the harmonies well and to be sure of what he was doing, he adopted a simplified, conventional, so-called classical style! Thus he limited himself to the use of conventional chords. The rest of Prokofiev's music is, of course, far from being neoclassical in the narrow sense of the word; it has grown too organically out of our time to be so.

Prokofiev had an excellent musical memory. I recall him

quoting themes of other composers — themes he had only heard once or twice, sometimes years before. He could sit down at the piano and play uninterruptedly for hours all kinds of music, Russian and Western European, some of which was little known or pretty well forgotten. He remembered such things as the early operas of Tchaikovsky and whole scenes from Moussorgsky's *Marriage;* he knew measure for measure all the harmonic and orchestral secrets of Stravinsky's *Rites of Spring.* He had an excellent memory also in another sense. I remember once making a few disparaging remarks about a piece of his called *Chose en Soi.* Several years later, when I had completely forgotten the piece and the incident, he played it to me again without mentioning what it was and asked me how I liked it. I said I liked it quite well, whereupon he laughed sarcastically and gave me an appropriate scolding.

In 1917 Prokofiev finally graduated from the St. Petersburg Conservatory. He was at that time fairly well known in the musical circles of both St. Petersburg and Moscow, and not completely unknown abroad. Diaghilev had commissioned him in 1914 to write a ballet, but when it was finally written it was not produced. The story of the ballet and, in many ways, its music were too closely akin to Stravinsky's *Rites of Spring,* which Diaghilev had just produced in Paris. However, Prokofiev made a symphonic suite out of the music for this ballet and called it *Scythian Suite.* This was finally performed in St. Petersburg in 1916 with tremendous success. In 1915 he had gone to Italy to discuss with Diaghilev another ballet, *Chout (The Buffoon),* produced in 1921. When he left Russia he had already started an opera on the subject of Gozzi's *The Love for Three Oranges,* suggested to him by Meyerhold, and this opera was produced in Chicago in 1921.

Prokofiev left Russia in the winter of 1917, right after the October Revolution. He was one of the first Russians to obtain a foreign Soviet passport and leave Russia legally, not as an *émigré.* He went to America via Japan for a tour of concerts. After a stay of nearly a year in the United States, he came to Paris and settled there, as did so many Russian intellectuals of both the pro- and the counter-revolutionary camps. In Paris he lived the life of a composer whose fame was rapidly growing and whose music was beginning to be performed all over the world.

During the early twenties he went repeatedly on extensive and lucrative concert tours to North and South America and all over Western and Central Europe. Almost everywhere he was acclaimed as one of the most outstanding modern composers and performers (for like many Russian composers, Prokofiev is a brilliant pianist and interpreter of his own music). In America he had met an attractive singer of Spanish extraction but of Russian upbringing, whom he later married and who became his close collaborator. Up to the early thirties the two Prokofievs frequently traveled together on recital tours, she singing his songs and he accompanying her.

In 1924 France recognized the Soviet Union and both countries exchanged ambassadors. One of the first visitors to the newly established Soviet Embassy on the rue de Grenelle was Sergei Prokofiev. Like other Russians in Paris he had become a "stateless person" and had taken out a refugee (Nansen) passport. Now he dug into the bottom of his trunk, found his old Soviet passport and went to the Embassy to start proceedings for his reinstatement as a Soviet citizen.

In 1925 he was granted Soviet citizenship and at the invitation of the Soviet Association of Proletarian Musicians went on an extensive tour of the Soviet Union. There he was triumphantly received as a famous Russian composer who was sympathetic to the Soviet regime and who, although residing in Paris, had rejected the ideological position of an *émigré*. His music was performed all over the country, and his operas and ballets were produced with great success by the best theaters of the two Russian capitals, Moscow and Leningrad.

What prompted Prokofiev to return to the Soviet Union and become a Soviet citizen? What sort of longing made him turn his back on his established position as a famous composer of the Western world? The answer is twofold: first, the Soviet Union of that period was not quite the same thing as the Soviet Union of today. Second, the feelings of a forward-looking and revolutionary-minded Russian intellectual toward his fatherland and its government were quite different then from what they are now and were on the whole rather mixed. In the middle twenties, the Soviet Union was going through the so-called NEP period, which to many outsiders and insiders appeared as a kind of reprieve or respite from the bloody horrors of the Red Terror and the civil war. A small number of Soviet citizens were for the first time allowed not only to travel abroad but even to reside in foreign countries. The demarcation line between the pro-communists and the anti-communists was not so clearly drawn at that time as it later became. Thus Prokofiev, although not a communist (so far as I know he has never been a member of the party), was clearly sympathetic to the Soviet regime, regarded it as the legitimate government of his country, and, like so many others at that time, excused its extremist and terroristic policies as caused by historical revolutionary necessity. On the other hand, Prokofiev, while he was living in Paris, mingled freely with many Russian *émigré* artists and intellectuals. He participated actively in artistic ventures which were run by men like Sergei Diaghilev whose personnel consisted mainly of Russian *émigrés*, and enjoyed all the advantages and pleasures of the Western bourgeois world. But such a dual position was by no means unusual at that time. The sight of the poet Ilya Ehrenburg, who at that time had just made his first about-face and from a violent antagonist of the Soviet regime had become one of its most ardent sycophants, sitting in friendly conversation with some anti-Soviet writer in a Paris café was quite normal and caused no surprise.

At that time Soviet writers, poets and musicians were visiting Central and Western Europe and famous Soviet theater companies (the Moscow Art Theater, the Meyerhold Theater, the Tairov Kamerny Theater) were giving performances abroad for audiences composed chiefly of Russian *émigrés*. It was only several years later that Prokofiev's position grew out of the ordinary and became a privileged one indeed.

The strange thing about Prokofiev's music is that it almost never changes. This fact was pointed out by a Russian critic, Sabaniev, some twenty-five years ago: "Impressionism, futurism have been succeeded by atonality, polytonality, and other tendencies, yet Prokofiev remains exactly as we found him at the beginning of his career: unresponsive to movements, his art is as naïve as that of Schubert, Chopin, or even Mozart." Leaving out the question of naïveté in the music of those three composers, I believe Sabaniev has caught something about the nature of Prokofiev's music which is intrinsically true. It is a kind of music which since 1914 and 1915 has undergone very little change. Prokofiev has much music of variable quality and dimensions, but if one were to listen to his early and late pieces and to try to find some developments, try to construct some form of chronology into the changes of style and fashion, I feel sure one would be quite at a loss. Since the publication of his three pieces, *Sarcasmes*, *First Violin Concerto* and *Visions Fugitives*, little has changed in either the style or the technique of Prokofiev's music.

At the outset Prokofiev himself and his music symbolized a reaction against an aestheticism burdened with philosophy, literature, and mysticism. His task was to bring music back to the world of pure sound. Hence, the cutting, direct, square, cheerful style in contrast to the "arpeggio-ridden" music of his contemporaries; hence the preference for simplified harmonic texture, a clear-cut melody, and the major character of the whole structure; hence also the sectional, sometimes almost mechanical, form of his music.

Certain particularities of his melodic line and certain harmonic relations used over and over again make his music unmistakably personal. Prokofiev loves, for instance — or at least did love until his recent works — to play a little game of melodic construction which could easily be discovered in any one of his pieces. The game consists of taking a conventional rhythmical pattern so obvious as to border sometimes on triviality, and then afterwards forcing this melodic line into a harmonic frame which seems disconnected, surprisingly arbitrary, and produces the feeling that the melody has been refreshed by having been harmonically mishandled. Another

(167)

little game in Prokofiev's thematic structure is the abruptness and unexpectedness of his leaps. A melody will start in a very stereotyped manner, and then suddenly will leap to an absolutely unexpected tone over seemingly unconnected intervals. These characteristics contribute a great deal to the joking, sarcastic nature of much of his music. The intentional breaking up of conventional patterns produces a series of audible shocks which in turn create the feeling of irony. In a certain sense, a similar game is carried on within his harmonic texture. Chords, generally very simple chords, are related in such an entirely unexpected fashion that the ear has always a new element of harmonic surprise to cope with. Of course, the arbitrariness of these relations is only superficial, for at the back of them there is an organic logic of relations which Prokofiev discovers and establishes in his music.

What is somewhat perplexing is the mechanical form of his music. In that, Prokofiev is traditionally Russian, for, with a few exceptions, most Russian composers fitted their music into an existing form and did not let the form grow out of the nature of their musical invention. Another puzzling thing about Prokofiev's music is that, despite all the squareness, conciseness of his rhythm, the rhythmical aspect of his music is unproblematic. His rhythm is usually quite conventional and although charming and attractive in itself it is for the most part devoid of the modern preoccupations with rhythmical problems of which the works of Stravinsky and Bartók are such typical examples. Prokofiev always used to say that his chief interest lay not in rhythm but in the invention of good themes, and by good themes he meant those melodies that one would recognize as indubitably his own. Formless and amorphous melodies are what he despises most in music. This emphasis upon melodic invention is most significant for the comprehension of Prokofiev's music.

It has often been said that modern pianistic style owes much to Prokofiev, and that Prokofiev was one of the first to discover the percussive use of the piano. Prokofiev, indubitably, is one of the major contemporary composers for the piano and one of the best technicians of this instrument, and he has exploited the percussive possibilities of the piano extremely well. Such works as his second, third and seventh piano sonatas, his third piano concerto, his *Visions Fugitives*, *Sarcasmes*, and *Suggestion Diabolique*, have become part of the regular piano repertoire. In his piano style Prokofiev does not shun the traditions of the nineteenth century. He is not unduly afraid of the Liszt-Chopin-Schumann heritage. Probably one of his most important achievements is the creation of a perfectly unified contemporary style of piano music which forms a synthesis of eighteenth- and nineteenth-century traditions with modern technical inventions. He is certainly one of the best piano composers since Debussy.

Personally, I think the best music Prokofiev ever wrote is not the ironic, joking music which is so well known in America, but rather those infrequent pages composed in a more lyrical mood: for instance, the nostalgic and melodically beautiful last pages of *The Prodigal Son* (the ballet produced in the last year of Diaghilev's reign in Paris in 1929), the second movement of his third piano concerto, his early songs on the poems of Akhmatova, even the *Lieutenant Kije* suite, and the somewhat overly simple yet tender and sincere themes of his *Fifth Symphony*.

Another peculiarity about Prokofiev's music is that its style lacks any consistent polyphonic development. Prokofiev seems to have a particular dislike for the style of imitative counter-point, and used to make fun of certain of his contemporaries for writing fugues and fugatos. He contended that this made their style necessarily derivative of and like eighteenth-century polyphonic music. This sounds somewhat paradoxical for someone who has made free use of the rather mechanical standards of eighteenth-century musical form and applied it to the very structure of his themes.

With all its individual characteristics, its urbanism and out-ward "classicism," the music of Prokofiev, particularly in its melismatic nature, is deeply rooted in the Russian past. Some-times it reflects Moussorgsky, sometimes Tchaikovsky. This is enhanced by a masterful orchestrational technique, a tech-nique born of the study of such Russian works as the ballets of Tchaikovsky, the operas of Glinka, and the late operas of Rimsky-Korsakov. His orchestration is much more conven-tional than that of Stravinsky. It is rougher, less polished, and it sometimes lacks the wonderful transparence of Stravinsky's scores.

But in spite of all the individual characteristics of Pro-kofiev's music, and its indebtedness to the Russian masters of the nineteenth century, there also exists a powerful interrela-tion between Prokofiev as an artist, as a human being, and the Russia of today. In particular, his art has served as a leaven among the younger generation of Soviet composers. In fact, few pages of the early works of Shostakovich, of Khatcha-turian, and of many others, are free from a specific relation to either Prokofiev's methods or his technique. In the Soviet constellation Prokofiev has occupied for a long time the posi-tion of an older master (a position shared with Miakovsky). Hence his works have been regarded as examples of artistic perfection, as objects worthy of imitation, and also as "signposts of the progress of Soviet musical culture." It is interesting to note Prokofiev's position in relation to that of Shostakovich. While Prokofiev represents (or represented, until the purge of 1948) the grand old master, Shostakovich is (or was) the "great glory of Soviet musical culture," a child of the new Soviet civilization, "the supreme fruit, borne by the tree of the October revolution."

While Prokofiev's music reflects the assumed outward qualities of Soviet life (optimism, simplicity of structure, and a certain uncouth roughness), Shostakovich's music attempts to illustrate the inward meaning of the revolution, of Soviet socialism, of the class struggle, of patriotism and heroism. Hence Shostakovich's long "descriptive" symphonies, his naïve and obvious attempts at "program music."

It would be perhaps worth while at this point to glance at the music of Dimitri Shostakovich in order to understand the relative position of both composers in the Soviet Union today.

It is as difficult to describe the music of Shostakovich as to describe the form and color of an oyster, not because this music by any means is complicated or "inscrutable in its profundity" (as Soviet Russian criticism used to put it) but simply because it is shapeless in style and form and impersonal in color. Yet the oyster has a very individual taste of its own which Shostakovich unfortunately lacks. For one of his chief weaknesses is absolute, eclectic impersonality. Even during his first period, when he still felt himself relatively free to choose or invent his own technique, his music was impersonal.

He still borrows other people's technical and stylistic inventions as if they were communal belongings. He still imitates indiscriminately (and I believe quite unconsciously) here Tchaikovsky and Beethoven, there Berlioz and Mahler; here again he tries out some device he learned from a score of Stravinsky or Prokofiev, or Ravel, or Hindemith, or from some minor composer of the twenties. During his first period he wrote a greater variety of kinds of music than later, using tricks, devices, and techniques taken from such different sources that they could not possibly lead to a unified style, and jumping from Tchaikovsky to jazzy rhythms of the *Mitteleuropa* variety. His operas are so different from his symphonies, his chamber music from his ballets, that one has a hard time recognizing that the same man wrote them; and it is the defects of the music, rather than its qualities, that are recognizable as his own. Thus, for instance, he writes few melodies in which the augmented fourth does not appear; yet this interval is essentially unmelodic and by association reminds us of very stale "melodies" of the late nineteenth century. His exaggerated liking for march rhythms of 4/4 and 2/4 time leads to a kind of wooden squareness in the fast movements of his music. His long melodic cantilenas are shapeless and awkwardly built. His "tunes" are often from very ordinary sources (in Soviet Russia they were called "marshy" during the years of his eclipse), imitating very common and uninteresting factory or army songs. One would probably not object to them if they had been treated originally; for Haydn, Beethoven, Stravinsky often used tunes coming from the gutter.

The two positive qualities I find in the music of Shostakovich are of a rather ambiguous order. The first one is his great versatility and efficiency in Conservatory training, which enables him to solve technical problems of a broad variety in a highly skillful manner. Shostakovich is undoubtedly an excellent craftsman and most of his inventiveness goes into such branches of musical craft as orchestration and efficient part writing (what the Germans call *Guter Tonsatz*). It is not infrequent among contemporary composers that such technical strength conceals a paucity of original musical ideas.

The second quality of Shostakovich, to foreigners so surprising, is the inherent optimism of his music. As everybody knows, the common view of Russian music and the Russian character is that they are by nature easily depressed and melancholy or just the reverse, boisterously and wildly gay — without any visible reason. This view, erroneous as it is, is well entrenched in people's minds. Hence when a composer from Russia is neither desperately melancholic nor in a state of frenzy, as in a Ballet Russe finale, he is believed to have lost his essentially Russian attributes. No one will deny that a completely new life has now been established in Russia, yet this has little to do with the national character of the people and their art, which at times in the past has been just as optimistic as the music of Shostakovich. Glinka, the father of modern Russian music, Borodin, Moussorgsky, and Tchaikovsky himself have numberless pages of the happiest, lightest, gayest music the nineteenth century produced.

Thus to a Russian there would not be anything particularly surprising in the optimism of Shostakovich. But his kind of optimism takes a redundant, blatant, and unconvincing form. One always feels a kind of compelling force behind it, a force of an extramusical order. It appears to be based on the official syllogistic formula: before the revolution life was desperate, therefore art was gloomy; now the revolution is victorious, therefore art must be optimistic. It is obvious that this *must* rings like a command of the gods rather than a logical conclusion of a syllogism. The result is that it often forces the composer into a great effort unnatural to his temperament and therefore unsuccessful.

What this *must* tends to do to Russian music in general and to Shostakovich's music in particular is lamentable. It drives the young composer to naïve and dated formulas such as an excessive and very conventional use of major triads, tunes and cadences in major keys, all of them describing the glorious and victorious events of the present in the most emphatic and banal musical language. (Minor modes are used to describe the dark and gloomy days of the past.) It steers the whole music into a verbose and brassy style which soon becomes dreary and monotonous. It produces that wooden 2/4 or 4/4 rhythm to which I have already referred, and which I suppose is considered "manlier" and "more virile" than the "effeminate" 3/4 or 6/8, and fills the thematic material with such commonplace metrical patterns as one eighth note followed by two sixteenth notes (or vice versa), which most good composers use very sparingly.

In Shostakovich's postwar music all these unfortunate characteristics come to full bloom. The substance of Shostakovich's compositions now tends to be of such obvious understandability that his music ceases to be an artistic language in which the adventurous human mind discovers new laws and new problems which it endeavors to solve in a new way. Every technique, every melodic line, every development, polyphonic or monophonic, every rhythm, every formal device is reminiscent of either contemporary or nineteenth-century composers, and is used in such an obvious fashion that after a while one begins to wonder if even the most uneducated masses will not soon tire of it. (I often ask myself if this *a priori* decision, so frequent among intellectuals and politicians, that the masses have a naturally low taste for the arts is not a proof of their own lack of discrimination.)

Simplification of music is in itself a salutary thing, but there is a moment when simplification becomes too obvious and absurd. Eclecticism is often the sturdy backbone of healthy tradition (was not Johann Sebastian Bach a great eclectic?) but when it pervades a man's music or stands in the way of the invention of a personal style it becomes deplorable. Objectivity should not be confused with impersonality, just as romanticism should not necessarily involve grandiloquent sentimentality and formlessness.

Composers of the older generation faced the crucial problem of their relation to the October Revolution. This problem never existed for Shostakovich. Every one of those older men had to make his own personal decision, to accept it, to reject it, like Stravinsky, or accept it only partially, like Alexander Glazunov. Shostakovich, on the other hand, was himself a child of the revolutionary years, a product of the Soviet environment, and hence to him the revolution represented the given terms of a theorem, a pragmatic, unquestionable reality.

Prokofiev accepted the Russian Revolution in its "totality" and saw in the new Russia the logical consequence of the old one, the result of a century-long process of emancipation. He was, and surely still is, a sincere and *instinctive* Russian patriot, who gives little thought to the question of justice or injustice of the Soviet government and regards its acts as the result of a kind of inexplicable historical necessity. In other words, he is a person whose political thinking never developed and who, not unlike many American artists, believed that his main job was to do his own work and leave political matters and entanglements to others. At the same time he felt very strongly his profound association, or rather his organic tie, with Russia, with the Russian people and Russian culture. Despite his long years abroad and his position as a famous composer in the Western world, he remained essentially Russian, in his habits, his behavior and his art.

When the early plans of the Soviet government concerning the future of Soviet music became known in 1930 and 1931, the drive *against* "formalist experimentation" (which was inaugurated by the first music purge in 1931), and the drive *for* a music "which would be acceptable and understandable to the broad proletarian masses of the Soviet Union," Prokofiev welcomed the official edict as a realization of some of his own ideas about the function of music. "I always wanted to invent melodies," he often remarked, "which could be understood by large masses of people — simple singable melodies." This he considered to be the most important and difficult task of the modern composer.

But there was another and more tangible factor which contributed to the return of Prokofiev to the U.S.S.R. in the middle twenties. To Prokofiev Russia represented at that time a vast field for the expansion of his artistic energies, a land of opportunity inhabited by millions of potential "consumers" of his music.

At that time Russia was impoverished by the loss of great numbers of her intellectuals who either had died in the war or during the Red Terror or had fled from Russia between 1918 and 1921. It was only natural that those intellectuals, friends of Prokofiev, who remained in Moscow and were working in the fields of music, the film and the theater, and with whom he had re-established contact as soon as he had settled in France, should be urging him to return to Russia. (Ironically enough, most of these friends of Prokofiev have since either been executed or have disappeared in concentration camps and insane asylums or else are leading the obscure existence of outcasts from Soviet society.)

In 1926, after his return to Paris from his first tour in the U.S.S.R., Prokofiev wrote his ballet *The Steel Leap*. It was one of those broad panoramas of Soviet life during the NEP, adorned by moments of satire and ending in a grandiose scene depicting the construction of a new Russia. He wrote this "heroic" ballet in the peaceful bourgeois surroundings of a respectable French villa in the Savoy mountains. The ballet was produced by the Ballet Russe of that same Sergei Diaghilev who has since become the archvillain, the corrupter of Russian art and artists and the prototype of the "pernicious, degenerate and rootless cosmopolitan."

From that time on, Prokofiev became a kind of representative of Soviet culture abroad: he was regarded as its best protagonist and its most useful propagandist. While the frontiers of Russia were slowly closing up and the cultural barriers becoming more and more apparent, Prokofiev's personal position as the unofficial ambassador of Soviet Russia abroad remained unchanged. He continued to reside in Paris, go yearly for three or four months to Russia and on extensive concert tours all over the world.

Nor did his private life change in any way. He saw the same circle of friends, freely expressed to them his ideas about the Soviet Union and his relation to it, his beliefs in the future of Russia and Russian culture, and seemed to enjoy enormously his peculiar and unique position as a famous man of two different worlds.

For it was really during that period that the separation of the two worlds became apparent. About 1932–1933 the Stalin reaction had gained control of nearly all the dissenting groups inside Russia and had developed its police network all over the vast Soviet land. It had imposed a ruthless system of compulsive collectivization and had liquidated and deported millions of Russian peasants and farmers. The "total state" became a pragmatic reality and the last vestiges of individual thought and independent cultural activity were being eradicated by Stalin's secret police.

Nevertheless, Prokofiev's position seemed to be well entrenched in the U.S.S.R. and he had there what is most needed in totalitarian states: protection in "the highest circles." In 1931 or 1932, he took an apartment in Moscow and started spending more time in the Soviet Union. According to trustworthy accounts, it appears that he had been "urged" to settle more permanently in Moscow by the "highest authorities." Prokofiev's privileged position must have naturally aroused a good deal of envy among his Soviet colleagues. Anyone who has lived in a totalitarian state knows what importance "privilege" can acquire and what overwhelming jealousies and hates it can arouse. It is quite possible that these suggestions were made to Prokofiev in order to quiet the feelings among his compatriots. But it may also have meant that while the "highest authorities" were ready to expend their special favors upon Prokofiev, lesser "high authorities" had become irritated and critical of a man who tried to live the independent life of a free artist.

Toward the middle of the thirties Prokofiev and his family

moved definitively to Russia. Whether he was mildly advised or ordered to do so is a matter of conjecture. The fact remains that he was obviously executing some kind of order and that he did so without much enthusiasm, hating to give up his independent and privileged position abroad.

All through these years his "instinctive patriotism" never wavered and he tried to conform in all aesthetic and ideological matters to the wishes of the party and the government. Thus, when it was suggested to him to write a piece for the fifteenth anniversary of Lenin's death, he obliged the "highest authority" by writing a *Toast Song to Stalin*. (He was unable to find a text in all the works of Lenin which would be suitable for a musical setting. Besides there are only two places in Lenin's voluminous works where he refers to Stalin, both times in a very slighting way. As a result, Lenin as a source of musical inspiration had to be abandoned and Prokofiev was compelled to use the safer and quite innocuous text of a drinking song.)

But has his music suffered from conformism? Does it show traces of creative deterioration which one could attribute to his having had to conform to the dictates of the party? Again this is a matter of conjecture. For we certainly cannot know or even guess what would have happened to Prokofiev's art had he stayed in Western Europe. On the whole one sees that his music has undergone a process of great and at times excessive simplification. Some of his melodies have become obvious to the point of being trivial, and in his harmonic language he has occasionally used devices of a defunct Victorian era. But how much of this is the result of conformism and how much the natural development of his art is hard to determine. It is certain, however, that throughout the thirties and the early forties he was the only Soviet composer whose music still preserved a great deal of genuine freshness, and had not left behind it that obnoxious odor of synthetic materials (like German ersatz gasoline) and the stamp of dull provincialism which are the trademarks of practically all Soviet contemporary music.

Until 1938, Prokofiev continued to make trips abroad, and came as far as America for his last visit to the Western world. When he met his noncommunist or his anticommunist friends abroad he put up an enthusiastic façade about the great achievements of the Soviet Union. But behind this mask of optimism and official praise, one could detect a feeling totally contradictory to the very nature of Prokofiev's character: the feeling of profound and terrible insecurity. He was more irritable than usual. He spoke about his many enemies among his colleagues and about the tension that existed between him and other prominent Soviet composers and critics. He admitted that he was worried during the purge of 1937, when the second big attack against formalism in music was launched and Shostakovich was put on ice for nearly two years. It is no secret that at that time Stalin personally intervened in his behalf, and Prokofiev was taken off the list of "purgees."

But above all he was worried about his art. All these years he thought he was doing exactly the kind of work his government wanted; that is, writing simple and easily "consumable" music. And he also thought that he was doing it quite well, better than most of the other Soviet composers, because his personal inclinations coincided with what he understood to be the wishes of his government. Suddenly he began to doubt his own interpretation of the government's decrees and to wonder what he should do next, what kind of music he should write in order to . . . conform. At the same time his remaining artistic integrity quite naturally revolted against the very idea of conformity for conformity's sake, a conformity which was not based on his own beliefs and ran contrary to his artistic freedom.

Nevertheless, Prokofiev continued to put up a façade. Soon his relations with his wife began to deteriorate and in 1940 he left her and his two children, and went away to the Caucasus with a young niece of Kaganovitch, Stalin's close friend and associate, herself an ardent communist and a prominent leader of the Soviet youth organization, the Red Pioneers. His personal drama preceded the war by only a few months. Soon after the war started, Prokofiev, like many other Russian artists, participated in various morale-building enterprises of his country. His position seemed secure and his reputation began to outrun and outclass all his rivals with the exception of Shostakovich. In fact, at that time, while Shostakovich was the "star" of Soviet music Prokofiev was its "dean." His new wife became his literary collaborator and in many ways served as a channel for his protection and as power in the higher ranks of the party.

Then late in 1943 or early in 1944, the news came of his sudden illness. He had fallen down a staircase, apparently as the result of a heart attack. He was unable to work for many months. But as soon as he got better he completed the voluminous score of his opera *War and Peace*. Despite his wife's collaboration as librettist and a lavish production in Leningrad in 1945, the opera was a failure. Another heart attack a year later compelled him to go for a prolonged rest to the Caucasus. In the meantime his *Sixth Symphony* was left unfinished. When he returned in 1946 he completed the score and it had a first successful performance in Leningrad and a much less enthusiastic reception in Moscow.

A third heart attack early in 1948 left him prostrate for another two or three months. While he was sick in bed, on February 10, 1948, he heard the ax fall. That was the day *Pravda* published the now famous and unique document in the annals of modern history: the point-by-point condemnation of the most prominent Soviet composers by the Central Committee of the Communist Party of the U.S.S.R. Prokofiev's name led all the rest.

The ritual of Soviet purges followed with scrupulous precision. Public meetings of Soviet composers were held all over the Soviet Union. At those meetings the composers recanted their errors, their ideological sins. Prokofiev wrote a letter of apology. In it he recanted in terms slightly more dignified than those used by other purgees. He regretted his obvious errors but indulged in a long explication of how difficult it is to invent good melodies. The letter was found inadequate. The next step in the purge ritual was the work of penance. Prokofiev chose a stilted patriotic short story about the life of a hero of the Soviet Air Force who had lost his two legs during the war. His wife concocted a libretto out of this "Soviet epic" and he wrote in record time a full evening's opera called *The Life of a Real Person*. After the first tentative reading of the opera by a group of singers and a Leningrad orchestra, it was thrown out as an "unpardonable distortion of Soviet reality" and a "base mixture of formalistic habits." Both Prokofiev and the conductor of the orchestra were reprimanded for having taken the orchestra's time to rehearse such abominable music. Prokofiev was compelled to write apologetic letters about the whole affair.

(182)

Again rumors of Prokofiev's ill health began to penetrate through the iron curtain while the Soviet press and some of his colleagues continued to attack him and his art with unrelenting ferocity.

Whether Prokofiev can achieve full redemption and regain his position as the dean of Soviet composers is doubtful. For in the eyes of those who rule the destinies of the Russian people, he is the symbol of Russia's former close association with the modern Western world with its great emancipatory tradition and its spirit of intellectual and artistic freedom. This the tyrants of the Kremlin cannot endure. It endangers the very foundations of their obsolete and reactionary state.

IX
Christmas with Stravinsky

DEAR NIKA DIMITRIEVITCH,

Yes, of course we will be expecting you for Christmas. You will stay right here with us. You will sleep on the sofa on which slept Nadia Boulanger, Olsen, Auden and others. Huxley was too long. I hope it will be long enough for you. (What is your height?)

You and Balanchine will probably take the Super-Chief, which gets you into Pasadena at 8:13 A.M. We will meet you *there.* (Pasadena is the last station before Los Angeles and closer to us.)

Please don't disappoint us this time — *come!* Vera sends greetings.

Yours,
IGOR STR.

THE LETTER was in Russian, written on one side of a half-sheet of airmail paper, in Stravinsky's jagged handwriting, and in very black ink. The sentence, "What is your height?" was in red pencil on the left-hand margin, with an asterisk following the previous sentence and a red-pencil tracer leading to it. The sentence about Pasadena was in blue

(184)

pencil, upside down in the top right-hand corner. A blue asterisk and a blue-penciled tracer connected it with the previous sentence. The word *zdȳes* (here) was underlined with a blue pencil; the word *tam* (meaning *there* and referring to Pasadena) was boxed in a blue-penciled frame; the word *priȳezjaïte!* (come!) was heavily underlined in red pencil. The whole little sheet gave the impression of compact and calculated orderliness and with its several colors looked like a gay and nervous drawing.

DEAR IGOR FËDOROVICH,
Please forgive this late answer, but I wanted to be definite and only yesterday did I decide to go *définitivement*. Also, Balanchine wants to "rest in a train" (*sic!*) whereas I want to fly, so we compromised: we go on the train, we fly back. We couldn't get any reservations on either "Chief." Balanchine's Dr. B. got us a drawing room in a "through" car on some kind of a "Limited." I believe it leaves sometime around 4 P.M. from Grand Central, but I don't know when it arrives in Los Angeles. My understanding is that this train doesn't go through Pasadena. We will wire you from Chicago.
Auden, who is back today, tells me that you need scores of Handel's operas. Do you have *Cesare* and *Rodelinda*? If not, I will bring them. How is the libretto? Much love to Vera Arturovna and yourself.

Yours,
N. N.

DEAR NIKA NABOKOV,
We are glad you are coming. Don't be late to the train. If you are going via Grand Central it is probably the Commodore Vanderbilt which has a "through" car. It makes connections in Chicago with the Grand Canyon Limited

(which is a *slow* train). The Commodore Vanderbilt arrives in Chicago at 8:30 Chicago time (I just verified it on the timetable), and the Grand Canyon leaves Chicago at noon. Thus, leaving the 19th at 4:30 P.M. (N. Y. time), you will arrive in Los Angeles (L. A. time) on the 22nd at 11 A.M. We will meet you at the station unless Maria Balanchine meets George in her car. In that case, she could easily drop you at our house, which is on her way anyhow.

We both liked Auden very much and I believe the libretto will be very good. Yes, of course, bring all you have of Handel's operas. All the rest we will discuss here. Come, come quickly. Greetings from both of us.

Yours,
I. S.

P.S. [on the left-hand margin in black pencil] Ask George to get [now in red and blue pencil] 2 bottles of Eau de Genièvre — it is *better* than vodka. I can't find it here. George will know where to get it. Come!

The drawing room of the "through" car disappointed me. In my imagination I had devised a luxury model bristling with chromium, beds sliding down or arising from under modern plush upholstery, and discreet invisible plumbing and air conditioning. Instead, our room was the usual wan green, fusty-smelling compartment of a tubercular Pullman car: coughing plumbing, clanking piping and wiggly, neurotic fan.

Balanchine, having "organized" the fancy-colored Christmas packages on the racks ("Best Wishes to Vera Arturovna — V. K."; "Merry Xmas and Happy New Year from the Sokoloffs to the Stravinskys"; "Merry Xmas, expecting you soon in New York — Vittorio," etc.), installed himself opposite me with a purrlike grunt. Soon his nose nodded to the rhythm of the car and the pages of the *Daily Mirror* wilted in his plantlike hands.

The train slipped out of the tunnel. The rush of haggard shrubbery and disconsolate housing abruptly shifted to the calm flow of the Hudson, its black surface chopped by slushy ice floes.

This was my first trip to California. I had never wanted to go. Up to the last minute I could not make up my mind whether to give in to the persuasion of a convenient neuralgia and send Balanchine off alone. The whole trip appeared silly and extravagant. To surrender oneself to some three night-days of boredom, restlessness, and insomnia in "through" cars, "luxury" diners ("Sorry sir, no more roast beef"; "Sorry sir, they forgot to put on the wine in Chicago"), and "strato-stuffed" airliners for the pleasure of four or five days in California (unfamiliar surroundings, dubious landscape) seemed capricious indeed.

True enough, at the other end of the journey there were the two Stravinskys, whom I liked so much and whom I had come to know so well during the years of their American "retreat." Auden had described to me how warmly they received their friends, how simple and gay Igor Fëdorovich can be in his tiny home. Then, too, I remembered the stern Stravinskyan warning, "Do not disappoint us this time. *Come!* [or else . . .]," and of course the relentless fascination which he held for me as for most of the musicians of my generation. To see him in his house, to observe him at work in his studio, to talk to him for long hours and follow the trail of his penetrating, agile thought, enlivened with succulent metaphor ("Can you imagine what it means for me to conduct in the City Center, with its orchestra pit like a men's room and no acoustics at all? It is like putting a new Rolls-Royce on Russian roads"; or about the Berkshire Festival: "It is perfectly all right, but why should contrabasses practice outdoors under pine trees? After all, they are not herbivorous instruments"), and above all, to scrutinize his latest scores — all this seemed enticing enough to outweigh the apparent absurdity of the tedious journey.

Taking a long train trip is like cooking a steak. Up to a point, while the steak is still rare, it preserves its identity with the animal of its origin; as soon as it turns brown it moves closer to the animal who will consume it.

Thus with my journey: Sometime in Chicago, between 8:30 A.M., when I peered out of our overheated sleeper and saw coats, hats and briefcases moving in wintry vapors towards the stairway in the LaSalle Street Station, and 12:30, when Balanchine and I, frosted by Lake Michigan winds, returned from a lonely tour through the Art Institute (where delicate French midsummers strip-teased from behind Renoirish nudes and iridescent Seuratic Sunday strollers), my thoughts had veered from New York and our hectic departure to the unknown Stravinsky home in Hollywood. Soon I began to wonder if they could really put me up, if it was convenient for them. It seemed a dreadful imposition to use their sofa, particularly during Christmas week, when they would surely have many guests. Would it have been wiser to stay at a hotel? I asked Balanchine.

"Oh, no," he said, "they love to have guests. He, in particular. Don't worry, he won't let you alone for a minute; he will talk to you day and night and ask you a million questions. They will drive you around Hollywood and take you to the best restaurants for dinner. In the morning you will have breakfast with him and his parrot and you will see him do his Hungarian calisthenics. You know he is well-built [George clasped his arms] and phenomenally strong, with a wrestler's biceps. He jumps like a ball, walks on his head and does push-ups with the ease of a twenty-year-old. And besides," he added sententiously, "he will play you his new scores: it will do you good to look at them carefully. Don't think of going to a hotel. You will offend him and he will never forgive you."

All along the way my thoughts buzzed around Stravinsky. I thought of his extraordinary destiny, how strange, how brilliant, and how perplexing it has been. A true and earthy child of that miscarriage of history, the Russian civilization of the nineteenth century, he reflected both its creative dynamism and its refinements.

Stravinsky has been one of the earliest "Great Refugees" of our ungrateful modern times. He left old-fashioned, miasmic Imperial Russia, which had no real use for him, in the first decade of our century and never returned to any of the Russias which have since appeared on the Eurasian plain. He has little use for any of them, least of all for the various Red ones, even for his memories, and he is altogether free of any romantic Ulyssean longing. For Stravinsky, Russia is a language, which he uses with superb, gourmandlike dexterity; it is a few books; Glinka and Tchaikovsky. The rest either leaves him indifferent or arouses his anger, contempt, and violent dislike.

In the years between 1908 and 1913, Stravinsky became famous in the old-world capital of Paris, where a wave of infatuation with exotics brought about the "discovery" of Russian music, painting, opera, and ballet.

These were the true *années des Ballets Russes*, as any Parisian old-timer will tell you. The astonishing success of Diaghilev's opera and ballet venture in Paris, which began in 1908 with the production of *Boris Godunov* and culminated in 1912 and 1913 with the productions of *Petroushka* and *The Rites of Spring*, turned the West toward the seventy-five-year-old Russian art, "the new Eastern enchantment full of rich, flashy colors and tempestuously wild or languorously melancholic music." This was approximately the time when in America musicians' names began to end in *ov's, itzky's* and *owsky's* instead of in *rosch's, ann's, er's, elli's* and *ini's;* the time of the first invasion of Sashas, Grishas, Mishas and Jaschas.

During these years, Stravinsky, a young man in his twenties from the land of the tsars, samovars, ballerina mistresses, and vodka attracted notice as the most famous *fauve* of Western music, the leader of its most radical movement.

In 1913 he shocked the congregation of Paris balletomanes by his *Rites of Spring*. The scandal of the first performance of this work at the Théâtre des Champs-Élysées, the yelling, whistling, and the ensuing scuffle (some fifty people got undressed to the bone and landed in the Commissariat de Police on the rue Havre Commartin), has never been surpassed, not even by the historical scandal of the first performance of *Tannhäuser* (that time the Jockey Club offered to its operagoing members elegant silver whistles with the inscription "*pour siffler* Tannhäuser").

From here on, Stravinsky's leadership of modern Western music became incontestable. As years went by he gained more prestige and received a greater and deeper respect, mixed at times with envy, jealousy, or limitless adulation. His reputation spread over the world in a similar and perhaps somewhat broader way than the fame of Picasso, his close friend and collaborator. Every new work of Stravinsky's was a major event; his Parisian adepts, the "inner circle" of his admirers, acclaimed him as the greatest composer of the time. His music was eagerly awaited by an enormous public and equally eagerly discussed. Hardly was there a music magazine in Europe which did not discuss his art in every issue; scores of books appeared about his music. Each of his new "lines," each attempt at a new style, became immediately the topic of fierce discussion and the musical fashion of the year.

No sooner did the chestnuts begin to burgeon along the boulevards of Paris than the international musical intelligentsia would be seething with rumors about the new Stravinsky ballet or concert piece which was to have its first performance each year at the end of May. I remember the unique, the unforgettably pure excitement (so totally devoid of any non-musical considerations) of these first performances of Stravinsky's music, the electric tension of the audience and the ensuing ovations.

A real commotion occurred when, in the early twenties, Stravinsky stopped using Russian folklore as subject matter and, turning toward the Western tradition, started to write music akin in style and spirit to the baroque period, the period of Bach, Handel, and Scarlatti. Numerous people were so deeply shocked at this new monster, half jazz, half Bach, half "modern man," half powdered wig, that they developed an intense and a prolonged heart-bleed. They bled at the loss of the "Russian Stravinsky" (the Stravinsky of *The Fire-bird*); they bled at the horror of this perverse new thing which, for want of a better term (or rather, for lack of imagination), was christened "neoclassicism." The bleeding persisted and in some cases developed into hemophilia. Traces of it can still be found, for example, in the pages of the *New York Times*. It manifests itself in an angry, resentful, and disillusioned denial of nearly all that Stravinsky has written since he abandoned the sacred soil of Russian subject matter.

Today, many still hate his music for many contradictory reasons. He deceived the congenital lover of Russia (not the new, but the exotic, fairy-tale Russia of wide spaces and *âme slave*); he enraged the extremists by his respect for and his return to tradition; he irritated those who saw in him the apostle of dissonance, of the percussion instruments, and of lush new tone colors. (This was approximately the time when various people, some real composers, more often unconscious charlatans, were experimenting with funny noises and the description of things mechanical. Pieces like Honegger's *Pacific 231*, Antheil's *Ballet mécanique* and Mossolov's [not Molotov's] *Iron Foundry* were typical examples.)

Despite his so-called neoclassical twist, Stravinsky nevertheless remained the unquestionable leader of modern music in Paris and the West throughout the early thirties.

True enough, in the second decade of the century, another figure became powerful and highly influential, this time in the waning and neurotic Central European capital of Vienna. This was Schönberg, the great atonal father, the inventor and practitioner of a new technique of composition: the "twelve-tone system." (Usually, to a layman, these words do not mean very much, but to his ears they certainly mean a great deal. They stand for the kind of music in which conventional frontiers between dissonance and consonance are completely abolished. In this music, such a distinction is meaningless. Everything sounds contrary to the habitual musical furnishings of our uncultivated ears and, instead of relaxing in comfortable, pretty music, we are invited to admire the supraphysical formulas of sound.)

Stravinsky is primarily an artisan, a craftsman, while Schönberg is a dogmatician, a theorist. Neither likes the other. And yet in the opinion of most musicians, both share the pontifical glories of our state of music. Since the death of Manuel de Falla and Béla Bartók, Stravinsky and Schönberg remain the lonely "founding fathers" of this strangely eccentric and highly anarchic state. To that anarchy, in which everyone seems to go his own way, they offer a certain amount of cohesion, a certain ideological meaning.

Curiously enough, as if to fulfill a fateful anachronism, both have found refuge in Hollywood, where a true eccentric looks like a sedate Baltic burgher and anarchy is a form of matrimony.

It was a little past noon on December 22nd when Balanchine's wife Maria stopped the car on an incline of winding North Wetherly Drive. On our right a low white picket fence was overtopped by a wall of tall evergreen shrubbery. Some two hundred and fifty feet behind the shrubbery, silhouetted against blue-brownish hills, stood a small and flat one-story house, rimmed by a narrow porch in front and a large terrace on its left-hand side.

Balanchine climbed out of the car. "Here we are," he said, helping me to get my bags and packages out of the back seat.

From behind the shrubbery we heard hasty footsteps and

Russian voices. A minute later both Stravinskys appeared at a small side gate near the garage. They were dressed in breakfast clothes — she in an impeccably white negligee, which made her look large and stately, he in a polka-dotted burgundy bathrobe, with the striking addition of a narrow-brimmed, wilted, black felt hat. Both of them smiled and gesticulated. We all began embracing.

"*Noo priyekhali* — well, finally you've arrived," said Vera Arturovna.

"*N-da . . . enfin*," echoed Stravinsky under his hat.

This vision made me suddenly aware of their extraordinary physical disproportion. There was something both touching and amusing in it. The tall, Olympian figure of Vera Arturovna, her broad and regular Scandinavian features, her wide-open and languidly smiling blue eyes, in such contrast to her husband's sharp facial contours, his beaklike nose and fleshy lips, and his short, totally fatless body, so surprisingly young, so agile and elastic.

I remembered that Tchelitchev called him a "prancing grass-hopper" and that Cocteau used to remark, when Stravinsky conducted, that he looked like "an erect ant acting its part in a La Fontaine fable." There is in effect something crickety, something insectal, about the movements of his body. They are swift, precise, and always well controlled, like the movements of an accomplished dancer or acrobat. Yet the moment I saw him in front of his garden in California, I knew that both Tchelitchev and Cocteau were wrong. He is neither a grasshopper nor an ant; he is not an insect at all: he is much more like a bird — one of those small birds with large, sturdy beaks, like cardinals or lovebirds, whose movements are quick, electric, and nervous.

"Give this to me," said Stravinsky, picking up my bag. "Heavens, what is in it? Someone's meat?"

"It's only music," I replied, "and a couple of bottles."

"Ah, you brought my scores. Good for you. Only — you know, I don't need them any more. I mean the Handel operas. I found most of them here and Hawkes promised to get me some more in London."

"Come, come," said Vera Arturovna, "let's go in."

We went through the gate and walked up to the house. The path led uphill through a patch of garden banked on one side by bushes, on the other by long-stemmed pink and cream-colored roses.

"Go to your right, *through* the living room," said Vera Arturovna as we reached the small entrance hall of the house. I crossed a spacious, sunny room filled with spring flowers, modern pictures, light-colored furniture, and several bird cages, and entered a smaller room, lined on two sides with bookcases. Across the room, turning its back to the terrace window, stood the sofa.

Vera Arturovna ordered me to take off my shoes. "The first thing we do," she said, "is to measure the prospective sleepers."

"Here they are, all of them," said Stravinsky, and he pointed to an array of marks and signatures written in pencil on different levels of the door frame.

"See, this is tiny Mrs. Bolm. She was the smallest of them all. And this is Olsen, the tallest."

We started deciphering signatures.

"And who is this?" asked Maria Balanchine.

"This . . . Vera, who is this? — Ah, yes, it's Elsie Rieti."

They were both relieved when my watermark did not exceed Auden's six feet.

"Oh," said Vera Arturovna in a disappointed tone, "I thought you were much taller than Auden."

"It's only his hair," commented Stravinsky. "Come here. Stretch out on the sofa. You see," he turned to George Balanchine, "he fits perfectly: from socks to hair. Like a violin in its case."

The Balanchines were leaving to visit Maria's family. They planned to pick us all up in the evening for dinner at the Napoli, Stravinsky's Italian *Stammstube*.

"I suppose you want to bathe and change," said Vera Arturovna.

"Why, he looks clean," said Igor, "*et il ne sent pas trop mauvais.*"

"Come, come, Igor; let's leave him alone." She dragged him by the sleeve. "When you're ready, we'll eat lunch."

"But I must show him where to wash," said Stravinsky and led me to the bathroom. Just before opening the door he turned to me and hugged me, his eyes full of pleasure and warmth. "I am really glad, Nika, that you finally came," he said. "I have so much to talk to you about and I want to see your new music."

He opened the door and let me into a small bathroom with a large black sink and a modern shower.

"This is my shower room. I hope you don't mind taking showers. I will use the other bathroom while you're here, so make yourself at home."

He closed the door carefully after having shown me how to operate the lock, the light and the shower door.

I had barely finished washing and changing when he returned. "Nika, if you're ready, come and have a drink. I have just received two bottles of marc from a farmer in Brittany. Let's have some."

We went through a short corridor to the living room. Just before entering it, he stopped in front of a small built-in cupboard and opened the doors.

"You see, this is my cellar. I have a few remarkable bottles here; both wines and brandies. What would you like to drink for lunch? What about a Mouton Rothschild 1937? I have only a few bottles left and it's a unique wine."

Stravinsky got out a bottle of marc and carefully extracted the cork with one of those double-decker silent French corkscrews which make one think of dental or obstetrical instruments. Having accomplished the operation, he fondly smelled the cork and, looking very earnest, said, "*N-da,* this is perfectly reliable marc," and added in English, "Not so bad!"

We gulped the marc, Stravinsky making a smacking sound with his tongue.

"Now, quickly, some proteins! Verotchka, where are the proteins?" he shouted excitedly. "Give Nabokov and me some proteins."

"Ah, here they are," he said as we entered the living room. He gave me a plateful of crackers thickly smeared with Camembert cheese.

The lunch tasted good after three days of Pullman cooking. The small and narrow dining room was lit by a northern bay window hung with long white tulle curtains. The pale light gave the entire room an atmosphere of neatness and airy coolness.

Before we sat down, Stravinsky repeated the cork-extraction ceremony, this time with more ritualistic concentration and a greater amount of cork-smelling, tongue-smacking and a more emphatic "Not so bad."

During lunch they asked me all sorts of questions, mostly concerning the political situation. I had quite recently returned from Berlin after two years with the U.S. Military Government. This, coupled with a general interest in politics, made me in their eyes an expert analyst of any political situation. Furthermore, as I undoubtedly had acquaintance with government secrets, I surely would be able to predict the course of world events.

The main question was whether there would be another war and consequently whether it would be safe to plan a European tour for the coming summer months. There was real anxiety in the way Stravinsky asked this question several times during the meal. I was of course aware of his profound distaste for any form of social upheaval, be it a war, a revolution, a strike, or simply a mild political demonstration. "How can one work in disorder?" he would say.

His former publisher, Gabriel Païtchadze, once described to me how perplexed and jittery he became when he was caught in Paris at the outbreak of the war. He could neither eat nor sleep, he could not work; an occasional bomb blast made him jumpy; he got angry, nervous and irritable. All he wanted was to get out as quickly as possible, out of Paris, out of Europe, into America where life was still orderly.

I remembered his departing remark to a mutual friend, shortly after Pearl Harbor, at the time when communication between the continents was nonexistent. Unable to keep in touch with his family and friends, Stravinsky felt very sharply the general war anxiety. On his way back to Hollywood after a tour in the East, he had had dinner with a few friends. Dur-

ing dinner the conversation had apparently been of such a concentrated gloom that everyone was overawed. As he was
leaving, Stravinsky took this friend aside on the platform at
Grand Central Station and asked him in a low, halting whisper:

"Tell me, quite unequivocally, will there be a revolution
in America, or not?"

The man squirmed, wavered and answered:

"How can I know? . . . Maybe, maybe not . . ."

"But where will I go?" said Stravinsky in an appalled and
indignant tone.

For Stravinsky social disorder of *any* kind is primarily
something which prevents him from doing his work — that is,
fulfilling his duty. He hates disorder with all the strength of
his egocentric nature. He dislikes even the terms *revolution*
and *revolutionary*, particularly when they are applied to
music. He is very angry when music historians use them (for
example in sentences such as: "The early *revolutionary* works
of Stravinsky . . ." or "The *revolutionary* discoveries of
Beethoven's immortal genius which swept etc. . . ." or,
somewhat Freudian and up-to-date: "The *revolutionary*
recognition of tonality as a traumatic condition"). "What
can they possibly mean?" he says. "*Revolution* is a term describing the overthrow of an existing order by means of violence. It is necessarily accompanied by disorder. Music is
the antithesis of violence and disorder. Music is order,
measure, proportion — that is, all those principles which op-
pose disorder. The only thing this term can mean is a cycle,
a span of time," and with a didactic emphasis on each word
he adds, "This is the only *correct* way to use it."

Stravinsky is equally fearful and contemptuous of conditions in which the creative work of the artist is subject to supervision or dictation (and possibly extinction) by the authorities of the state.

"Tell me, please," he would say with intense irritation, "what can these gentlemen [the authorities] know about how to write music? I don't try to tell them how to be a *tchinovnik* [bureaucrat]."

Hence Stravinsky's deep disgust for the situation of the artist in the Soviet Union, "where every *tchinovnik* can tell you what to do."

"I ask you," he says, "what is the difference between conditions today and the time of Glinka, when Nicolas I had to approve the libretto of *A Life for the Tsar* before the music was written? At least Nicolas did not try to tell Glinka what kind of music to write.

"No, my friend," he would say, lifting his shoulders and grinning sardonically, "let them stew in their own juice. I don't want anything to do with it. Let them make their music *à la* Mr. Syerov and others of his ilk."

Stravinsky usually follows up such a tirade with one of his most typical remarks in Russian: "*Noo, komoo ēto noozhno?*" (Who, after all, needs all this?)

Hence also his spontaneous and sincere attachment to the United States, where he can work in peace, earn a comfortable income, and feel secure and happy. "America is good for me," he often says.

"He has become softer and is less frequently angry," echoes his wife.

Stravinsky does not permit criticism of America in his presence. He usually interrupts and changes the conversation or, in an aside, says, "As far as I am concerned, they can have their generalissimos and Führers. Leave me Mr. Truman and I'm quite satisfied."

After lunch, in the living room, Vera Arturovna introduced me to the lesser (only in size, not in affectionate standing) members of the household.

"Here is Pópka," she said, taking a small gray parrot out of a cage and seating him on her husband's shoulder. "He is two years old. Did you see his picture in *Time* magazine? He usually eats with us at the table when we are alone."

"Look, Vera, look!" interrupted Igor Fëdorovich as the parrot flew toward me, landed on my shoulder and began climbing up on top of my head. "He is already flirting with Nabokov. *C'est un grand amoureux.*"

"It's Nika's mane," said Vera Arturovna. "You're a Mélisande for him."

"Pópka is after vermin and lice and not after Mélisande," remarked Stravinsky caustically, and he added, "Be careful; you know what birds do on people's heads."

Besides the parrot, the feathered household consists of a weather-beaten and henpecked-looking canary, whose name is Lyssaya Dushka (Bald Darling), and a flock of about eight lovebirds.

Bald Darling and Pópka are friends. The parrot opens the canary's cage, lets it out and both fly around in circles in the living room. Stravinsky likes the parrot and the canary but is quite indifferent to the lovebirds. Hence Dushka's and Pópka's cages stand in the living room, each near a window. Opposite a large white mantelpiece, as if to tease them, hang several engravings of falcons, eagles and other birds of prey with large protruding beaks.

(201)

The lovebirds' cage stands outdoors on the porch. Vera Arturovna took me there to see them. As we were examining them, she told me their names.

"These are Beauty and Pretty," she said, showing me two pale-blue birds seated tightly together on the upper rung of the large cage. "They were the first — given to us by Emil Ludwig. And this one here with her sexy eyes is Lana Turner; near her is her youngest brother or lover, Whit-Whit. They all intermarried and now it's one happy incestuous family."

She turned away from the cage and pointed at a big black cat stretched out in the sun. "And this is our only quadruped — Vasska. His full name is Vassily Vassilyevitch Lechkin: he was described in the *New Yorker* and also in *Time*. When I used to run a picture gallery, I always sent him a printed invitation and wrote on it: 'Please do come — fishbones, cocktails.' "

Stravinsky appeared on the terrace and called me. "Nika, if you aren't too tired, come and show me your music."

"But Igor, let him rest," remarked Vera Arturovna. And to me, "You must be tired. Why don't you take a nap till teatime?"

I said I wasn't tired. I wanted very much to go to his study.

"Perhaps I could show you my music some other time," I said. "Now I would rather look at your *Orpheus* and at your Mass."

"All right, come with me," said Stravinsky. He led me to his study at the other end of the narrow corridor, where we had had a drink before lunch.

He sat down at the piano, carefully wiped his glasses with

a Sight Saver, and opened the orchestra score of *Orpheus*. A moment later we were both absorbed in it.

I stood behind him and watched his short, nervous fingers scour the keyboard, searching and finding the correct intervals, the widely spaced chords, and the characteristically Stravinskian broad melodic leaps. His neck, his head, his whole body accentuated the ingenious rhythmical design of the music by spasmlike bobs and jerks. He grunted, he hummed, and occasionally stopped to make an aside.

"See the fugue here," he would say, pointing to the beginning of the Epilogue. "Two horns are working it out, while a trumpet and a violin in unison sing a long, drawn-out melody, a kind of *cantus firmus*. Doesn't this melody sound to you like a medieval vielle [a viol]? Listen . . ." And his fingers would start fidgeting again on the keyboard. Then, coming to a passage in the Epilogue where a harp solo interrupts the slow progress of the fugue, he would stop and say, "Here, you see, I cut off the fugue with a pair of scissors." He clipped the air with his fingers. "I introduced this short harp phrase, like two bars of an accompaniment. Then the horns go on with their fugue as if nothing had happened. I repeat it at regular intervals, here and here again." Stravinsky added, with his habitual grin, "You can eliminate these harp-solo interruptions, paste the parts of the fugue together, and it will be one whole piece."

I asked him why he introduced the harp solo. "What was the point of cutting up the fugue this way?"

He smiled maliciously, as if he were letting me in on one of his private secrets. "But didn't you hear?" He turned the pages to the middle of the score. "It is a reminder of this — the Song of Orpheus." And he added thoughtfully: "Here in the Epilogue it sounds like a kind of . . . compulsion, like something unable to stop. . . . Orpheus is dead, the song is gone, but the accompaniment goes on."

Several months later, listening to the first performance of *Orpheus* in New York, I remembered this last remark of Stravinsky's and understood its full implication. The Epilogue seemed to me to be one of the most effective pieces of dramatic music since the Prelude to the last act of Verdi's *Otello* (to which, of course, it bears no resemblance whatsoever). Yet the musical devices of this Epilogue are as simple and even as obvious as the dramatic situation of the ballet plot.

Orpheus has just been ripped to shreds by the Thracian women; or rather, as Balanchine's choreography and Stravinsky's music suggest, they have completed a bloodless, inevitable, and dispassionate surgical operation on the body of hopeless Orpheus. Orpheus is no more; Orpheus is dead. The world is without song, mute and desolate. Apollo's hymn to the memory of the dead hero and his attempt to play his lyre enhance the melancholy realization of Orpheus's death. The lyre (or harp) in the hands of Apollo sounds like the forlorn accompaniment of a song which is lost forever. This translation of a simple dramatic situation into an equally simple musical form is executed with incredible lucidity and with the microscopic precision of the laboratory scientist.

Stravinsky's devices are always the same: a remarkable economy of means coupled with an infallible sense of proportion, time, and form.

The ingenious instrumental combination of this Epilogue, the slow and majestic flow of its polyphonic lines, are both at the service of the dramatic situation. The very choice of the instruments which sing those expressive, sad melodies is significant; two French horns and one trumpet (the unison of the solo violin melting in the timbre of the trumpet), purposely *not* bowed string instruments.

These melodic lines could, of course, have been distributed to other instruments — violas and cellos, for example. And in a sense their character and general outline suggest bowed string instruments. Yet had Stravinsky chosen such instruments, he would never have given to these somber, medieval-sounding themes that tense quality of anguish which is evoked by two bleating horns and one lonely trumpet. For no other instrument of our modern orchestra can equal brass instruments (horns, in particular) in this special evocative power. When horns sing a sad lyric melody in their upper register they sound strangled, precarious and tragic.

Here, once again, Stravinsky revealed to me his uncanny sense of the individuality or, better, the personality of each instrument of the orchestra. It is this sense which enables him not only to find for each dramatic situation (when he is concerned with a dramatic subject) the most suitable and therefore the most expressive instrumental combination, but also each time to discover a new and surprisingly fresh mixture of orchestral sound. All this, as I said before, is accomplished with the greatest economy of means — few polyphonic lines, a minimum of tones in chords, a minimum of instruments to each melodic line, and the most astute use of the specific qualities of each instrument. Stravinsky is, I believe, unquestionably the greatest living investigator of instruments as "individuals," perhaps even the greatest since the middle of the eighteenth century.

The experimentation with instruments in the nineteenth

century was primarily concerned with the extension of their range and their dynamic power. The specific expressive qualities of each individual instrument were a secondary consideration. The motive was not so much a craftsmanlike interest in the technical possibilities of each instrument but the need of finding the necessary so-called "tone colors" on the orchestral palette, in order to suggest or describe the extra-musical images, expressions, ideas, or objects with which romantic music was preoccupied. Only towards the end of that century did composers show a renewed concern with instruments as individuals within the orchestral unit. Previous to this time, instruments were constantly added to the symphony orchestra. The orchestra devoured them with an ogre's appetite and grew bigger and fatter in volume. The individuality of each instrument, however, was being drowned out by the mammoth sound, by impersonal mixtures of this newly invented engine of musical warfare — the 100-piece symphony orchestra.

In retrospect, this "development" added little to musical culture. The new symphony orchestra was a delight to those who like to bathe in a sea of mushy sound, and of course a delight to the orchestra conductor, but it was an abomination to all those who cared for clarity, precision and transparency in the art of music.

Naturally there were exceptional composers who continued to be interested in the individuality or personality of musical instruments, such as Tchaikovsky (mainly in his ballet scores) or Verdi or even, at times, Richard Wagner, normally the greatest offender against the mores of the individual instrument.

Today, in the middle of the twentieth century, the attitude

of the composers towards the instruments of the orchestra, and hence towards the art of orchestration, has definitely changed. Composers know that *orchestration* is not *registration* (not like pulling the stops on a huge electric organ in order to acquire impersonal and "phony" mixtures of sound), but that it is rather a highly complex art, in which the intuitive or imaginative faculties of the composer's mind are combined with the logical and critical faculties. Thus, this art can be completely successful only when the composer thoroughly understands the individuality, and hence the limits (in terms of technical possibilities), of each instrument in the orchestra. On this knowledge he must base his own art of orchestration.

This does not mean, as people often think, that the composer should be able to play most of the instruments of the orchestra. His is a different ability than that of the performing artist. The ability to perform has little to do with the composer's work; it may even sometimes be a handicap; that is, it may lead the composer to estimate the possibilities of the instruments by his own standards of performance. This will inevitably result in a timorous and bland orchestration.

The primary importance the art of orchestration holds in contemporary music is largely due to the influence of Stravinsky. If we consider that at least two thirds of the quality of an instrumental piece is in its adequate orchestration, we must give credit to Stravinsky's approach to and his discoveries in the instrumental field.

His approach is based essentially on his knowledge of the technical limits of each instrument. Hence his imaginative and extremely skillful exploitation of these limits. In other words, Stravinsky treats every orchestra musician as an accomplished performer, a master craftsman of his instrument. He requires of him the ability to play at extreme velocity and at the same time to be at ease in the most complicated rhythmical design; he must be able to intone with mathematical precision in all the ranges of his instrument and at all possible dynamic conditions of the music (from very soft to very loud); and finally, he must strive to extend the high ranges of his instrument beyond the conventionally accepted limits.

This is why most orchestra musicians, despite its difficulty, like to play Stravinsky's music. When we ask a modern-minded orchestra musician if he likes Stravinsky's music, he usually replies that he does, because it is *interestingly* written for his instrument.

Thus by using unexploited registers of instruments, by discovering new technical devices, by employing certain instruments to perform melodic outlines usually associated with other instruments, or by combining instrumental sounds that are considered unsound and unorthodox by the orchestral canons of the nineteenth century (according to the treatises on orchestration by such pundits as Berlioz, Richard Strauss and Rimsky-Korsakov), Igor Stravinsky achieves an incredible variety of orchestral combinations which always sound new, fresh and, at the same time, persuasive. In these last twenty-five or thirty years, the orchestral texture of his music has acquired a degree of transparency, lucidity and crystalline fragility unequaled by any of his contemporaries. At times, it is a kind of orchestral tightrope walking, precarious and precise. . . . Diaghilev once remarked to me while we were listening to a new work of Stravinsky's (I believe it was the octet for wind instruments) that it was so transparent "one could see through it with one's ears."

X

Stravinsky and Hollywood

S TRAVINSKY AND I spent most of the afternoon looking at the score of *Orpheus* and at the two parts of the Latin Mass he was writing at the time.

After a while I grew tired of standing, and flopped down on a soft, narrow couch that stood behind the piano in his study. On one end of its dark silk surface lay a neatly folded plaid rug, and on the other a dainty little pillow. By then he had entirely forgotten my presence and was absorbed in one of the pages of his Mass. He was playing the same passage over and over again. It looked as if he were testing the quality of what he had written. He was remeasuring the interval relations and recalculating the rhythmical patterns. His head and body jerked and bobbed and he was quite distinctly humming the words of the Mass.

I suddenly caught myself following his movements with a special kind of interest. Often before, I had been captivated by the movements of his body. They are always so personal and profoundly revealing of his personality and of his music. Frequently, in fact, while listening to his music, I have closed my eyes and seen in front of me a characteristic Stravinskian gesture. At other times, when seeing him pace the floor on tiptoe in the middle of a discussion, his upper body bent forward like that of a frog-fishing stork, his arms akimbo, I would be struck by the parallel between his physical gesture and the inner gesture of his music. His music reflects his peculiarly elastic walk, the syncopated nod of his head and shrug of his shoulders, and those abrupt stops in the middle of a conversation when, like a dancer, he suddenly freezes in a balletlike pose and punctuates his argument with a broad and sarcastic grin.

Not only does Stravinsky's music reflect his bodily movements and characteristic gestures; it also reflects succinctly and convincingly his whole mode of life — his attitude towards his environment, towards people, nature, and objects. Above all, it reflects his love for order and his stern work discipline, so totally devoid of self-indulgence and self-pity. It reflects his penchant for all sorts of mechanical gadgets, from thumbtacks to stop watches and pocket metronomes, his passion for hardware stores and the pleasure he derives from fitting a message into the prescribed twenty-five words of an overnight cable. (On December 23, we spent nearly an hour at the Western Union office while he "tailored," as he called it, two Christmas cables to his sons.) It reflects his attitude towards money, for which, as everybody knows, he has a "profound respect," which some people mistake for avarice.

Sometimes he makes amusing comparisons between music and money. For example, once during one of his habitual, bitter attacks against contemporary composers, he said, "Why they've lost all sense of the interval. They don't hear intervals and have no respect for them. One should treat intervals as if they were dollars."

But perhaps, in an even stronger way, his music reflects his nervous and acid hates; his hate of all kinds of stupidity (stupid people, stupid art, stupid letters), his hate of stuffy rooms, of dirt or disorder, of dusty furniture and bad odors. The wittiness of his caustic remarks about people and, chiefly, about bad music is the same kind of wit one finds in some of his scores — in, for example, his ballet *Jeux de Cartes* or the dances from his *Histoire du Soldat*, or his ballet *Renard*. It is a scathing, pitiless kind of humor which knows no compassion. He will often, for example, distort the name of a person or a piece of music he dislikes (usually because the person or the piece of music is a bore), or else he will invent a funny nickname for it. Thus Richard Strauss's *Rosenkavalier* is usually called the *Sklerosenkavalier*, and the music of Shostakovich is an "old oyster." (This nickname, which I have already mentioned, is derived from an article of mine on Shostakovich in which I compared the flabby structure of his antediluvian symphonies to that of an oyster. Stravinsky loved this comparison and at the time wrote me a warm congratulatory letter.)

In general, Stravinsky likes precise, picturesque, or onomatopoeic remarks. His talk as well as his letters is full of them. Once in New York a cold bothered him. He complained: "*J'ai un porte-monnaie dans ma nossoglotka.*" (I have a change purse in my larynx.) Another time we were discussing his new opera, *The Rake's Progress*. He was explaining how he intended to treat Auden's libretto: "I will lace each aria into a tight corset."

People often irritate him when they stop him in a store

or on a street corner and ask him, "Excuse me, aren't you the composer of *The Firebird?*" after which they produce an autograph book. "You know," he says, "I'll hire a secretary and call him Mr. Firebird, and when people ask me this I will be able to say, 'Oh, no, *this* is Mr. Firebird — in person, flesh and bone.' "

Stravinsky's love for clear terms, for laconic definitions and adequate translation, manifests itself in his enthusiasm for dictionaries, with which his study is filled. Of all of them he prefers the French *Grand Larousse*.

"You know what sex is?" he would ask, opening the *Larousse*. "Listen: *le sexe est une conformation particulière de l'être vivant, qui lui assigne un rôle spécial dans l'acte de génération.*" (The sexual organ is a formation peculiar to living beings, who delegate to it a special role in the act of procreation.) "Isn't this a superb definition?"

His own remarks generally have a Laroussian precision as well as wit and imagination. When, for example, someone is in a hurry, he will say, "Why do you hurry? *I have no time to hurry.*" But particularly sharp and picturesque are his remarks about people. An overemotional conductor, who bristles with exuberant gestures, reminds him of a "*danse du ventre vue par derrière* — an Oriental belly dance seen from behind," while his arms are a pair of "egg beaters."

Conductors in general readily incur Stravinsky's wrath and his most scathing remarks. In a filing cabinet under his piano, in a separate folder, are collected some choice pictures of conductors in highly contorted poses. Most of these pictures are taken from publicity releases or newspapers.

"Look at him!" says Stravinsky, pulling a conductorial extravaganza out of the folder. "Look at the dandy! Look at his idiotic expression, his frothy gestures. Is all this nonsense necessary to conduct an orchestra?"

His workroom is another example of the precision which orders his music and his language. An extraordinary room, perhaps the best planned and organized workroom I have seen in my life. In a space which is not larger than some twenty-five by forty feet stand two pianos (one grand, one upright) and two desks (a small, elegant writing desk and a draftsman's table). In two cupboards with glass shelves are books, scores, and sheet music, arranged in alphabetical order. Between the two pianos, the cupboards and desks, are scattered a few small tables (one of which is a kind of "smoker's delight": it exhibits all sorts of cigarette boxes, lighters, holders, fluids, flints, and pipe cleaners), five or six comfortable chairs, and the couch Stravinsky uses for his afternoon naps. (I saw him on it the next day, lying on his back, with an expression of contained anger on his face, snoring gently and methodically.)

Besides the pianos and the furniture there are hundreds of gadgets, photographs, trinkets, and implements of every kind in and on the desks and tables and tacked on the back of the cupboards. I believe Stravinsky has in his study all the instruments needed for writing, copying, drawing, pasting, cutting, clipping, filing, sharpening, and gluing that the combined effects of a stationery and hardware store can furnish (and yet he is always after new ones). A touch of nature in the midst of all this man-made gadgetry is provided by a bunch of fresh roses in a white china vase which stands on his desk. His wife cuts them for him every morning from his special rosebushes.

Yet despite this mass of objects and cluster of furniture,

Stravinsky's study is so well organized and so functional that it gives one a sense of spaciousness and peaceful comfort. One feels as if one were surveying a chessboard, with its black and white figures arranged in exact relation to each other, ready for a long musical game.

At the same time the room seems as compact as an ant-heap. When its owner moves cagily through the little corridors formed by the various pieces of furniture, he gives the impression of a busy and diligent ant crawling through the orderly labyrinth of his citadel. In fact, Stravinsky's own attitude towards his study is very much like that of an ant. He loves to carry objects of all kinds into his study. If someone brings him a present, as I was able to observe on Christmas Day, he will not open it in front of his wife, or anyone else. He will wait for a convenient moment and then quietly slip away with it to his study. There he will unwrap it and, if he likes it or it appears useful, he will find a niche for it among his other souvenirs and gadgets. . . .

While I was still sitting on the couch and Stravinsky was puttering at the piano, Vera Arturovna appeared in the entrance to the study and announced that the Balanchines had arrived.

"George and Maria are here," she said, "and Genia Berman is waiting for us with vodka and *zakousska* [hors d'oeuvres]. It is time to go, Igor. Come, Nika."

"*Seytchas, seytchas,*" answered Stravinsky.

I got up to join her while Stravinsky, without changing his position at the piano, said to me, "Nika, please go and tell them that I'll be out in five minutes." And he went on playing.

Half an hour later we were driving down to Eugene Berman's apartment. On the front seat of the car, squeezed in between Vera Arturovna and myself, was Stravinsky's tiny figure, dressed in a pea jacket and a yachtsman's hat. (He bought the pea jacket at a navy surplus sale and is both proud and fond of it.) The Balanchines followed us closely in their own car.

Eugene Berman, the painter, is one of the few members of Stravinsky's Hollywood "family circle." A gentle, soft-spoken, and somewhat melancholic man with a wistful sense of humor, Berman is devoted to the Stravinskys and they in turn to him. While I was in Hollywood, Berman came nearly every afternoon to the Stravinskys', stayed for meals and long into the night. One felt that Vera Arturovna and Igor Fëdoro-vich, with their warm and attentive friendship, had made their house a home for Berman.

We entered the hall of Berman's apartment house and went to the desk. Vera Arturovna announced our arrival. The telephone operator, an elderly lady with glasses, looked at Stravinsky and, recognizing him in his nautical apparel, said, "Aren't you the author of . . . *Firebird?*"

"You see?" whispered Stravinsky. "It never fails."

He smiled charmingly and answered, "Yes, madam, *Firebird* is a bird of mine."

The dinner at the Napoli was gay and happy, like one of those dinners of the twenties when we used to get together with Diaghilev, Prokofiev, Picasso, Derain, Balanchine, and other collaborators of the Ballet Russe at Giardino's restaurant on the top of the hill in Monte Carlo. Stravinsky was in wonderful form — voluble, witty, and at the same time extremely attentive to all of us. As usual, he ordered the best food and, especially, the best wines, and he had the waiter play funny, sobbing old Caruso records on the juke box.

Gay and happy as the occasion was, both Balanchine and I couldn't keep from yawning — so much so that Vera Arturovna and her husband (who usually can sit it out till the early hours of the morning, provided he is with close friends and there is Scotch around) started to urge us all to go to bed as soon as we had finished coffee.

But by the time we came home and I fitted myself comfortably on the three cushions of the famous sofa, my tiredness was gone and I felt just as wide-awake as when I had arrived that morning at the Los Angeles station. I looked around for books and found a few rare Russian editions on a shelf that contained a pell-mell assortment of French novels, Russian classics, murder stories, and biographies. There were no books on music except Mozart's *Letters*. Among the books were the epigrammatic works of that peculiar and quite unjustly forgotten Russian thinker and writer of the beginning of this century, Rozanov (whom I knew Stravinsky liked very much and whose works he rereads and quotes constantly, comparing Rozanov's ideas and style to Gogol's and Dostoevsky's). I took down a volume of Rozanov called *Fallen Leaves*, and tried to read, but soon discovered that I could not concentrate and that my eyes were wandering senselessly over and over the same sentences. I was still too much under the influence of my afternoon with Stravinsky in his study, and all my thoughts were concerned with his work. Somehow I felt that I had to find answers all over again to essential questions about his art.

What, after all, does his art mean to us contemporary musicians of the younger generation? What is its value in the general evolution of music history? What are his essential discoveries?

It is difficult to say something new about Stravinsky's music. All seems to have been said. There has rarely been a composer whose work has been as much discussed during his lifetime as the work of Stravinsky. He himself in his two books — his *Autobiography* and his *Poetics of Music* — has stated his point of view on the art of music and thus by inference discussed his own art. Everything one might say seems redundant and commonplace.

And yet, lying on his sofa in his house, surrounded by his warm friendliness, I felt overcome by an enormous sense of gratefulness for his art — the kind of gratefulness an apprentice feels towards his master craftsman. I felt that I owed Stravinsky much of my understanding of how to use the materials of music — intervals, rhythms, melodic outlines. I felt that it was his art that opened my eyes to the decay of impressionist harmony and the corruption or the emotive paroxysms of late romanticism. Above all, I felt that it was his example that had brought me to admire the continuity of the classical tradition, the beauty of polyphonic technique, and to understand the necessity for a clear-cut, well-defined formal structure.

At the same time it was Stravinsky's art, I believe, which showed the musicians of my generation new horizons in the domain of rhythm, new possibilities in the use of musical instruments, and a new concept of harmony, fuller, broader, and nobler than the sterile harmonic concepts of the late nineteenth century. Yet to me the most important discoveries of Stravinsky lie in his artful perception and measurement of the flow of time by means of the most complex and beautiful rhythmic patterns and designs.

Who else, I thought, among contemporary composers can

exhibit such a continuity and such a variety of admirable works of art (or should I say solutions of "problems")? Who else has *successfully* used *all* forms, *all* styles, *all* techniques, and integrated them in an unmistakably personal art of his own? Who else in our time has written pieces so easily understood and of such immense popular appeal as *The Firebird*, *Petroushka*, *Histoire du Soldat* (in the twenties in Central Europe thousands of schools performed the latter to the general delight of teen-agers; my own son, when he was about seven, loved this piece more than anything else and always wanted me to play the records of it over and over again), *Symphony of Psalms*, and *Apollon*, and at the same time has produced such hermetic masterpieces as the symphony and octet for wind instruments, or the *Serenade* for piano solo (which is the joy of a skilled music lover)? And finally how few, how very few, composers of our time can produce a record of such total devotion to their craft, so completely devoid of any concession or compromise, so intransigent and conscientious.

When . . .

I was suddenly interrupted in the middle of my thoughts by soft footsteps in the living room. The door opened and Stravinsky appeared, in his bathrobe.

"Why aren't you sleeping? Put the light out. It's late," he said reproachfully. He walked over to the window. "Don't open it so wide — especially with your neuralgia. Our California nights aren't warm at all." And having shut the window to a small crack, he left.

The days in California went by much faster than I would have wished. The weather was exceptionally sunny and warm, even for old Hollywooders like the Stravinskys. The soft, gentle air, the roses and carnations in the garden, the accumulation of neat, fancy-colored packages in the living room and the deluge of Christmas cards on the mantelpiece; all of this made me feel happy and carefree. They brought back holiday memories of my childhood: the smells of the French Riviera, the lilac-colored sea of Yalta and the tuberoses in my mother's room one Easter morning in Odessa. In fact, this Hollywood holiday seemed more like Easter than Christmas.

The days were filled with music, talk, enjoyment, and gaiety. I had rarely seen Stravinsky so happy and so full of fun. Balanchine was right. He did not leave me for an instant. He upset his normally rigid work schedule to spend all his time with Balanchine and me. We went marketing and Christmas shopping. He helped me choose one of those artsy-craftsy silver bracelets for my wife. (When the salesgirl brought out a tray filled with all sorts of silver jewelry, I said to Stravinsky, "What should I buy?" "First of all," he answered sententiously, "I must know how much money you are ready to assign to this purchase.")

One afternoon they took me to the ocean via the interminable Sunset Boulevard, where I was to "salute" the Pacific by dipping my finger into its waters. In doing so I got my feet wet and was ordered to take off my shoes, for fear of a cold. The next day they drove me all around the avenues and hills of Hollywood, past those curious blue, pink and silver Christmas trees which stand on its street corners and in gas stations.

We went to the well-known lunch market to have lunch with the Aldous Huxleys and a few other friends, and I got lost in the maze of Italian, French and Spanish food counters. One entire evening was spent listening to the Toscanini records of *La Traviata*, which N.B.C. made especially for Stravinsky at his request (of Verdi's operas, Stravinsky likes *La Traviata* and *Aïda* best of all; he is less fond of *Otello* and *Falstaff*), and the Glyndebourne recordings of *Don Giovanni*. This opera is Stravinsky's special love; particularly now that he himself is busy writing an opera.

"Listen to the length of those lines," he would say. "Listen how clever they are, *quel souffle, quelle clarté!*"

On Christmas morning Stravinsky, at my request, exhibited his Hungarian calisthenics. Not knowing anything about gymnastic exercises, I was unable to see how they differed from the usual calisthenics or the German "Dr. Müller's *Koerperliche Morgenauffrischungs-Uebungen*" (Dr. Müller's bodily morning refresher exercises), which were popular in Russia during my childhood. It seemed to me, however, that some of the exercises had a kind of Turkish or Magyar flavor, perhaps because Stravinsky when doing them rolled his eyes like a dervish in a trance.

The calisthenics were interrupted by the doorbell. Stravinsky, who was in bathing trunks, ran to his room to dress. I opened the door to a middle-aged gentleman with a Christmas present in his hand.

"I'd like to see Mr. Stravinsky," said the gentleman, pronouncing the name Straw-windsky. "I'm from the X. Blueprinting Company."

When Stravinsky appeared, the gentleman took off his hat and wished Stravinsky "a very merry Christmas." And he added, "And here's a little token of our appreciation."

Stravinsky thanked him politely and ceremoniously and

took the present. The gentleman put on his hat and said, "Why don't you open it right here, Mr. Straw-windsky?"

Stravinsky unwrapped the gift, which was one of those commercial calendars with semi-nude teasers on each page.

"How d'you like our calendar?" said the gentleman with a wink.

Stravinsky shook his head in approval. "Very nice, very nice. Thank you very much."

"Wait a minute," said the gentleman. "Turn to April."

Stravinsky turned to April.

"How d'you like *that* gal?"

"Very pretty, very nice young lady," replied Stravinsky.

"Now take a look at October and tell me what you think of *that*," said the gentleman, taking the calendar out of Stravinsky's hand and proudly exposing to our view a pair of succulent, cream-colored female buttocks.

"Very good, very true to life," said Stravinsky, with even greater sobriety.

At this, the man approached Stravinsky, tweaked his left ear lobe, and with a clubman's smile said, "You rascal!" After he had gone, Stravinsky roared with laughter and shouted, "Vera, Vera! Look what I've received."

That same evening the small circle of Stravinsky's family and friends gathered at his house for a party. There were just a few people: Stravinsky's daughter and her French husband, the two Bolms — the famous dancer and his tiny wife — Eugene Berman and Stravinsky's physician, Dr. Edel, with his broad Austrian accent and equally broad, friendly smile, and, finally, the two Balanchines. We all had a quiet and happy dinner with lots of wine and each of us received a carefully "premeditated" present (Balanchine and I had silver goblets for drinking vodka). During dinner the conversation, out of deference to Maria Balanchine, lingered in a kind of pigeon English, but after dinner and late into the night the linguistic wind blew stronger and stronger in the Russian direction, to the mutual disappointment of Maria Balanchine, Dr. Edel and Stravinsky's French son-in-law.

The next day, December 26, I had to go back to New York. We drove to the airport through the darkening hours of the evening, long in advance of take-off time (an old Russian custom). At the TWA counter we were told that the plane was one hour late and that all planes in the East were grounded or delayed. (It was the day of the big snowstorm in New York.) I somehow hoped that the plane would not take off and that I could go back with them to North Wetherly Drive.

We sat in the waiting room unnoticed by anyone. A fat man passed by and went to the traffic counter.

"You know who that is?" said Vera Arturovna. "It's Alfred Hitchcock."

"And there," added Stravinsky, "is Henry Fonda. It looks as if you're going to have lots of famous men on the plane with you."

Near the exit gate stood someone whom I thought I knew. He was dressed in one of those movie-star specials: an overly long and broad polo coat. He was talking to a pretty woman wearing a felt hat and a cabbage-size orchid. Her face also seemed familiar. I asked Vera Arturovna who she was.

"I think it's June Havoc, the sister of the famous stripteaser."

Finally the plane was called and we started moving towards Gate No. 2 The man in the polo coat turned to me and said,

"I think we have met in Vienna. Aren't you Nicolas Nabokov? My name is Helmut Dantine."

"Oh, yes," I said. "How are you?" ("One more famous man," whispered Stravinsky.)

We parted at the gate and I walked with the crowd of passengers through a tunnel to the plane, leaving the two Stravinskys on the platform in front of the terminal. But we were kept waiting for about twenty minutes before we could board the plane.

As I was going up the steps of the gangplank, I looked back toward the terminal. There in the bright California moonlight I saw a small figure frantically waving his hat. I waved back and entered the plane.

Helmut Dantine approached me and asked in a quaint Viennese accent, "Excuse me, who was that man with whom you came to the airport? His face looks so familiar."

I explained.

"That's what I thought," he said. "But what is he doing in Hollywood? Oh, yes, on second thought I heard that he was here. Is he doing a picture?"

I answered that he was not.

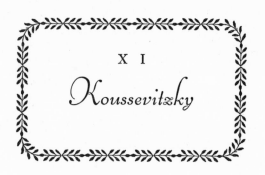

X I

Koussevitzky

T HE CLERK at the desk of the New York hotel rolled
his pre-chewed cigar to the other side of his mouth
and mumbled through his teeth: "No, Mr. Thomson's
not in . . . he's out of town until Monday . . ." "But didn't
Mr. Thomson reserve a room for me?" I asked. Grudgingly
he picked up the reservation book. "Ah, yes . . ." he remembered, "he *did* reserve a room . . . let me see . . . here's the
name of the party . . ." And glancing above his spectacles
at my unshaven face and my crumpled uniform he asked:
"Are you Mr. . . ." He hesitated and followed up the "Mr."
with an Irish-sounding deformation of my name: "Are you
Mr. Nab O'Cough?"

The only "available" room was dark and tenant-beaten. It
had the same smell of old food and older dust that had struck
my nostrils in the lobby of the hotel. But I did not care; I was
glad to have its bed, its bath, its privacy. I was glad to be out
of airport waiting rooms, shabby army hotel lobbies and
messes, communal washrooms and iron-clad bucket seats. "I
will sleep," I thought, "I will sleep for the first time in five

days, since the Azores, since Paris. I will get the drone of the motors out of my ears and the bucket-seat bend out of my back, and no one will wake me at 4 A.M. shouting: 'Flight Number 84 will depart at 4:20 A.M., all passengers . . .' or: 'All flights canceled until tomorrow.' "

I tipped the porter, undid my bulging Valpack, ran the bath and . . . the telephone rang . . . once . . . twice . . . I picked up the receiver and was about to utter one of the juicier cusswords that had singed my ears during my eight days of army-sponsored journey, but the voice on the other end forestalled me. Familiar, calm, and business-mannered it said: "This is Western Union. We have a telegram for Nicolas Nabokov from Lenox, Massachusetts. Are you he?" "Yes, I *am* he," I replied and asked her to read it to me. I turned off the bath, found a pencil and wrote: "Welcome back. Hope you can come this week end. Must see you at once. Call Lenox. Best regards. Sergei Koussevitzky." "Will you take a reply?" I asked, when she had finished reading. No, she could not. I had to give it to the hotel operator. Could she at least tell me what time and what day of the week it was? The Western Union manners disappeared and she answered in an irritated, high-pitched bark. "Friday, May 9 . . . 1:35 A.M.," she said and hung up. I called the hotel operator and gave her my wire: "Sorry cannot come today. Must sleep. Will call Saturday morning. Regards."

The Berkshire Express is, as everybody knows who has ever been bounced by it, a slow and sulky train. It sulks for a long while at every one of its many stops and each time I take it it seems to have added a new one. Between stops, it crawls, shakes, and rattles. But I did not mind its slowness and shakiness when I boarded it on Sunday morning, May 11, 1947. I was free from the pleasures of the army, I was on leave, I was going to the country, and I was eager to see Sergei Alexandrovich Koussevitzky, to visit him at his "musical fun grounds" as someone in the *Stars and Stripes* had termed the Berkshire Music Festival. I had never been in Lenox or seen its famous "Shed," its open door auditorium, the opera workshop and other buildings of the Music Center, except in publicity folders or in magazines. Now I would see it all and spend a quiet two or three days with the creator of this extraordinary musical project.

Besides, it was May, the weather was balmy, the windows were open, and as the train passed Danbury and began winding along narrow valleys, the smell of young leaves, of pine and of honeysuckle filled the car and gave me the taste of the springy countryside. Though shaken and dandled about I felt happy, as I began to think about the man I was going to visit, about his life, his work, his achievements, and his fantastic, unique success. I had never visited Koussevitzky before, nor had I seen much of him since I had come to America in 1933. Even before 1933, in Europe, despite the fact that I was one of "his" composers (my music was published by the publishing house for Russian music that he had owned until 1948) and that Koussevitzky was the first important conductor to perform my music in America, I had seen him only on rare occasions, when, after his American season, he came to Paris and spent a month or two in his comfortable home on the edge of the Bois de Boulogne. In fact, I had had little opportunity to become a friend and intimate of the Koussevitzky household in Europe. When, in the early twenties, he lived in Paris, I studied in Germany. When I moved to France in 1923, I was an obscure, struggling aspirant to the compositorial profession, with very little to offer, while he was already a very famous man, a man whose name has been ringing in my ears for more than a decade and who was known not only as a conductor but as what the Russians call an important *obshchestvennyi deyatel* (a public-minded person), and as a rich Maecenas. I had little chance of meeting him before I had something concrete to offer in terms of music. Besides, Koussevitzky soon went to America and except for the spring months in Paris, when he gave his famous series of concerts, there was no way for me to meet him.

I think it was Prokofiev who brought Koussevitzky and me together for the first time. He took me to a tea party at the Koussevitzkys' residence sometime in the spring of 1928. It was a large affair with many composers, famous performers, critics, and important hostesses of the Parisian musical salons. Prokofiev introduced me to Koussevitzky as Diaghilev's latest "find." He used to say the word *nakhodka* (find) teasingly, as if I were an old piece of Roman pottery Diaghilev had dug up in some dusty museum. Koussevitzky grinned broadly, and asked me why I didn't come and show him my music. I said that I had very little to show, but he insisted. I should come the next day, he said, for after that he was leaving for Plombières, the summer resort in the Vosges Mountains, where he used to go every year.

The next day I came and brought the score of *Ode* and banged it out on the piano and howled the parts of the chorus and soloists. Despite my outrageous performance he seemed to like the piece. He listened to it very attentively and asked me to repeat some parts of it. "Too bad . . ." he said after I had finished playing, "that I can't play this in Boston . . ."

"It's too . . . Russian, and besides it needs too many singers." And tilting his head he asked me: "Have you something else . . . for orchestra alone?" "But this is the only thing he has written," interrupted Prokofiev, who had come with me to give me courage and see what happened. "Well," remarked Koussevitzky, "why doesn't he then sit down and write something new?" He shrugged his shoulders, raised his eyebrows and smiled; and, as if giving me a classroom assignment, he added: "You write a symphony for me and I will play it everywhere."

A year and a half later the symphony was written and he played it in 1931 in Boston and New York. After the New York performance he sent me a warm, two-page cable. I received it in my summer quarters in Alsace and the postman who brought it remarked in total amazement: "This isn't a telegram; this is a huge letter!" When I came to America and settled in New York I had occasion to see Koussevitzky several times in the Green Room of Carnegie Hall. Each time he greeted me warmly and graciously, but somehow I felt that in the excitement of the post-concert bustle, he did not quite connect me with the young man he had seen in Paris and whose music he had performed. Although by 1933 or 1934 I was no longer a struggling aspirant, but had become a full-fledged struggling composer who, as such, needed Koussevitzky's help and support very much indeed, I did not press the matter, nor call him, nor try to see him, nor go on pilgrimages to Boston.

I have always felt a certain difficulty and reticence in approaching and becoming friends with prominent performers and in particular with famous conductors. In a curious and quite instinctive way, I feel that disinterested, human relations between famous conductors and composers are not only extremely rare and difficult but are of necessity unreal and precarious. The state of affairs in our world of music is such that conductors can easily afford to dispense with the "services" of most of the contemporary composers. Being in possession of a vast repertoire that conforms to the so-called "average taste of music lovers," they can build (and 75 per cent of them do) most of their programs out of this repertoire. Only an occasional acknowledgment of the existence of contemporary music is necessary to satisfy the proprieties and exhibit the good manners of a symphonic orchestra. Thus the conductor, instead of being a helper, a channel of communication between the contemporary composer and the public, becomes an insurmountable obstacle to the development of a composer's career.

True enough, in the last five to ten years things have somewhat improved (thanks to the courage of conductors, chiefly Koussevitzky and Mitropoulos, and composer-critics like Virgil Thomson), but still our symphonic repertoire continues to be clogged by the big B symphonies and the antediluvian monstrosities of Sibelius and Richard Strauss, and other *demivierges* of Western musical culture. The percentage of new music that the public should hear is just the reverse of the present state of musical affairs. Yet we are handicapped in obtaining it by the inordinate reverence we feel towards the treasures of our culture, the treasures of the past, some of which, on calmer and closer view (especially the nineteenth-century ones), are far from being treasures and could readily be dispensed with, to the benefit of everybody concerned. As a result of this situation, a cleavage exists between the famous performing artists and the so-called "serious composers." The conductor is like the banker from whom the composer expects to obtain the favor of a small loan.

When I meet a famous performing artist I always have the feeling that he knows that I want something from him, that I have wares to offer and consequently that at some point I am going to pounce on him and ask: "Would you like to see my latest . . ." Embarrassed, he will have to find excuses. He will say that he has already received over a thousand new scores that at present clutter his piano, that his manager won't let him play more than four new pieces a year, that he has no time to look at new scores, and that anyhow his programs for the next season are already made. The very possibility of such situations makes me feel uneasy and this is why (like many other contemporary composers) I live and move in a quite different world from that of performing virtuosi. I see only a few of them, only those who are proclaimed and enthusiastic missionaries of the music of our time. I may be somewhat quixotic in my hesitancy to form friendly relations with famous virtuosi. It might in fact prove useful if I could overcome my reticence and feel free to pounce at them at every opportunity. But then one couldn't call such relations *friendly*. They would resemble the relations of a salesman and his boss or of a banking clerk to a bank director, devoid of all warm human feelings.

Koussevitzky, however, is one of the very few famous conductors to whom this reticence of mine should not have applied, for not only has his life been dedicated to the fight for the music of his contemporaries, but on a quite personal level he *was* after all the first famous conductor to perform my music in America, he was my publisher and he was also my compatriot. Yet, curiously enough, the habit of

(230)

reticence once established worked even here. Instead of calling him on the telephone, as Mme. Koussevitzky suggested
at one of the encounters in the Green Room, I did not call and
instead of sending him my new scores or visiting him in Boston,
I remained aloof and silent. Perhaps quite unconsciously I
sensed that, as a newcomer to America, I needed his help and
support very badly and because of this very fact I felt uneasy
and would not do anything about it until, as I secretly hoped,
he himself would stretch towards me his helping hand. But
soon a change in my circumstances made the possibility of
direct contact with Koussevitzky, and in general with the
musical life of the metropolitan areas of America, difficult if
not utterly impossible.

As I have intimated, I am a so-called "serious" composer,
and as everybody knows, composers in America are divided
into two categories: the "serious" ones and the "popular" ones.
The popular ones write commercial music and make a lot of
money. The serious ones write music which by and large does
not sell and, with a few exceptions, they do not make a living
and remain poor. Thus, using the terminology of the thirties,
the popular composers are the "haves" while the serious ones
are the "have nots."

As Virgil Thomson pointed out in his charming book *The
State of Music*, the "serious" contemporary composer has several alternatives if he is to earn money and continue to compose: (1) rich matrimony; (2) the films; (3) teaching. I chose
or rather drifted into the last category. I took a teaching job
and for five years was buried like a hibernating mole in a small
college in the more or less desolate regions of northern New
York State. I taught counterpoint, harmony, music history,
led choruses, directed plays, and did all sorts of things I was

neither prepared for nor really equipped to do well at the time.

I often reflected during those musically lean years what would happen if suddenly the taste of the public should go berserk and, led by managers, night-club owners, juke-box builders, record-company directors, and radio sponsors, should demand Schönberg instead of Rodgers, Stravinsky instead of Jerome Kern, and Nabokov instead of . . . Would then the heavy "haves," the stars of popular music, become "have nots" and take jobs in schools and colleges and teach the same musty nonsense the "have nots" have been teaching for the last fifty years?

Contacts with the "outer world" in upstate New York were limited to the periodical concerts of visiting artists and occasional trips to New York City. Under those conditions it was hard to start any new friendships or even keep up with old ones. My world had suddenly shrunk to a small and homogeneous community. Living isolated as I was, far away from the active centers of music, important and famous people like Koussevitzky seemed quite remote and totally unreachable to me.

But towards the end of the war, having removed myself from my pedagogical slavery to an even more fantastic enslavement, the "great books" St. John's College in Annapolis, Maryland (here, besides my usual music chores, I was compelled to indulge in the reading, teaching and discussion of the "great books"), I received an unexpected assignment to go overseas as an employee of the War Department. Once in Germany a chain of accidents moved me into the position of a Deputy Chief of the American Military Government's control of German music. Although I occupied this venerable post for only a very short time and soon drifted into more important bureaucratic occupations and acquired a more imposing nomenclature, I was able during this short interval to do something in the line of duty which seemed at the time of vital importance to the Koussevitzky publishing house.

The center of the publishing house since its foundation had been Berlin. During the bombing, the building in which the publishing house had its offices and where the main records (such as contracts with composers, manuscripts and other documents) were kept had been reduced to rubble. Moreover, the Berlin director of the house had lost contact with the main director of the firm, who lived in Paris. In short the latter asked me to find the former, give him food and help and also find out whether the scores, parts and documents were intact in Germany. I did all of those things, and even arranged a two-week-long digging expedition at the desolate site of the destroyed publishing house in order to unearth or rather unrubble a steel safe in which the contracts were kept. We did not find the *Schrank*, as the German diggers called it, but my "activities" were duly reported to S.A.K. and several weeks later I received a very gracious letter from him thanking me for my trouble and asking me to visit him in Boston as soon as I returned home.

Yet I knew at least one person in the Koussevitzky household, his niece, who soon was to become his wife, Olga Naoumov. Before coming to America she had lived with her parents in the South of France, in Nice, where the Naoumovs owned a villa surrounded by a large garden on one of the lovely hillside streets. My mother's apartment was only a fifteen-minute walk from the Naoumov villa. We used to go there for tea or lunch when I came home from Paris to visit my mother. Olga and I became friends during one of my Easter visits, in 1924 or 1925. I liked her at once. She was so different from the usual uneducated girls of the wealthy Russian upper classes. She looked slight and fragile and spoke in a thoughtful subdued tone of voice of earnest matters. We used to find a bench in the lovely garden of their villa and there, in the mild afternoon sun, we would sit until dinnertime having endless Russian talks. We talked of Russia, of her future, of the great Russian writers and poets, of philosophy and religion (Olga belonged to a devout Greek Orthodox family and was herself deeply religious), of Russian music, and of her uncle Sergei.

I was therefore happy to see Olga waiting for me at the Lenox station, greeting me in the subdued voice I remembered, and, as we drove past the gates of Tanglewood, telling me how busy Sergei Alexandrovich was, how much work had to be done in preparation for the festival, how little time he had to rest, and how exhausting was the Boston season with its four concerts a week and its harrowing tours. A moment later we drove past a sign marked "SERENAK − PRIVATE," and stopped under a wooden canopy in front of a rambling white house.

"Sh . . . sh . . ." said a white-haired lady in a mauve silk dress, trying to quiet the bark of an old black cocker spaniel: "Beema! be quiet!" It was Henrietta Leopoldovna Hirschmann, a close friend of the Koussevitzkys, who, during the summer months, stayed at Serenak and worked for him as a secretary, a confidential assistant and an all-round helper. "Sergei Alexandrovich is still in conference," she said and pointed to the drawn curtain which hung across the bright broad corridor of the lobby. "Why didn't you come yester-day?" she continued in a hushed tone. "The weather was won-derful yesterday and now, you see, it's raining."

We went out on the covered porch to see the view. The rain had stopped for an instant. Heavy cumulus clouds cov-ered the skyline and hung low above the landscape. Between them, here and there, were patches of deep blue. The distant hills, bathed by a shadow of the rain, were barely visible. The earth was warm and damp, and in the stillness the odor of the grasses, flowers, and fruit trees smelled intensely of an abun-dant spring.

The house, Serenak (an anagram made up of *Ser* from Sergei and *Na* from Natalya, Koussevitzky's late wife and forty-year-long companion, and *K* for Koussevitzky), stands on a terraced hillside, about a mile to the west, and high above the festival grounds. It is a large two-story house dominating an extraordinarily broad and panoramic view. From its terrace one can see a vast horizon filled with the blue rolling pattern of the Berkshires and, at its feet, encased between these hills, like a huge oval mirror, lies Lake Mahkeenac, the Stock-bridge Bowl. The back of the house is protected from the north winds by a high forested hill. In front of the house, the hillside descends in a sharp incline to the Lenox-Stock-bridge Highway, planted with large old apple and plum trees. The whole gives the impression of great serenity, a peaceful detachment from the busy life down in the valley, near the lake. And as one learns the mode of life of the inhabitants of the house, the feeling is pervasive, infinitely restful for visitors. Everything in Serenak is unhurried, calm, subdued repose. Even during the hectic days of the festival season this atmosphere of serenity and peace remains unchanged.

Inside the house the rooms are large and airy, softly car-
peted and softly furnished. Decorated in a neat and well-
mannered way, it resembles the somewhat bulky style in
which the wealthy St. Petersburg merchants of the early nineteenth century furnished the interiors of their large Finnish
dachas (the suburban villas) or the style in which the indus-
trial magnates of the Rhineland adorned their comfortable
houses near Düsseldorf or Cologne. But Serenak has its own
style, very personal and very Russian. Russian not only because its inhabitants, with the exception of one or two maids,
are all Russian and constantly speak Russian, but because
the mode of life, the habits of its master and both of its successive mistresses have molded the environment around them
and given it a distinct flavor of an old Russian *Oussadba*,
the country home of a wealthy squire, with all of its charm
and quiet simplicity.

The curtains opened and Koussevitzky came towards me
with a broad smile on his face, his eyes shining with pleasure
and friendliness. In his broad Russian he exclaimed: "Where
were you all these years, where were you hiding?" in the
tone of a stage father scolding his disobedient child. "We
looked and looked for you *everywhere* until we finally
tracked you down in Germany." And he looked me over
as if he was appraising me. "*Noo, poydem, poydem,*" he
said, "it's late and you must be hungry. Olya, Guenia, where's
lunch?" The meal was long and relaxed. Koussevitzky bom-
barded me with questions about Germany, about our relations with the Russians, about my experiences with the
army and the military government, and listened with avid
interest to my detailed account of the new music I had seen
or heard in France, in Austria, in Berlin, and in particular the

music at the closed concerts of the Soviet military authorities, to which I had been occasionally invited. He wanted to know whether I had news from Prokofiev, and whether it was true that Prokofiev had been so terribly ill that he couldn't compose for more than a year.

At the end of the meal, as we were getting up from the table, he turned to me with a glint in his eye and said: "And now I have to talk to you privately about something which may be quite interesting to you." He led me ceremoniously to the living room as if he had prepared there a surprise for me. "What I want to talk to you about," he began as we sat down, "is . . ." he paused: "a commission . . . yes, we were looking for you all over the place last winter to . . . give you a commission. But we couldn't find you!" And he threw his arms in the air. I apologized for having been such a needle in the haystack and explained that I had been overseas and thus of necessity completely divorced from music and musical life in America. "No, no," he exclaimed, "I do not mean now, I do not mean these last years since the war . . . I mean before. Where were you before the war? Why did you hide from me? What did you do? What did you write?"

I hesitated, not knowing whether I should answer. Somehow I felt that he really did not care for answers, but that these questions were rhetorical, giving weight and impact to his Maecenaic proposal. "Well, anyhow," he continued after a moment's silence, "what would you like to write for us, for the Koussevitzky Foundation? We have put money aside to commission you to write a piece."

I had suspected when I received Koussevitzky's wire that something in the nature of a commission might be on his mind. At least, I hoped that this was the meaning of the phrase "must see you at once." I had thought about it on the train and decided that if he offered me a commission I would suggest writing the piece which, at moments of relative leisure between bureaucratic routine and official parties, I had begun sketching at the blond piano of my Berlin billet. I thanked Koussevitzky for his offer and began explaining. "Yes," I said, "I have a piece in mind, Sergei Alexandrovich. I even started working on it while I was in Berlin. It has to do with a long poem of Pushkin and I don't know yet whether I should write it for orchestra alone or set the text of the poem to music for tenor voice."

At the mention of the name of Pushkin his face beamed. But he did not approve of a solo tenor voice. "The public does not like long solo pieces for tenor," he explained, "they are hard to place because there are few good tenors nowadays. Here in Tanglewood we have a marvelous young tenor, David Lloyd, but elsewhere I know of almost no one . . . Besides it is difficult to write well for tenor and orchestra. The orchestra is always on top of the tenor part . . . like an elephant." He paused for a moment and, as if a splendid idea had just struck him, he began speaking excitedly, his face growing crimson and the veins on his forehead swelling: "I tell you what you do. You write a concerto for soprano and orchestra. No one has ever tried it and I always wanted someone to write one. It will be a real novelty. And you should treat the voice as if it were an instrument; like an oboe . . . or a . . . flute." And getting more excited at his proposal he exclaimed: "Write me a good concerto for this combination, and I will find you an excellent singer and play it everywhere. As for the text . . . it does not matter what kind of a text you use, you can take a poem of Pushkin in Russian . . . you can take a poem in . . . Burmese, or anything you want. For a piece like this the text doesn't matter. It would be like the words of a . . . Handel aria. What is important is that it should show off the voice and be interesting musically."

He paused again and added in a quieter tone: "You know who should sing it? The little Marina . . . do you know her? Marina Koshetz, Nina Koshetz's daughter. She has a wonderful voice and her mother's schooling." I answered that I never had heard Marina but that I knew that her voice was very good, nearly as good as her mother's had been.

"But . . . but . . . Sergei Alexandrovich, my idea is different from yours," I tried to explain. "To me the meaning of Pushkin's poem is paramount. The words express something very intimate, something terribly close to my heart. In fact it is a kind of personal confession . . . a very grave and important thing to me." At first I was afraid that he would be annoyed but, on the contrary, as I went on his expression changed and he became visibly more and more interested. Finally he interrupted me.

"But what poem of Pushkin is it?" he said. "Can you recite it?"

"Yes, of course I can," I answered, "but before reciting to you I must tell you how I came about choosing this particular poem so that you know what it really means to me . . . but it will take a long time and you probably should go and have your afternoon nap." He looked at me with a gentle, friendly smile and said:

"Go ahead, Kolyenka, tell me your story. Never mind the siesta. I can rest later. Go ahead."

"You see, Sergei Alexandrovich," I began, "it's a long story. It has to do with my childhood in Russia and my love for

Russia of the past. It has to do with this war and the circumstances that brought me to Germany at the end of it. It has to do with my knowing Russians in Germany, all kinds, in uniform and out of uniform, generals, soldiers, officials, D.P.'s. It has to do with all these things and with much more, with something which is hard to put into words."

He continued to look at me with warm attention and occasionally he nodded his head as if to give me a silent signal of his understanding. "Go ahead, go ahead, try and say it. I want to hear every bit of it."

"Every exile," I said, "carries for a long time within himself a nostalgic vision of his native country, a deep-rooted, irrational hope that somehow, by some miraculous process of history he will be able to find a road back, a new communion with his native land, its people and its culture. Shunted around from country to country, passportless, not knowing where to go and where to settle, he is constantly aware of his exiled condition. Not belonging to the culture of the countries to which his exile takes him, even such cosmopolitan cities as Paris cannot make him forget. He is haunted by memories, by images of his childhood, by familiar smells, sounds and tastes.

"During the early years of my exile, in Germany and in France, this nostalgia took hold of me at times with unbearable intensity. I was haunted by the vision of the streets and bridges of St. Petersburg or by the smells of the forests of Byelorussia or by the endless horizons of the Taurian Steppe, or the exuberant, fragrant springs at the Crimean seashore. Like a drug addict I would throw myself on the poems of Pushkin, of Tiutchev and Lermontov, avidly reread Tolstoy's *War and Peace* and Chekhov's short stories, thereby only increasing my nostalgia, only intensifying the haunting power of my wish-dreams. I would go to even greater lengths in nursing my 'illness.' I would try to meet travelers who came from 'over there,' even those who came as heralds of the new Socialist Fatherland and proclaimed the glories of the Bolshevik regime. Even though they intimated that people like myself were the scum of the earth, deserters, who had fled their country out of fear for their 'egoistic bourgeois interests,' they attracted me because they came from there, from tortured, tormented Russia.

"Thus in Berlin, in the early twenties, I met the poet Yessenin. Utterly confused and debauched he was being toured around Europe by his mistress, the fat and disintegrating matron, Isadora Duncan. One night in a Berlin café he got drunk and violent and began yelling at me: 'Get the hell out of here, you little bourgeois bastard . . .' And I left, bitterly sad, because I admired him as a true Russian poet and because I felt that he himself was close to the end of his journey. Two years later, in total despair, he hanged himself and joined the many silent poets of his now totally poetless country. I met Meyerhold, the famous theater director and close friend of Prokofiev and Eisenstein, the great pioneer of modern cinema, and the writers Pilnyak, Katayev, Ilf and Petrov. Avidly I asked them all about Russia. How was it there now? Was life getting easier? Would the regime mellow, or be replaced by another, more humane government?

"Then I came to America, thanks to the help of Archibald MacLeish, a friend, and collaborator on my ballet *Union Pacific*. I obtained the rare privilege, the treasure of all treasures for the exiles of the twentieth century, the American immigration visa. Now I had a home again, a status, a country. I received my first papers and I swore allegiance to this new home, this new country, and soon I became one of its citizens, with all the rights of a free human being. I was proud of my new state and grateful to my new country for making me again a full-fledged member of the human community. The old nostalgia, the wishful dreams that haunted me in those early years of my exile, died away.

"At the same time things began to be clearer about conditions in the Soviet Union. In the lingo of Stalinism, certain 'concrete' facts could not be explained away by hopes and wishes. I saw that instead of changing, instead of mellowing and humanizing, life in Russia became harder and tougher. There was only more famine, more fear, more deprivation, more silence, and more murder. The poets, writers, theater directors, in fact most of my acquaintances from Russia, began to disappear. Names that had been heralded as the greatest in Soviet culture were dismissed, showered with abuse, or imprisoned. No, nothing, not an iota of improvement, occurred in the tortured lives of my former countrymen. No statistics of increase in the production of tungsten or of improved breeding of tomatoes could change the facts: exile, prison, violence and murder.

"Then came the war. Like most Americans, I followed the battles of Moscow, the siege of Sebastopol, the great battles of Stalingrad and of the Don bend with enthusiasm. And with the turn of the tide in the war, there seemed to be a vague glimmer of hope for the fate of Russia. 'Maybe,' I thought, as did so many idealistic Americans, 'maybe now the people of Russia will take their destiny into their own hands, maybe the Party will not be able to re-establish its authority over the army, maybe those rumors about revolts in the

Ukraine and in the Caucasus are true, and are preludes to the disintegration of the Soviet power . . . maybe . . . maybe . . . maybe . . .'

"This is why I wanted to go overseas and see for myself whether my new hopes, shared by all my American friends, were founded on reality. I wanted to meet Russians, speak to them, see what they are like, what they think, how they behave, what they say. Thus driven anew by a different form of 'idealistic nostalgia,' I was full of hope, full of great expectations. I was going overseas to see my hopes confirmed and the wishes of many long years come true. Instead, I found a final cure for my nostalgia in the bitter recognition of the hard, morbid truth. Yes, I did get to meet Russians and talk to them but before I met the Soviet officials, the counselors, marshals, generals, civilian advisors or colonels of the M.V.D.; before I saw all these 'active' Soviet citizens, I saw thousands of others, 'non-active' victims of the Soviet state, debased, dejected, exploited and hunted human beings, who lived in crowded camps in an agony of fear and despair.

"They were heroes of escape, these gray masses of Russian people, and they were being sent back into slavery and into death. We were packing them like sheep, whole families of them, into cattle cars and delivering them by the thousand to the Russian border posts, right into the death camps of the M.V.D., as horrible and as murderous as Dachau and Auschwitz. Only ten months after the end of the war did our military government half-heartedly back out of this crime by association. By that time more than half of this miserable humanity was returned to its 'rightful owners' — the bosses of Stalin's secret police.

"It did not take me long to see, to hear, and to understand

(243)

the truth. By August 1945, when I moved to Berlin and began to take my minor part in the Chinese ceremonial known as the Allied Quadripartite Government of Germany, my old nostalgia, my deep-rooted illness, had left me. I knew then that my Russia, the Russia of an exile's wish-dream, had been wiped out, and that all that remained of it were these tragic human beings, each one of whom had the same story to tell: misery, hunger, abuse, and violence. I also knew that those other men, the men who wore big stars on their epaulettes and medals on their chests and stomachs, and the M.V.D. 'civilians' in blue serge suits (later replaced by porterlike uniforms) had nothing in common with what was once a real culture, a burgeoning civilization, the hope and the dream of our childhood. They were another breed of men, men from a ghastly inhuman world. Hard, treacherous, cruel, they did not even speak the same tongues, not our mellow, warmly modulated Russian, but a belchlike, abrupt, ugly-voweled dialect.

"Among the officials of the Soviet military government in Berlin there was one couple to whom I took a sincere liking. They were both young, gentle and friendly and hence very much unlike the usual run of Soviet puppets and bores with whom the Americans had to entertain polite business relations. We used to see each other occasionally, at first, on neutral territory. Then, quite often, either at my billet or at their tiny villa in the Russian sector of Berlin, Karlshorst. After the barriers of false pride were overcome and the propaganda slogans swept away, they acquired a certain amount of confidence in my discretion, and began to talk to me with increasing frankness. First they made one or two critical remarks about the Soviet regime, bathing them each time in a shower of awkward smiles and furtive glances, or Tania, the pale, slight wife of the officer, would take me aside and, after begging me not to repeat it, and not tell her husband, she would tell me a joke about Stalin. Finally after several months of frequent long talks, their reticence melted away and they talked boldly and bitterly.

"It was the same old story, the one I had heard before from hundreds of D.P.'s: fear, and an enormous, all-consuming and totally impotent hatred of the Soviet regime. They wanted to know what America thought of them. They listened eagerly to all my stories about America. They wanted to know how I felt in America, I, a former Russian, in a land that had adopted me as its citizen. I told them about myself. I told them about the nostalgia of exile that had burned in me, and how I now felt at home and at peace in America, with no need, no wish for the past. I remember the night I spoke to them about it all, I remember their wretched little drawing room cluttered with its ugly, German furniture and a worn upright piano. The blinds were closed and their chauffeur was asleep upstairs in his cubicle above the staircase. When I stopped talking there was a moment of awkward silence. It seemed as if we did not dare look at each other for fear of disturbing what each of us felt. Then, quietly, without raising her head or looking at anyone, Tania said: 'You know, what you just said is all in Pushkin, in one of his long poems. Do you remember? The one in which he describes how he came back to his country after a long absence, and how he finds that none of the things he loved are there any more, that all has changed. Do you remember?'

"The next day, in the late afternoon, a tiny car stopped in front of my billet and a man from the Soviet bookstore delivered a package. It contained a brand-new *odnotommik* (collected works) of Pushkin. I opened it, found the poem, and indeed it was my story, the story of exile, with all of its longing, its nostalgia, its bitterness and its resignation. Of course it did not have the same ending, the discovery of a new life, the change of heart . . . its America. And while reading it I felt that this must become my last tribute to my childhood, to its lost dreams and thwarted hopes. That same evening I sat down at the piano and began to compose. I searched for themes and sketched them on the last sheets of music paper I had brought with me from America."

Koussevitzky listened very attentively to every word of my long story. "I know . . . I know how you felt, Kolyenka," he said with a sob in his voice and he put his friendly hand on my shoulder. "Yes, you should by all means . . . you must write your Pushkin, and Marina must sing it. And now tell me . . . recite me the poem."

> . . . I have seen again
> that corner of the earth where once I spent
> in banishment two years of time unnoticed;
> another ten have now gone by, and many
> have been the turns and changes in my life,
> and I to nature's law conforming also
> in many ways have changed; but here again
> the past envelops me, so near and vivid
> that I, meseems, but yesternight among
> those groves have wandered. . . .[1]

Koussevitzky has always been a pioneer, a builder, a man with a keen sense of progress, a devotion to the growth of musical culture and an awareness of the importance of the art

[1] Alexander Pushkin, *The Return of Pushkin*, first stanza, translated by Vladimir Nabokov.

of music in modern society. Long before he came to this country, as a young, beginning conductor in Russia, he was filled with a sense of the cultural mission he must fulfill for the welfare of the community. In this, he was not unlike those liberal, progressive members of the Russian intelligentsia of the nineteenth century who, against incredible odds and the stubborn inertia of the decaying tsarist regime, were trying to build the foundation of a free democratic culture.

Born in a poor Jewish family, he was able to rise far above his circumstances, and with the help of his wife, the daughter of a wealthy Moscow merchant, who became his energetic collaborator in all of the cultural work he was engaged in, he quickly rose to the position and acquired the stature of one of the most important, most forward-looking personalities in Russian music from 1909 to 1921. He built a symphony orchestra in Moscow and took it on extensive tours all over Russia. He founded the first publishing house in Russia where composers were partners of the enterprise, and where profits were divided in such a way as to bring the composer a share of royalties far more generous than those of any other music publishing house of its time. He patronized young composers and promoted their music with a persistence and a zeal unequaled by other conductors of his generation. He propagandized Russian music, first in Russia and then all over Europe, in a manner equaled only by Sergei Diaghilev. He encouraged, helped, advised, worked incessantly, avidly, enthusiastically.

I remember well, as a child, looking at a photograph of bearded and mustached musicians in heavy fur coats and hats boarding a Volga steamer; and another, representing all sorts of instruments: contrabasses, harps, cellos, being loaded on the same steamer. I remember my amazement when I was told that this was Koussevitzky's orchestra going down the Volga to play in all of the Volga towns from Nijni-Novgorod to Astrakhan. It sounded like a fairy tale. I recall my first Koussevitzky concert in Berlin in 1922 or 1923. He conducted Stravinsky's *Rites of Spring* with the Berlin Philharmonic Orchestra. It was my first encounter with this extraordinary work, and I believe it was the first time it had been performed in Berlin. Dazzled and dazed I returned home and wrote Koussevitzky an anonymous "thank you" letter, the first and last fan letter of my life. Later I went to the Koussevitzky concerts in Paris and heard their yearly stream of novelties and the performances of extraordinary pieces of music rarely or never heard in the regular repertoire of Paris symphony concerts. Then he went to America and gradually the news of his achievements there began to seep into Paris and I envied the inhabitants of the city of Boston for having such a great orchestra and such a forward-looking, courageous conductor. Yes indeed, Koussevitzky's career was unlike the career of other conductors. It is not only the success story of a brilliant virtuoso, it is an important part of the history of musical culture in our time.

It was evening when we returned to Serenak from a visit to the Tanglewood Festival grounds and the lights were on in the house. Olga took me upstairs to show me my room and told me that dinner would be served in ten minutes. I had just time enough to wash my hands and comb my hair when Koussevitzky knocked at my door, came in and asked me whether I had brought any sketches for the Pushkin piece. "You know," he said, "I think it's a splendid idea, I'll ask Guenia to write to Marina Koshetz about our plan tomorrow." Unfortunately I had nothing with me to show him but promised that before the end of the summer the piece would be ready. "Well if it isn't ready I won't play it," he said, "so it better be ready . . . but . . ." he added in a teasing tone, "don't you start hurrying and spoil a splendid idea. The music has to be good, you know." As we were going down the broad staircase to join the rest of the household for dinner, Olga appeared at the foot of the stairs and in her calm, unhurried way said: "*Ach,* Nika, I forgot to tell you. Somebody has been calling you from Washington. Why don't you call the operator now, before we sit down to dinner?" It was a friend from the State Department, urging me to be in Washington for a conference the next day.

The dinner was simple and quietly gay. Koussevitzky was in excellent form. He told amusing stories about his concerts in Russia, about his first encounters with Scriabin, with Schönberg, with Stravinsky. He related in detail how he met Debussy and how Debussy came to Russia and stayed at his house for three weeks in 1913. He spoke of his first years with the Boston Symphony and how shocked the habitués of the Friday concerts were by the quantity of new music he played. "Then," he said, "I told the trustees: 'This is only the beginning of my plans. The *public* will have to learn to like new music and develop its taste — not *me.*'" He spoke with enthusiasm of contemporary American composers and told the story of his "discovery" of Walter Piston and Aaron Copland, and described the first performances of their music. Most of his stories were told with an awareness of the eminent role he had played, and the important effect of his activity upon most of the musical events of his time, yet they were told with such candid conviction and so much enthusiasm that I felt a constantly growing sympathy with the storyteller himself.

After dinner, when we were having coffee in the living room, and Koussevitzky his cup of hot water with a slice of lemon in it, he asked me how long it had been since I had heard the Boston Symphony. I replied not for at least five years. "Well, my friend," he said with the tone of a farmer who is about to show you his prize-winning Guernsey bull, "then you have a great pleasure in store for you when you come to Boston next fall. You will hear something which is like nothing else in this world."

It was late in the evening when we finally went upstairs to our rooms. For more than an hour Olga had been giving me silent signs that it was time to go to bed, but Koussevitzky did not want to leave. He was again questioning me about politics, about Europe, and Russia, and wanted to hear every scrap of an answer I could give. He took me up to my room and stopping at the door he said: "*Noo, Kolyenka, ni poukhou ni pyera*, much luck to you and don't come back to me without a good piece of music. Good night."

All during the summer I worked at my Pushkin poem, spending as much free time as I could glean from a very crowded schedule. I had left the military government and was participating in a new and quite fantastic venture: I was helping organize the Voice of America to Russia, then in its precarious infancy. But I did get three weeks of leave in August and I spent them in a quiet place in France where I finished my Pushkin piece. I called it *The Return of Pushkin*,

(250)

an "elegy in three movements" and sent the copy of the first
movement to Koussevitzky.

It was agreed that I would come to visit the Koussevitzkys
at the beginning of the concert season in October, and that I
would stay at their house in Brookline, Massachusetts (a town
which I nicknamed in his honor Nijni-Koussevitzk). I was
eager to play my new piece for him, but I was also excited at
the thought of hearing the Bostonians play. Unfortunately I
was unable to get away from New York to be in time for
the last rehearsal. I arrived at Symphony Hall just as the
musicians were packing their instruments into their respective
black coffins, and found the "good Doctor" sitting in his
black cape in the Green Room sipping tea out of the cap of
a Thermos bottle. "Well, how did you like the rehearsal?"
he asked, after we had embraced. "Didn't you think we played
well?" And he looked with pride at Mr. Burk, the program
annotator of the orchestra, who had come into the room with
me. Not wanting to disappoint him, I mumbled something
made up of "splendid, magnificent, superb." While we drove
to his home, he spoke to me with great excitement and in great
detail about the *Fifth Symphony* of Prokofiev, which he was
studying at the moment, and about a new work by David
Diamond, written for the Koussevitzky Foundation.

After lunch, I played my piece for him for the first time.
He seemed to like the second and third movements of the
elegy, but he frowned at the first. He was annoyed at my
writing it in half notes to a beat instead of quarter notes to a
beat, and changing time at certain movements from 5/2 to
9/4. "This is utterly unnecessary," he said. "No one will play
it right. Everybody will play it much too slowly." But at a
second hearing he began to like it better, and finally after its

(251)

first performance he liked it as much as the other movements.

In the evening we all drove to the concert. Olga and Mrs. Hirschmann sat with some friends and I had a ticket at the extreme right of the front row. As soon as the orchestra began playing I realized that Koussevitzky was right: there was nothing quite like the sound of the Bostonians. I had not heard an American orchestra since 1941 and for the last two years in Germany I had been treated mostly to the sound of decalorized and denazified orchestras. I had forgotten what a first-rate orchestra sounds like. Besides, this was not just a first-rater, it was one of the most perfect symphonic ensembles ever put together; an instrument of extraordinary beauty and precision, the result of careful selection, daily practice, and decades of a tradition of stringent discipline.

The round sensuous tone of its strings, the power and precision of the brasses, the clarity and transparency of its wood winds, and the internal balance among the various sections make it one of the finest sounding symphonic groups in the world, capable of achieving effects which composers like Beethoven or Schubert never heard except in the silent performances of their imagination. I thought, as I listened to the orchestra and watched its conductor, that Koussevitzky's contribution to the construction of this extraordinary ensemble was immeasurable. It became clear to me that his profound knowledge and uncanny ability to recognize the worth (the technical and musical abilities) of each individual musician must have come, in part, from his early training as a double-bass virtuoso. Good conductors often grow up from orchestra players. But Koussevitzky had not only been an orchestra musician, he had also been a fabulous soloist, a virtuoso of one of the most difficult and most ungrateful instruments. But this, of course, is only a part of the story. Tenacity, persistence, the ability to work and make others work, enthusiasm, the spirit of youth and optimism in overcoming all kinds of difficulties and handicaps, constant merciless self-discipline — all these qualities of character created the Boston Symphony Orchestra.

The last number on the program was Tchaikovsky's *Fifth Symphony*, a famous piece of Koussevitzkiana. Curiously enough I had never heard him conduct it; hence it was a revelation to me. Whatever his detractors, his critics may say about his performance of this work, it was certainly the most inspired, the most romantic, the most Tchaikovskian performance of the *Symphony* I have ever heard. Since that time I have heard him conduct the *Fifth Symphony* twice and each time I marveled at the broad and generous sweep of his interpretation.

When he ended a storm of applause broke in like thunder. I looked at him as he was taking his bow. He looked young and happy. I applauded gratefully to the small figure with its crimson face, its veins ready to burst, and its proud, content, and triumphant expression. As he was going off stage he caught a glimpse of me from the corner of his eye and winked — slyly, happily, like a child. I went backstage and there he was standing mopping his forehead, while Victor tried to adjust the black cape on his shoulders. "*Noo*," he said anxiously, expectantly. "How was it? Was it what I told you it would be?"

XII
Music Under the Generals

MR. NABICALF, Mr. Nabicalf, hurry up, we're late," came Blintz's voice from below. "*Es ist schon nach halb vier.*" "Damn that German and his creaky voice," I grumbled, rubbing my "pinks" with lighter fluid, trying to remove a big stain and instead producing a bigger halo around it. I threw the pinks back into the closet, picked up the "olives," brushed and put them on and buttoning up my coat ran down the staircase. Blintz, a placid GI of Hamburger origin, stood at the bottom of the stairs and shook his head.

"Always late, always late," he mumbled as we walked to the garden gate. "*Wenn der Körnel Nicholson da wäre . . .*" he went on in German.

"Oh stop nagging, Blintz," I cut him off, "and for heaven's sake, why don't you speak English!"

Looking sulky he slipped into the driver's seat of the worn Ford sedan, our so-called "staff car." "It is not I who is going to the opera," he began sulking again, as we drove towards the Königin Luisen Strasse, "*und* you know how long it takes

to get to the Russian sector; *ausserdem,* we have to pick up
the two Körnels and the Herr Major Borowski." Blintz had
been sulky ever since my friend "Körnel" Nicholson and I
inherited him from the General. He had banged up the General's "super-de-luxe, left-drive, streamlined O. W. I. P. W."
Buick and now, reduced in status, he was driving a "Körnel"
and a "cifilian" — meaning me. *"Und was ist* a cifilian in de
army?" he would ask rhetorically. *"Dreck!* Worse than a
T/4!"

We stopped to pick up the "Körnels," but they had already
left with the General and "Herr" Major Borowski had a hang-
over. "Besides," he said, "why the devil do I have to go and
sit through an opera!" We drove to the gray arcades of the
ruined central Radio Station and turned into the main artery
leading from the west straight into the Russian heart of Berlin.
I looked at my watch. It was 4:05. The opera began at 4:30.
There was time enough, I thought, but Blintz grumbled on.
"You know how it is *mit die Russen,"* he said, "dey don't
know how to handle traffic. And today all de generals will be
dere: from us, from de British, from de French. We will never
get trough." We drove into the desolate Bismarck Allee, past
heaps of freshly cleared rubble, and reached the Tiergarten,
Berlin's sumptuous, shady park, now a barren wasteland.

"How quickly they've done it," I thought, looking at a wet
tree stump being hauled away by two disheveled women. It
was only two months ago that the Allies graciously acceded
to the Bürgermeister's request and permitted the Berliners to
saw off what was left of their big park. Now it was all clear,
hauled away, eaten by the little iron stoves in the broken hall-
ways and damp kitchens. The Tiergarten lay like an empty
morgue under the low winter clouds.

We passed the Victory Column with its French flag flapping furiously in the wind, through the Brandenburg Gate, and entered the Russian sector. Here the Generalissimo's icon framed by mossy garlands and wet red flags guarded the entrance to the ruins of Unter den Linden, the lime-tree avenue of Berlin. On the right stood the monstrous cavity of the Adlon Hotel; on the left, a sea of ruins and rubble. A vision of the same spot six months before passed through my mind:

The entire avenue is clogged with debris. In front of the Adlon stand two trucks. The first one contains a mountain of brass: tubas, trumpets, and trombones covered by heavy Bokhara rugs. On top of the rugs sit three sullen-looking Mongoloid soldiers. Their uniforms are tattered. They are eating bread. The second truck stands half-cocked on three wheels, blocking the traffic. It contains thousands of naked typewriters, and standing in their midst a cow moos. Two youngish Russian officers have taken off the fourth wheel of the truck and, watched by a silent crowd of ragged kids, are testing an inner tube in a basin of muddy water. . . .

As soon as we turned left on the Friedrichstrasse we got into a fierce traffic jam. Blintz was right. The narrow passageway in the center of the street (a winding river bed between high banks of rubble) was filled with cars of all denominations: American and British staff cars with stars on their backs; huge black Horch limousines filled with Russian uniforms; jeeps, U.S. army busses, nondescript German sedans, tiny Opels, and B. M. W.'s sporting the French Tricolor. All of them, in an endless file, were stalled, honking, their drivers cursing in four different tongues. When we finally got to the Wintergarten (the old Berlin Music Hall that housed the Prussian State Opera Company) the courtyard was nearly empty. Only a few latecomers were jumping out of cars and hurrying towards the entrance. At the door two officers in long gray coats with blue bands on their caps (the colors of the M.V.D. Security Troops) asked for the invitation: *"Bitte sehr . . . Einladung?"* I produced the large, engraved card with its golden hammer and sickle and its uneuphonious text: "The *Glavnokomandouioushchyi* [C.I.C.] of the Military Forces of the U.S.S.R. and the *Glavnonachalstvouioushchyi* [Governor] of the Soviet Military Government for Germany has the honor to invite *gospodin* N. Nabokov . . ." I crossed through the empty lobby and as I climbed the plush and gilt staircase two adolescent soldiers in dark green parade uniforms saluted me. The hall was dark. The curtain was up. The music had begun. "My God," I said to myself, recognizing the oily tunes of *Madame Butterfly* and remembering the program, "not that old thing!"

The stage, a labyrinth of bedragoned screens and bamboo shades, was lit from the back by the indigo blue of the Nagasaki harbor. On the left of the stage, in rocking chairs, sat Lieutenant Pinkerton, U.S.N. (tenor), and the American Consul, Mr. Sharpless (baritone). Between them a small wicker table held two glasses, a water pitcher and a Vat 69 bottle in a bucket of ice. In high-pitched German (the lingua franca of Berlin) Lieutenant Pinkerton invited Mr. Sharpless to *"Milch,* punch *oder* whisky?" and then resumed his loud bravado about "Yankee *Freuden"* (pleasures) and "Yankee *Reisen"* (travels).

Stepping on boots and shoes, I made my way to a seat in

the center of the eighth row. Oddly lit by the interior of Lieutenant Pinkerton's Nagasaki dwelling, the hall was a strange and perplexing spectacle. Hundreds of rows of oversized eggs, with noses, mouths and eyebrows painted on them, rested on top of glimmering epaulettes, colored lapels, beribboned and bemedaled chests, and vertical rows of golden buttons. All was motionless. From every direction and level of the enormous dark hall the eggs were staring at the stage. It was the inside of a gigantic incubator, the monstrous hatchery of a war lord, each of his fantastic eggs held by a gaudy mannequin.

"Hy'-you, Nick. I'm sure glad *you're* here," said a voice on my left in a loud whisper and a perceptible Southern drawl. I turned around and saw the bald anteater's profile of General X. "You know Colonel W. don't you?" and he introduced me to his neighbor. "Nick here," whispered the General to the Colonel, "works for Bob McClure in Information Control. He's hep on music and tells the Krauts how to go about it." He chuckled with his whole body and added: "He'll be able to tell us what this G. D. thing is all about."

Trying to be as quiet as possible, in order not to interfere with Lieutenant Pinkerton's enumeration of the advantages of a Japanese marriage ("*Es kann monatlich anulie-jert werden*," it can be annulled each month), I began explaining that this was *Madame Butterfly*, an Italian opera with music by Puccini, adapted by two Italians from a story by Long and Be—

"I don't care who wrote the damn thing," interrupted the General, "what I want to know is who are those guys up there, and what's this German doing," and he pointed at Lieutenant Pinkerton, "in an American uniform?"

(258)

"They're drinking whisky," remarked Colonel W. dryly.

"Whisky my eye!" said the General. " 'Orse-piss. Plain, German 'orse-piss."

"*Silence, s'il vous plaît,*" whispered an angry uniform in front of us. "*Ah, ces Américains!*"

"Go on, never mind the Frenchie," said the General and turned his ear closer to my mouth.

I started explaining the story of *Madame Butterfly*, and as I went on, his face began to change. From cheerful, it turned earnest, from earnest, grave, from grave, angry, from angry, outraged. "Why it's an insult!" he burst out in a loud whisper. "You mean to say that an American officer knocks up this Jap girl" — and he pointed to Cho-Cho-San — "and then goes back home and marries somebody else? It's outrageous!" His face was livid with fury. "Don't you think so, Bill?" and he turned to the Colonel. The Colonel nodded, his face adopting the grave mien of the General. "Don't they know that an American officer, if he did such a thing, would get court-martialed?"

"*Wollen Sie bitte schweigen,*" said another uniform in a hoarse whisper and a broad Russian accent. A big egg turned around on its short, stocky stem and remarked sententiously: "*Wir wollen Musik hören,*" and turned back in a tinkle of medals.

"Oh, damn it," mumbled the General. He turned away from the stage and stopped looking at it. We sat through the rest of the act in awkward, frozen silence. Only towards the end, when after a great deal of slobbery singing and perfunctory necking, Pinkerton and Cho-Cho-San were about to withdraw to their so-called "marriage chamber," did the General look at the stage again. "Why the G. D. S. O. B.'s," he grunted as

the curtain went down and several thousand pairs of uni-
formed arms began to flail about producing a drone of applause.

I sneaked out quickly before the lights went on and my
neighbor had time to notice my disappearance. I hurried upstairs to the loges, trying to find some friend who might hide
me in his box. But I found no one. A dense crowd was moving
slowly down the stairs towards the lobby. I followed it. Downstairs, I found a small side door and stepped outside.

Slow, big snowflakes were streaking past the light of a
crooked lamppost. Groups of Allied military stood around
smoking, and talking in subdued voices. Beyond the lamppost
all was dark and silent. I went into the darkness towards the
street. I turned right and walked through the slush to the Spree
River. There, at the edge of its absent bridge by the dim light
of a lantern (OBYEZD, MOST VZORVAN; VORSICHT,
BRÜCKE GESPRENGT; ATTENTION, PONT SAUTÉ;
STOP, BRIDGE OUT), I tried to light a cigarette. But the
matches were wet and would not burn. So I stood for a while
in the silence of the evening, breathing in its cold, dank air
tarnished by the ugly smell of decay. When I started back, a
figure bolted out of the dark and picked up the cigarette
I had thrown away.

I cursed to myself, coming back to the theater and finding
that the intermission was still on. "Now he'll see me and I
won't be able to get away from him." I stood outdoors and
waited, but the bell rang, and the last smokers began piling
into the lobby. I followed, and propped up by the crowd I
moved towards the entrance to the orchestra seats. I was about
to slip inside the theater when a familiar voice shouted, "There
he is," and pulled me by the sleeve into the corridor. "Where

have you been?" said General X. in an irritated tone. "Bill
and I looked all over the place for you! You vanished among
those Russkies. Come on, I have to talk to you." He took me
to an empty corner of the corridor. "Say, Nick," he started,
"did *you* know about this G. D. thing," and he pointed in the
direction of the theater, "before you came here tonight?" I
replied that I had; it was printed on the invitation. "You mean
to say that you *knew* about it!" he exclaimed. "You knew that
they were going to permit the Krauts to put on American
uniforms and go through that . . . insulting . . . that slan-
derous rigmarole! And you didn't *do* anything about it! You
didn't protest?"

I explained that I believed there was nothing to protest.
"After all, General," I said in as soothing a tone as I could
muster, "*Madame Butterfly* is performed in New York at the
Met and all over the United States. It's a famous opera . . .
it's a classic . . . its music is known to — "

"I know, I know," he interrupted, "I've heard that G. D.
music played by our band in Fort Worth, and better than
those Germans, too. I don't mean the *music*. I mean the *play*.
I mean that these stinking bastards did it on purpose. It's a
calculated insult to America and its armed forces. We *must*
protest. Don't you think so, Bill?" and he turned to the Colonel. The Wrigley-trained jaws of the Colonel moved acquiesc-
ingly. "If you let these Russkies get away with it," continued
the General, "you'll soon have them . . . they'll soon be . . .
they'll soon have us by the . . ." And not finding the proper
words he turned on me in a rage and started shaking his finger:
"I'm going to call Bob McClure and tell him to lodge a protest
tomorrow and demand an apology." He put on his cap, but-
toned his coat and started towards the stairs. "And if Bob

McClure won't do anything about it," he barked, "I'm going to see Lucius Clay."

Yes, musical life in Berlin was indeed complicated in the winter of 1945–1946. But it was hardly better than elsewhere in Germany during the first months of occupation. Berlin was only the focal point of a disaster which the generals inherited from the *Gauleiters*, from the work of the United States and Royal Air Forces, and from the Yalta decisions. Berlin was only *more* corrupt, *more* decadent, *more* degenerate than the rest of Germany, and its ostentatious morbidity was more apparent, because it was the seat of the most emasculated government in the world: ineffectual, cumbersome and absurd.

When I arrived in Berlin in August 1945, the Allies had divided their musical Germans among themselves and were controlling their activities with various degrees of severity and encouragement. The three big music-making organizations, the State Opera, the Berlin Municipal Opera, and the Philharmonic Orchestra, went respectively to the Russians, the British and the Americans (*their* Germans, *your* Germans and *our* Germans). The French, having come too late for the prize-awarding ceremony, got nothing. They had to be content with occasional gifts from the other Allies, in the form either of concerts by the Philharmonic Orchestra in their part of the sprawling Berlin ruin, or of the loan of the Municipal or the State Opera House for performances of the Comédie Française or the Conservatoire orchestra.

The control of German music by the American generals was, on the surface, reasonable enough. It was based on the principle so well expressed by the late King of Saxony, who, having abdicated, turned to the delegates of the Constitutional

Assembly and said: "Now you can make your dirt all by yourself."

Officially we were supposed to be concerned only with the following:

1. To eject the Nazis from German musical life and license those German musicians (giving them the right to exercise their profession) whom we believed to be "clean" Germans.

2. To control the programs of German concerts and see to it that they would not turn into nationalist manifestations.

3. To guard and protect the "monuments" and "treasures" of Germany's culture which had by virtue of conquest fallen into our hands.

All the rest was supposedly left to the Germans and was none of the concern of the officers of the Music Control Branch of the Information Control Division of the United States Military Government for Germany, whose activities I was supposed to represent as an advisor to General McClure on what was called in the Berlin jargon of the times a "quadripartite level." Of course, like most policies, ours was far removed from reality. Though we did a good deal of successful Nazi-hunting and put on ice a few famous conductors, pianists, singers and a number of orchestral musicians (most of whom had well deserved it and some of whom should be there today), the work as devised by our policy would have taken up only a small part of the time of the zealous, enthusiastic young Americans in uniform, the Music Control officers all over our zone of Germany (most of whom were, in civilian life, professional musicians or intense music lovers) who were trying to help the Germans re-establish a semblance, a modicum of culture on the ruins of twelve years of the Nazi *Reich*.

Unofficially we had to find halls and houses for the orchestras, operas and conservatories, coal to heat them, roofing and bricks to patch up the leaks and holes, bulbs to light them, instruments for the orchestras, calories for the musicians (questions raised at staff meetings included such ticklish problems as whether a trombonist is justified in getting more calories than a string player — that is, whether more calories are needed to blow the trombone than to bow the double bass). The bombed-out orchestra libraries needed parts and scores; composers needed music paper and ink; opera houses needed performers and costumes; and everybody needed shelter, food and fuel. Fortunately "our" general was a very good general, and he backed up the work of his officers and let them do the thousand and one chores needed to put things in shape. He fought with his superiors about the narrowness, the shortsightedness, of our policy and got his ample share of worry in that citadel of frustration which was Berlin of 1945–1946.

The Russian policy differed from ours. The problem of "clean hands" in regard to Nazis and collaborators did not worry them. In the beginning, they put thousands of Nazis in M.V.D. camps, raped and murdered a number of others while putting Berlin and other German cities through a monstrous medieval sack, but once all this was over they began to use the Nazis (Nazi conductors, performers and singers) whenever and wherever they found it useful. They agreed with us perfunctorily on the need of denazification but, as in most other cases of "quadripartite agreements," they disregarded them completely whenever they found them to be obstacles to their independent policy in regard to Germany.

Overtly, towards the Germans, they began from the very outset to play the role of patrons of German art, German music and German culture and as a corollary to this propagandistic *Kulturtraegertum* (carrying the banner of culture) they began at first secretly, then openly, to castigate the Americans and the British as suppressors of German culture, pointing at our "hands-off policy" with an accusing finger. While we kept aloof, the Russians pushed the Germans around, told them what to do and how to do it, ordered them to resume opera and ballet performances on incredibly short notice, told them what to play and what not to play, made them join the Socialist Unity or the Communist Party under the threat of losing their jobs or the inducement of getting better rations, and presented to them as supreme examples of the Great Soviet culture, Russian choruses, troops of dancers, singers and virtuosi, brought to entertain the Soviet occupation troops and the officials of their military government.

These "closed" concerts for the Soviet military, by imported Russian artists, were curious affairs, reflecting average Russian tastes and hence fascinating to see. I would occasionally go when invited by my "opposite numbers" of the Soviet military government (which included the following series of names: Major Dymshitz, Mr. Fartuchny and General Popov). Once after a concert these gentlemen took me to a kind of Junior Officers' Club in Karlshorst, the northeastern part of Berlin, where the S.M.A., the Soviet Military Administration, had its headquarters. Besides my O.N.'s, there were other Soviet citizens in the party—Russian artists and actors, both male and female, military and civilian.

The concert had been long and dreary. It had begun with the famous Russian tenor Kozlovsky, who sang the two famous arias from *Eugene Onegin*, the *Song of India* from *Sadko* and lieder by Tchaikovsky, Glinka, Arensky and Rachmaninov. The voice was small but lovely. Like many Russian tenors it had a warm lyrical quality. He switched from his full tone to a soft falsetto with ease and grace. His breath was controlled and completely inaudible. His dynamics were smooth and his intonation perfect; but . . . but . . . his interpretation! The awful provincial taste in delivery, its greasy outmoded sentimentality reminiscent of the worst habits of the American radio crooner. After each of his numbers the audience clapped, and cheered furiously. Their faces got red and their eyes wet. The stocky pomaded little colonels and their round middle-class wives dressed in prewar evening gowns, a plump brooch keeping the V-shaped neckline from bursting out under the heavy milk-farm equipment, jumped to their feet and bellowed the names of famous Russian songs they wanted to hear and yelled: *"Bi-is . . . Bi-is . . . Bi-is."* He sang innumerable encores, each time interspersed by the same kind of bellowing and clapping until finally, after he had made a gesture of vocal exhaustion, they let him go.

During the next two numbers on the program, the *Second String Quartet* by Borodin and the oozy *Andante Cantabile* by Tchaikovsky, played by the famous Moscow Beethoven String Quartet, the audience sat in respectful, though fidgety silence. They looked just a touch bored and restive; and as I glanced at the meaty faces of the men and the talcum-powdered complexions of the women, they seemed so flat, so bland, so provincial and so terribly bourgeois. The next attraction was a cubical lady pianist. (I forget her name but she must have been well known; she was greeted with booming applause.) She played the *Twelfth Hungarian Rhapsody* of

Liszt, two hackneyed nocturnes of Chopin and the painfully boring *Polichinelle* by Rachmaninov.

After a long, long intermission, Kozlovsky reappeared and gave us some more of the stuff he had sung before. He topped that off with a few gay and boisterous pseudo-Russian pseudo-folk songs. Then a troupe of Ukrainian singers and dancers in national costume and headgear appeared and did what Ukrainian singers and dancers are supposed to do and have been doing whenever and wherever they are on the stage of a theater, a concert hall or cabaret. The male dancers kicked about on the floor in crouched positions, surrounded by a flock of bouncing girls who zigzagged between them waving colored kerchiefs. The chorus, in a semicircle behind them, bellowed and clapped to the strumming of three bandura players. The last and longest entertainment on the program was the singing of the famous and superlative Red Army Chorus. The army boys started off with Russian sentimentalia (akin in spirit, period and quality to the American barbershop-iana), then branched into three or four old patriotic songs of the time of the late Emperors Alexander III and Nicolas II. They concluded with a "splendid rendition," as the *New York Times* would say, of the three celebrated patriotic Soviet songs of the last war: *Broad Is My Fatherland, The Song of the Red Pioneers,* and the unavoidable *Red Cavalry Song* with the thumping of horses as background.

Throughout the evening I kept being reminded by the program and the whole atmosphere of the concert of the "patriotic" benefits that were held in the beginning of the First World War in St. Petersburg's large Circus Chiniselli. It was the same kind of music, the same kind of performance and the same kind of enthusiastic reaction in the audience. In fact, the parallel was so great that at moments it seemed that a whiff of the old nostalgic circus odor was coming at me from the stage. What seemed particularly significant, and it was not the first time I had noticed it, was the absence of any kind of new music throughout the evening's entertainment. With the exception of the banal Red Army songs, there was not a single piece of music that had not been composed long before the Revolution of 1917, nor the name of a single famous Soviet composer on the program.

My O.N.'s, in particular the *Kultur* Major Dymshitz, as the Germans called him, and some other *Kultur* colonels, majors and captains, were always declaiming about the new "great masters" of Soviet music, their "glorious achievements" and their "unsurpassed genius." In committee, at inter-Allied parties, and in private conversation, they cited such works as Shostakovich's *Fifth* and *Seventh Symphonies* as examples of the unheard-of high standards of Soviet music. But all these fervent declarations sounded forced, stilted and reminiscent of the style of the letters to "great Stalin" printed daily on the first page of *Pravda*. Only once did I see one of the *Kultur* boys seem sincerely moved by a piece of new Soviet music. It happened after the first performance of Shostakovich's *Fifth* (or was it the *Seventh?* I can't seem to tell Shostakovich's symphonies apart in my memory) by the Berlin Philharmonic Orchestra. Captain Barsky, the Soviet officer, had tears in his eyes and for a while could not speak. But a moment later he was again pouring out his "lesson" in the best epistolary style of the one-way *Pravda* correspondence.

Now, I thought, as I entered the officers' club after the concert, I may have the opportunity of asking a few questions of my Russian hosts and for once getting straight answers. I sat down at an oblong table, covered with a worn white cloth, in a large, crowded and smoke-filled dining room. My neighbors at the table were a pleasant-looking Russian captain (I had never seen him before) and a girl in a lieutenant's uniform with a pale, sad face and black unkempt hair. The cubical pianist and a few other artists of the evening's performance also sat with us. The watchful ears and eyes of my O.N.'s were at another table, in another corner of the room. After some small talk I turned to the nice-looking captain and asked him why the evening's program did not contain at least one work by a contemporary Soviet composer. Realizing that I was some Russian-speaking kind of foreigner (and at that time such foreigners were not all labeled "blackguard beasts" and "Wall Street lackeys") who wanted an explanation, instead of giving me the propaganda line he said quite frankly: "You see, we don't really *like* the music of Shostakovich and Proko-fiev . . . It's strange to us . . . its language is unfamiliar . . . it's too complicated, too dissonant . . . and not enough *melodichna*." While he talked, the lady pianist and some of the other artists nodded approvingly.

"But isn't this just your personal feeling?" I insisted. "Don't the majority of the Russian people admire Prokofiev and Shostakovich?"

"Yes, we do . . . *admire* them," he answered, making a special inflection on the word "admire," "but admiring and liking are two different things, aren't they?" and he smiled disarmingly.

"Most of us in Russia," broke in the girl lieutenant on my right, saying *Rossia* instead of the usual *Soiouz* (Union), "don't like to listen to this new music. When I go to a concert, I want to hear exactly the kind of program we heard tonight. Didn't you think this was a splendid concert?"

I heard these opinions often, especially at those occasions when after some drinking and eating, Soviet citizens would unbend and forget about the presence of a foreigner or the eager ears of my O.N.'s. Later, when the music purge took place and the best Soviet composers received a public whipping by Mr. Zhdanov, the opinions of the average, semi-educated Russians that I had heard in Berlin, in Leipzig, in Dresden, came back to my mind. It occurred to me how much their point of view conformed to that of the Politbureau and Stalin, or rather how closely their taste and opinions in regard to music (as represented in the edict of the Central Committee of the Communist Party) reflected of the incredibly old-fashioned provincial and parochial taste of the new uneducated middle strata of Soviet society.

But the main purpose of my coming to Berlin and working on General McClure's staff had little to do with the recalorization of German trombone players or the observation of Russian tastes in music. My task was different, and on the surface appeared simple and urgent. I was expected to find (or rather track down) those Russians in the Soviet administration whose task was the same as General McClure's — that is, the control of German press, publications, radio, film, theater and music. After finding the recalcitrants, I was to persuade them of the urgent need and the general usefulness of establishing a Quadripartite Directorate of Information Control with the British, the French and the Americans. Such a directorate would then be adopted as the thirteenth or fourteenth child of that happy military family called the Allied Control Commission.

The task which seemed so simple and clear-cut turned out to be intricate, complex and infinitely arduous. If it had not been for the fun I got out of it, I would have given up a fortnight after I arrived in Berlin. At first my difficulties in unraveling the structure of the Soviet military bureaucracy in Berlin seemed normal. It appeared to be just another form of the pentagonal mystery I had encountered in our own bureaucracy. From experience, I knew that the secrets of bureaucracy have to be penetrated gradually and that the technique of penetration should be based upon (*a*) tenacity, (*b*) constant pressure on sources of information, and (*c*) luck.

First I went to see a man called Bezpalov, who supposedly controlled the German press and who I hoped would enlighten me and discuss the matter with me. He was cold, polite and noncommunicative. He smiled a great deal with his steel teeth and invited me for red caviar and a drink of vodka. Next, I went to see a man named Filipov, a short furtive little creature in an M.V.D. blue serge suit, a typical Soviet *tchinovnik* (routine bureaucrat) of the amiable type. He was a little more voluble and although he had no caviar to offer, he drew me a chart of the Soviet Military Administration and thus gave me the first clue to my mystery. He turned out to be the censor of German newspapers and when I left him I saw several gray, flatulent Germans in his waiting room, with ear-ache or stomach-spasm expressions on their faces. Next in line was the editor of the official Soviet German-language daily, the *Tägliche Rundschau*, Colonel Kirsanov. He was suave, cold and polite. He invited me to a pressed caviar lunch and tried to dissuade me from continuing my investigations. I left him, unconvinced by his arguments, and drove out to the farthest outskirts of Karlshorst and there, in a dingy old villa near a potato field, I met Professor Ignatiev. He was old, shy and wiry and looked terribly frightened by my visit. He knew nothing. He explained that he was only concerned with the control of music and that now he was about to go on leave to Moscow. While we talked he was wrapping hard-boiled eggs in newspaper. "You see, I'm going to Moscow by train," he said, "and it takes five long days."

And so from Bezpalov to Filipov, from Kirsanov to Ignatiev and from *-okev* to *-enko*, from *-enko* to *-adkin*, from *-adkin* to *-yi*, I went on and on for two weeks. At the end, I knew very little. I knew that the Russians had no organization like ours and that they did not wish to co-operate with us in any form or manner. I also knew that all Russian bureaucrats are divided into a caviar hierarchy: on top are the fresh caviar Russians, below them the pressed caviar Russians, next the red caviar Russians and last the great mass of noncaviar Russians.

One day after nearly two months of frustrated efforts, the uncommunicative Colonel Kirsanov tipped me off. He informed me that two important personages had arrived from Moscow and that both of them were to reorganize the information control bureaucracy of the S.M.A. He promised to introduce me to the august arrivals at the party Marshal Zhukov was giving in Potsdam on the seventh of November, to which all of our generals and colonels were invited.

On November seventh, our general was out of town, so a friend, an American colonel, and I pocketed his invitation and drove to the party. Although this was my first visit to an official Soviet gathering of the freshest caviar class and although the party was well stocked with marshals, generals, brigadiers, colonels, suckling pigs, turkeys, geese, venison, ducks, sturgeon, salmon and goose-liver pâté, I was not fully impressed, as I had already heard too many detailed descriptions of such parties, and because I was looking out for Colonel Kirsanov and his arrivals from Moscow. The crowd of hosts and guests got drunk and noisy an hour after we had arrived. The only men who remained sober were the glum M.V.D. guards who stood by the doors and looked down at the crowd from the balcony under the upper row of windows. I could not find Kirsanov anywhere and began to think that his tip was another one of those deceptions and evasions to which I had become accustomed in Berlin. I went despondently through all of the halls of the Crown Prince's palace where the reception was being held. I inspected every corner, looking behind every group of red, roaring faces. He was nowhere to be found. My colonel-companion (a nondrinker) suggested that we leave.

"It's no use," he said, "your colonel pulled another one of his usual tricks." We went towards the exit. In front of the palace, their backs turned to the entrance, three Russian generals were silently relieving themselves.

I had forgotten my coat and went back to the check room. There, helping someone out of his fur coat, I recognized Colonel Kirsanov. He turned around and said: "Ah, Nikolai Dimitrievich, here he is! This is Colonel Tulpanov and this," and he directed me to another figure standing behind him, "this is General Bokov." The General seemed to be the open-stock pattern Russian general: stocky, short, round-faced. The Colonel was different. His face, his manner, his whole appearance immediately arrested my attention. He was bald, or rather his head was clean-shaven and had large protruding ears. It sat, totally neckless, like an oversized billiard ball, on a short, well-built body. His features were Mongoloid, but no more so than the features of most peasants from Central Russia. His eyes were narrowly slit, his cheekbones protruded and his nose was flat and turned up at the end. When he smiled, as he did when he greeted me, his eyes took on a shy and somewhat foxy expression. His whole manner of greeting me was both polite and reticent, awkward and friendly. I was struck by the absence of rows of medals on his worn-looking khaki coat — only one or two little patches of ribbons and a small red star dangling near them.

I did not know what to say and how to begin but he helped me: "You don't mean you are leaving so early," he said, "from such a . . . gay party?" and his eyes squinted. I replied that I had to, but that I was full of regrets because I had hoped so much and for so long to see him.

"But could I perhaps call on you . . . tomorrow," I said, "and extend to you at that time an invitation from my general, General McClure?"

"*Noo . . . noo*" — he started — "not tomorrow. Tomorrow we will be resting and digesting," and he looked up at Kirsanov and laughed. "Besides, General Bokov and I have just arrived . . . and," he continued, forestalling any further questions, "I do not know *anything* about the things you want to talk to me about. Better give me a ring in a few days. Colonel Kirsanov knows my number. He will give it to you."

"Call me up tomorrow," said Colonel Kirsanov as the group moved towards the party.

I felt elated, as if after long days of frustrating fishing I were pulling out of a dark, slime-covered pond a fat, golden carp. "Now," I thought, "things will clarify, and we might perhaps find a way to . . ." and I did not know how to finish my thought.

He *was* a carp and a fat one, as we soon began to find out. In fact, he was the prize carp of the S.M.A., but he wasn't on my line . . . and the pond he swam in was far beyond my reach. Tulip, as my British colleagues christened him when they discovered the derivation of his name, was a big-time operator, and belonged to the freshest caviar stratum of the Soviet hierarchy.

By training and official profession Colonel Sergei Ivanovich Tulpanov (now Major General) was an engineer. He was of Great Russian peasant stock, from a village somewhere in the neighborhood of the city of Kalinin. One of his aides told me that he joined the revolutionary movement as a very young man. At any rate, when the Revolution of 1917 overthrew the tsarist regime, he soon became a member of the Leninist wing of the Social Democratic Party. While a student at the St. Petersburg University (or of the Technical Institute of St. Petersburg) he established close and friendly relations with the late Alexander Zhdanov (who was to become the party boss and the creator of the Cominform). He fought well and hard in the civil war of 1919–1921 and, so it seems, during those years established a permanent connection with the Tcheka, the ancestor of the M.V.D. Surviving all trials and purges, he rose slowly in power and importance, chiefly because of his friendship with Zhdanov. Officially he occupied innocuous posts, first as instructor and later as professor of engineering at the Technological Institute of Leningrad. According to German sources, Tulpanov visited Germany in the middle or late twenties, studied the German language and traveled widely all around Germany. In those years, he was supposed to have established close contact between the Soviet O.G.P.U. and the security organization of the German Communist Party. During the war he took part in the defense of Leningrad and, it is said, participated in the construction of the ice road across the Ladoga lake which saved the city from complete starvation. Tulpanov was Zhdanov's logical choice for the job of chief of Agitprop (Agitation and Propaganda Administration) for Germany. He and another friend of Zhdanov's, General Bokov, arrived in Berlin to become the propaganda whips of Germany, and the eyes and ears of the Politbureau in the S.M.A.

But all these things were unknown to us at the time. Only gradually did we come to know the importance of the Tulip. To us, in November 1945, he was just another Soviet colonel, who had been sent to Berlin to put some order in the disorganized Soviet control of information media; and, we hoped, come to terms with us and begin co-operating in our dreamland organization: the Quadripartite Directorate of Information Control.

Although I obtained the Tulip's telephone number I could not reach him. The other end of the wire would either not react at all or after endless ringings a bland voice would answer: "I am listening to you . . ."

"Is Colonel Tulpanov there?"

"No . . . he's out!" and the receiver would be slammed down.

Finally I decided to go to Soviet headquarters and find Tulpanov in person. After a great deal of labyrinthine exploration, insistence, and persistence, patience and mock indignation, I succeeded in tracking him down and obtaining an interview with him. He greeted me like an old friend, excused himself

(276)

for having been "so terribly busy" and promised to call "next week" on General McClure. He also explained that from now on his new office, the Office of Propaganda of the S.M.A., would control, on the Soviet side, all the media which came under the control of General McClure. "Next week," surprisingly enough, occurred in ten days. He called on General McClure with two of his aides and agreed to meet with him and the British and French chiefs of Information Control on an "informal" basis to discuss "the points of common interest."

For the next three or four months, instead of lessening, our frustration was to grow stronger and more intense. We met at regular intervals at so-called "informal" meetings of an "informal" committee to discuss "informally" our "informal" business. The decisions of such a tenuous organization could neither be binding nor of any value whatsoever. Tulip came to most of the meetings and even acted as "host" at one of them (no caviar); but when either his British or his American colleague asked him when we would be able to drop this ballast of "informality," his answer would be: "I am expecting new directives from my government."

In the course of these months, I grew to know him quite well and, so it seemed to me, he started to take an interest in, if not a liking to, me. He would invite me to visit him at his H.Q., or at his house in the suburb of Weissensee, where the villas of the big bosses of the S.M.A. were situated. At every opportunity for a private talk he would ask me questions about myself. Where did I live before the revolution? Who were my parents? Was I a relative of Vladimir Nabokov, the Russian liberal leader? Did I know Soviet musicians? Did I know Prokofiev? When had I last been in Russia?

(277)

He was always very careful not to make his questions appear too ostentatious, and thus circumlocuted with shock-absorbing general talk. I knew that my "position" in the United States Military Government was not quite clear to the Soviet authorities. Through the grapevine of our intelligence I was informed that the hierarchically minded S.M.A. had an exaggerated idea of my importance. Because of that I understood the Tulip's "questions" and interest in me to mean that he wanted to find out who I was, what I was doing, and what my duties really were.

General McClure was pressing me to get the Tulip to come and have a "quiet" dinner with him at his villa on the Wannsee (the American version of the Russian Weissensee). In the good old American way, he thought that the way to do business with a tough customer was to invite him to a party, have a couple of Martinis (vodka would do) before dinner, follow them up with a hearty meal, then have more drinks, and in the course of it all settle some "mutually profitable" business. The Tulip, after much nagging and prompting, accepted the General's invitation. But being a busy man (he was organizing the Eastern German unions and sponsoring the formation of the Socialist Unity Party) and a "forgetful" man from the other side of the world where rudeness is law, he either conveniently or intentionally forgot about the General's dinner party and at the appointed hour did not appear.

I was sitting in my office, waiting for him to arrive. It was arranged that I would guide him from our H.Q. to the General's house. Six-thirty passed. My telephone rang every five minutes. The General was on the phone, getting angrier by the minute. I and a colleague of mine were working two phones, calling every Soviet number we knew. From every-

where came the same sullen answer: "I am listening to
you . . ."

"Is Colonel Tulpanov there?"

"No, he's out."

While this frustrating and absurd search was going on, I
kept seeing before my eyes the General's Martinis dissolve
in ice, the roast shrink in the oven, the soup grow opaque
and the salad wilt. Finally at 8 P.M. we tracked down Major
Dymshitz and by talking alternately we made him feel as if
he were confronted with an ultimatum: "If Colonel Tulpanov
is not going to come then . . ." etc. etc. Curiously enough
(and I still cannot understand why) it worked. Ten minutes later the Colonel called me. "But I thought it was the
eighteenth and today is the sixteenth," he said in an unper-
turbed voice. I replied dryly that he must have on his desk
a "reminder" which had been sent to him only two days ago.
"*Noo* . . . all right," he said, "if it isn't too late and I won't
disturb the *gospodin* General McClure I will come." Half an
hour later he arrived in my office in his long greatcoat and a
Papakha, the tall gray Astrakhan fur cap of the Cossack cavalry. He smiled slyly and said: "*Noo*, Nikolai Dimitrievich,
poydem [let's go]. I'm awfully sorry, but I assure you I
thought it was the eighteenth. I hope your general will forgive me."

The first part of the dinner was icy and all my premonitions
about the Martinis, the soup, the roast, and the salad came
true. It took General McClure some time to control his indignation and decide to make the best of it. The Tulip, on the
other hand, was all charm. He talked about the war and his
wounds during the defense of Leningrad and the way the
Germans were beaten in the battle of the Don. He asked the

General about the landing in Normandy (a topic which no American general can resist) and the liberation of Paris and . . . by the time the dinner was over the General's ire had melted down. No business, however, had been discussed and there was not a glimmer of hope left that it would be.

When we got up from the table and went to the living room the Tulip, pointing at an upright piano in the corner of the room, turned to me and said: "Ah, now I've caught you! Get down at the piano and start playing." And he turned to the General: "*Gospodin* General, please order him to play." I had the feeling that, by that time, the General knew that the game was up. So I played the General's favorite gypsy songs, and then the Tulip began to sing some new Soviet ones, and the General told me to write down the words; but the Tulip wanted me to provide accompaniments for his songs, so that every time I would start writing he would start singing another, and I would have to start banging the piano again, and then I had a Scotch and soda, and then another Scotch and soda. The songs grew louder and louder and I banged the piano more and more . . . playing accompaniments for the Tulip . . . and then . . .

It was dark when we slipped into the Tulip's big black Horch. "Where do you live? I will drop you," he said. I gave the driver my address, and we started bumping on the worn, narrow road. He hummed for a while the last song of the evening. Then he stopped and it seemed, in the dark of the car, as if his eyes were observing me, watching me, looking me all over. "Well, here we are," he began in a low, slow voice. "You, a Russian, and I, a Russian. Only you . . ." And he stopped for a moment as if searching for words. "You

. . . are in this strange uniform and I . . . I wear our old Russian Cossack *Papakha* and the epaulettes of the great Russian army." He stopped as if waiting for me to say something but I kept mum. "Ni-ko-lai Di-mi-tri-e-vich Na-bo-kov," he continued, pronouncing with care every syllable of my name. "Na-bo-kov — what a good well-sounding old Russian name. And here you are . . . in *that* uniform."

I felt suddenly that I had to speak, that I had to say something simple, something definite and true. "In this uniform," I said, "you can't do anything to me. If I didn't have this uniform on now . . . if I had stayed *there* I wouldn't need any uniform. I would be dead. I would . . ."

He laughed quietly, slyly. "All of you *émigrés,*" he remarked in a didactic, paternal way, with a barely perceptible overtone of contempt, "all of you have a thwarted, a distorted idea about our Fatherland. You think in terms of 1918–1919, but we have gone ahead and a new world has been born in Russia. The revolution has receded into the dialectical process of history. The doors are open again for *all* Russians *everywhere.*" And again I felt his eyes look me all over, as if baiting me: "A man with a name like Nabokov should be in Russia, working, toiling for the new life, for the future. You are a musician aren't you? A composer?" And he stopped, waiting for my answer. But I couldn't speak; I had nothing to say.

"We need composers in Russia," he continued, "and you know what has happened all over Russia? New towns have sprung up all over the place, and each one has a new university and a *technicum* and a conservatory. I saw some of these wonderful new towns in Siberia. They were built by the Red pioneers, during their summer vacation." The tone of his voice began to mellow. It grew emphatic and lyrical. "In the middle of the town stands a factory, say a tractor factory, and around it are clean, neat workers' dwellings. The whole town lives for the factory. Imbued with pride at its rising production, it follows the statistics of the factory's output with intense excitement. When a tired father comes home from a day's work in the factory his children jump all over him and shout:

"'Tell us, tell us, Father, how high was the output today?'"

The car stopped and the driver rolled down the window and asked for directions. I told him where to turn and proposed that I sit near the driver and guide him to my billet.

"No," he answered, "he will find his way," and again I dropped back into the darkness of my seat. "Yes, Nikolai Dimitrievich Nabokov," started the Tulip, picking up the thread of his talk where he had left it, "a man with your name and your intelligence should be wearing *our* uniform or should be teaching in one of *our* schools or *our* conservatories. We need people like you. Of course," he continued, and again I felt the contempt so well concealed by the quiet paternal tone, "of course you wouldn't hope to find right away a teaching post in Moscow or Leningrad, or even Kharkov or Kiev but . . . but in one of those new Siberian towns . . . there . . . there you would have a good place to live, to teach and to work."

I waited till the car had stopped in front of my house, and the chauffeur had come out and opened the door. In the pale light of our door lantern I looked at his face. I saw his bare, naked forehead, his protruding ears and the sly, foxy eyes. He was looking at me, smiling, laughing, full of brazen scorn and contempt. "Thank you, Sergei Ivanovich," I said calmly and slowly, "but I prefer the climate of New York," and I shut the door of his car.

As I tiptoed upstairs to my room I heard the quiet snoring of Colonel Nicholson. "Thank God," I said and went straight to bed.

Index

(285)

INDEX

(287)

(289)

INDEX

(291)

INDEX

(294)

DATE DUE

#47-0108 Peel Off Pressure Sensitive